Life in The Faith Lane

Living the supernatural life in a natural world

Jennifer J. Swanson

To my mom and dad,

Who I love and appreciate very much.

To Jonathon, Cristina, Laura and Matt,

Who have filled my life with such joy.

And, of course, to my dear husband, George,

Who is the love of my life.

Thank you...

To Teri Powell, for prompting me to finally write this book.

To Bob Tillman, for your many hours of labor toward
editing, even during the time you were writing
your own book.

To my wonderful sister-in-law, Dona White, for your
professional touch of proofreading, and your encouraging
words to help me move forward.

To Dr. John Evans and Pastor Erik Powell, for your
doctrinal expertise in the epilogue.

To Robert and Jessica Bloemendaal, and Sharon Whitmore,
for helping me with the final details of the book, and the
photography.

To my precious husband, George, for your close walk
of faith with God, and your sacrifice during my time of
writing, and pitching in with the things that needed to get
done that I just couldn't seem to get to.

And especially to Jesus for inspiring, directing,
and guiding me each step of the way.
I love You!!!

The names throughout the book have been changed to
protect the privacy of the individual.

TABLE OF CONTENTS

Prologue

It was just another ordinary Sunday afternoon for George and me, except that millions of Americans across the nation were celebrating Super Bowl Sunday. This particular year we had been invited to a big family gathering at our friend's house. After an exciting afternoon of eating and fellowshipping, we decided to dart out early and catch the late afternoon matinee before heading home. We planned to follow this by a comfortable, relaxing evening together; or at least that's what we had hoped.

Within fifteen minutes of arriving home, George jumped up from the couch, not understanding why his thumb was moving in an uncontrollable manner unlike anything he had ever experienced before. Then his hand started closing itself into a fist. "Jennifer," he yelled, "Grab my hand so it won't clamp shut!" I had no idea what was happening, but I knew from the urgency in his voice that something was seriously wrong. I quickly grabbed his hand. His grip became so tight that I had to forcefully pull my fingers out. His arm then began to shake involuntarily as he slowly fell to the ground. As he sank down, he managed to say weakly, "Throw me a pillow, and . . . call Lori." At this point he went into a full seizure. Suddenly a deep sense of terror swept over me. I had never seen him go through anything like this before. Was he having a heart attack, or maybe a stroke? George's request that I call Lori cut through my panicky thoughts.

Chad and Lori lived next to us in Sandia Park, New Mexico, on a twenty-acre lot. Not only were they our landlords, but we also had the privilege of becoming very close friends. An added bonus to our relationship was that Lori was a registered nurse. Whenever we experienced any kind of medical issue, she was always there to assist us. I immediately called her to come and help. After that, even in my terrified state of mind, I was able to think clearly enough to then call 911. When the call was answered, I nervously cried out, "Please help, my husband is on the floor. I think he's having a seizure and I don't know what to do!" Even as I stared down at George, the seizure stopped. Noticing that he was not moving at all now, fear gripped me like never before. The operator spoke up as she heard me cry out, "Oh no, he's not moving!"

"Take his pulse," she directed. When I knelt down to find a pulse, there was none.

Frantically I replied, "I can't feel his pulse… Is he… is he…?"

She must have sensed my fear and shock. "Ma'am, stay on the line with me, we're on our way there."

At that moment Lori came running into the house. She brought an oxygen tank with a mask attached. I was never so relieved to see her as at this critical moment. I told the 911 operator that I would be all right, that my friend who was a registered nurse was now with me and we would wait together for the emergency medical technicians to arrive. As Lori began administering oxygen to George, we both prayed to God for His help. George suddenly opened his eyes. Relief flooded me that he was still alive. I asked anxiously, "Honey, are you all right?"

"I can't move my body," he said. At that moment the paramedics came barging through the door, and immediately began to get George up on the gurney. As they were lifting him, he started to get feeling back into his body. They were asking me question after question about his previous health. After I assured them that he was in good health before this evening, they turned to him and asked, "Have you ever had a seizure before?"

"Never," George said.

"Did he have a stroke?" I asked fearfully.

"Oh, no, it wasn't a stroke. It's something else. We're not sure just what's wrong," answered the medic. He shifted the conversation. "What hospital do you want us to take him to?" After a considering, George suggested a hospital near the home of some dear friends in Albuquerque.

On our way to the hospital a million thoughts raced through my mind. I found myself beginning to feel a bit numb. My next thoughts focused on our children, who were living in Flagstaff, Arizona. I realized that I must call them and tell them the shocking news of what had happened to their father. I picked up my cell phone and called both Jonathon and Laura. Of course their questions, like ours, couldn't be answered yet. I left them with, "I'll let you know more when I know more. You don't need to come right now. I'll call you in the morning."

Everything had seemed to happen so quickly until we arrived at the hospital. Now it seemed as if time were suspended. With test after test being taken, along with blood work and the many other things that go along with being in the emergency room, we continued to wait and wait and wait.

I decided to walk to an area in the hospital where my cell phone would pick up service. I wanted to call the children again to assure them that everything would probably be all right, but instead I found a message that Jon, his wife and son, and Laura were on their way from Flagstaff. "Mom... Laura, Cristina, Jordan and I are on our way there to see dad. Even if he's going to be okay, we want to be with him." None of them had peace of mind waiting in Arizona for my phone call. While I appreciated that the kids would drive 350 miles at such late hours of the night to be with their dad, it seemed unnecessary to me; I was beginning to feel more confident that whatever strange thing that had happened to George was over. By this time he was talking and laughing, and seemed to be his own self again. But our children had made up their minds. They were on their way. There was no stopping them.

But when I made my way back to the emergency ward and re-entered George's room, I immediately could sense something was not right. Maybe it was the expression on George's face, or the way the nurse looked at me when I walked in. "Is everything all right?" I asked nervously. The nurse immediately turned her back to me and walked to the other side of the room as if to act busy. "George?" I looked into his eyes.

"Honey, sit down," he said. "It isn't good. They found a cancerous tumor lodged in my brain the size of a golf ball. It has metastasized from my kidney."

I don't think anything can prepare us for such horrific news. My mind was rejecting all of this and not willing to process what was really happening to us. I fell onto the bed beside George and began to cry out to God. "No, no, don't let this happen!" Somehow I hoped that I would find myself awakening as from some terrifying nightmare, to find that it was only a dream. Struggling to come to grips with my emotions, I sat up, wiped my tears, and knew that somehow in this new tribulation that we were going through, God would work it out for the good as He always had in the past twenty-five years of walking our Christian walk. The supernatural strength of God that somehow passes all understanding at that moment kicked in.

The situation got worse the next few days. If the brain tumor hadn't been bad enough news to swallow, the doctors in charge also informed me George only had a short time to live. "As we are talking, the cancer is spreading throughout his system rapidly," they added. The oncologist told George to get his house in order. My only recourse was to literally force myself to stand on the scripture that I quoted so many times to others in their time of need, taken from Romans 8:28, "And we know that all things work together for good to those that love God, to those that are called according to His purpose". I had been able to stand on His promises before; would I be able to stand as I walked through this valley of the shadow of death that we now found ourselves in?

In the journey on which we were about to embark, I found myself reminiscing about all the adventures the Lord had taken us through. I always knew that life with George was not ordinary. Even though many times I would have settled for the ordinary, especially during those moments I couldn't imagine life getting any stranger, I always came back with the realization that our life together had taught me over and over that there truly is a God out there who is real and alive. We weren't just playing a religious game. He's the only God who's personal, powerful, in control, and above all, the God who loves us more than we can even fathom.

This was a time of reflection for me. It was hard to believe that life with my husband was all coming to an end. My partner, my buddy, my best friend... I could never have imagined that to part this way would be the last chapter of the script for our lives. God had taken us through so many years and struggles together to teach and equip us for the work of the ministry. Why would He now allow something like this to creep into our lives? None of this was making sense. Or was it?

Let me tell you what the Lord took us through. Well... Maybe I should start from the beginning...

Jesus answered and said to him,
"Most assuredly, I say to you,
unless one is born again,
he cannot see the kingdom of God."

John 3:3

I have come that they may have life,
and that they may have it more abundantly.

John 10:10b

1
The Road to Salvation

No matter how hard we try to plan our lives, they never seem to go that way. If someone had told me I was going to be a missionary when I grew up and live a life contrary to the American dream, I would have laughed.

Even though I was raised in a religious home and attended a private Catholic school for part of my life, it was far from my nature to be interested in becoming a missionary. By the time high school came around, I was having the time of my life, doing what pleased me, partying with friends regularly, just getting by with my grades, and putting my dad and mom through a lot of turmoil during this rebellious time. In my junior year of high school, feelings and desires to pursue change and experience life beyond what St. Paul, Minnesota had to offer drove me to want to see the world and meet new people. I knew that coming up with a plan to present to my parents was in order. For one thing, there was no way that they would allow me to travel without first graduating from high school. I was determined to work very hard during regular school hours to get good grades, while simultaneously attending night school five nights a week to earn credits needed for my senior year. By thereby speeding up the process, I would be able to graduate a year early and get on with life. I imagine my dad and mom were so happy to hear my enthusiasm to push myself to get good grades and finish high school that they were willing to go along with my plan. Looking back, I still don't know how I actually pulled it off. Maybe my determination to leave Minnesota and travel to other parts of the country where I had never been gave me the push I needed.

After graduating in 1975, a good friend and I left Minnesota to begin our journeys. Before leaving we decided it would be a good idea to fix on a final destination point after all of our traveling. My friend wanted to settle in Phoenix, Arizona, and my desire was to settle in Denver, Colorado. We flipped a coin to decide: heads said we end up in Arizona, tails said we go to Colorado. Heads it was! Imagine choosing your destination by the flip of a coin! So we were off and running, and before long found ourselves in Phoenix.

I remember my excitement at renting my first home and purchasing what every teenager buys to furnish that first home — a new stereo and speakers. Within one month the reality of life was setting in. With no job and very little money, rent due, and groceries to be bought, life on my own was not at all like I had imagined it would be. Being broke and eating white rice every day, while diligently searching for a job with no offers forthcoming, was not my definition of fun. But my pride had kicked in. To call my parents and ask them to bail me out was not an option in my book. It was important to prove to them that I was responsible and mature enough to live on my own. To this day, they probably don't know that I went hungry for an entire month before finally getting a job. Calling them on the phone periodically (collect, of course) and telling them how wonderful life was treating me and what a great time I was having, wasn't exactly the truth.

My life continued with the party scene. I worked and played. After almost a year of doing the same things that I had done back home, I became bored with my surroundings and wanted to move on. My friend Jess had decided to attend college at Northern Arizona University in Flagstaff and asked if I wanted to move there too. I agreed. Actually, neither of us could afford to travel much farther than one hundred and fifty miles away anyway. So, off we went to the little college town that it was, back then.

Coming from the Twin Cities and then living in Phoenix made Flagstaff look like a tiny hick town to me. My thought the first day we arrived in Flagstaff was that boredom would set in quickly. My premonition came true. After working and partying most of the time, my hopes that there was more to life than what I was presently experiencing were growing dim. Maybe going to college would be the answer. I soon found myself enrolled at Northern Arizona University, and my life started to take on some purpose for a while. But again, life took another turn.

One night after drinking and partying, I got into the passenger seat with a drunk driver. The next thing I knew I was being pulled out of the car by paramedics and hauled off on a gurney to Flagstaff hospital. It wasn't until the next day that I was told that the driver of the vehicle had hit the curb and over-steered, resulting in the car flipping over three times. (To this day there isn't any recollection of this accident in my memory bank. In the aftermath of this accident, though, panic still comes over me when I'm in a car and the driver gets close to a curb.) The diagnosis was two cracked vertebra in my upper back; I was also left with a severe cut on my head that was filled with glass. The pain in my ribs was intense. It took several months before I felt good again. Needless to say, school attendance ranked low in priority, forcing me to make up credits through activities my professors had assigned for me.

The following semester the school made a mistake on the grant previously given to me, which meant having to come up with the tuition on my own to continue. Not at all sold on college at the time anyway, it seemed like a good idea to me to quit and go find full-time work. Working brought in more money than I had ever made, and before long I was enjoying myself by buying all the goodies life had to offer. Purchases of clothing, jewelry, frequent flights back home, eating out at some of the finest restaurants, relishing and indulging in it all, seemed to be the answer.

As time went on, though, that became old too. Once again life was boring. It seemed that everywhere I went and everything I did left me feeling empty inside. Turning to yoga looked like an interesting path to travel; that only left me feeling self-righteous. The thought that maybe the drinking and drugs might have altered my thinking entered my mind. When I made the decision to give up those things, my perception became a lot clearer. I began to eat a healthy diet and exercise, which was beneficial and kept me interested and busy for a while, but after a while that became monotonous too. Nothing was bringing satisfaction. My aim became to search persistently for something that would fulfill me. Hopefully there was something out there that would satisfy my appetite.

Someone had given me a Bible on my journey. Maybe the Bible might give me the answers I was looking for. Not understanding most of what I read, my goal was to continue to read it anyway, just to be able to say that I had read it. It seemed appropriate to start attending a local church during this time also. Between Bible reading and going to church, my party lifestyle was eliminated altogether. I was now feeling pretty religious, and yet still not able to escape that nagging, empty feeling inside.

During one of my many trips back home to Minnesota, my sister Connie invited me to her church potluck. What I really wanted to do on this gorgeous summer day was to go water skiing with my friends, but Connie was quite persistent about my attending. She talked me into it. Reluctantly I went, with a bad attitude.

When we arrived, the "critique" mode set in. I found myself internally criticizing almost everyone there. Each person had at least one wrong thing about them. It was when the pastor asked everyone to go outside to sing hymns that I was convinced I was surrounded by a group of nerds. It was a dumbfounding thought to believe that Connie was able to talk me into being involved in such an event as this. When we all gathered together in the back yard, however, observation told me that these people were actually happy at what they were doing. I didn't get it. How could this scenario make a group of people so excited? What did they have or know that I didn't have? It was a sobering thought.

This was a subject that needed addressing, because I earnestly wanted to obtain happiness and fulfillment in life. I prayed, "God, I must be missing the mark somewhere, because personally what these people call fun seems totally ridiculous to me." Pausing, my prayer took on a more personal tone. "Lord, as much as I have been searching for truth and direction for my life, it's nowhere to be found. My lifestyle of partying doesn't exist any longer, you've seen my faithfulness in church attendance lately, and the Bible is being read. Hopefully you've noticed the ten percent tithing of my earnings too, not to mention being baptized twice; once as a baby and now as an adult." Laying out all my good works and credentials to the Lord one by one, it suddenly dawned on me that none of this mattered to God. A very vulnerable feeling came over me; talking to the Creator of the Universe was no light matter. Deep down inside, I felt the reality of God being present. I knew somehow He was really there, meeting me right where I was at. It was such a surreal moment. For the first time in my life, my talk with the Lord was very profound. It wasn't just a nice religious talk we were having. This was genuine heart-to-heart talk. I continued with my prayer. "Lord, this religious game can't go on any longer. There isn't any strength left in me to try and do this on my own. If You're as real and powerful as the Bible claims You are, then please come into my life and change me. Make something of my life and become personal to me; going through the motions of religion to be religious isn't working. Our relationship needs to be a reality! Trying to live righteously on my own isn't working either." I ended my prayer, saying once more, emphatically, "So if You are really real and can change my heart, then I'm all yours!"

The next moment was one of the most awesome spiritual experiences I had ever encountered. God's presence literally came over me after that prayer. Gazing around the back yard, it suddenly looked very different. The detailed colors emblazoned in the flowers, how beautifully they were arrayed in the flower beds, everything was so pronounced. Glancing up to the sky, I noticed the magnificent hues of blue. There was so much joy in my heart. Something extraordinary had happened to me. In my joy, I thought of jumping up on the picnic table where we were sitting and yelling at the top of my lungs, "Praise God! He's really real!" I managed to control the urge, but it took everything in me not to do it. Still I knew that day my life would never be the same. How could it be, now that the Holy Spirit had entered my life? (John 14:17). This was just the beginning of what God had in store for me.

*

The road that George took was much different than mine. Even though we had some things in common, such as our middle class families and Midwest backgrounds, our lifestyles as adults were one hundred and eighty degrees apart.

George grew up in Aurora, a suburb outside Chicago, Illinois. He joined the Navy after graduating from high school, serving four years, with one tour of duty in Vietnam. Returning home after serving his time, he became a mechanic by trade. Getting involved in the drug and alcohol scene for a time ultimately led him down the path to becoming a bona fide hippie. He traveled around, getting odd jobs here and there, until he eventually stumbled upon a hippie commune outside of Albuquerque, New Mexico. His comfort with the laidback lifestyle of living off the land soon provoked him to give up his vehicle, buy himself a horse, and just hang out. He even started making his own beer. His friends soon nicknamed him "Wild Man George."

Then, like me, after so many years of empty living, he decided to leave the commune and search for meaning to his life. He sold his horse and began to hitchhike west, ending up at a rescue mission in Nevada. For those of you who have never been to a "rescue mission" in the United States, it's a safe haven for the homeless. Ministers share the gospel message of salvation to those that come, prior to feeding them a meal and giving them a hot shower and a safe place to sleep for the night. Many of the people that enter through the doors of a mission have been out on the road wandering around, looking for purpose. Some come from broken homes and have never experienced a normal lifestyle.

One particular evening George found himself at one of the services. As the preacher was giving an altar call, asking those who wanted to surrender their lives to the Lord to raise their hand, George was experiencing an internal battle in his mind. Trying to convince himself that he needed to clean his act up first and then approach God with a clean heart, he emotionally locked up. He decided, "I will not raise my hand. I'd be a hypocrite to do so." But up went his hand, in spite of his struggle. Again, the pastor requested those who raised their hand to come forward, because he wanted to pray for them. George's prideful thoughts told him, "No way am I going to walk forward in front of all my peers and make a confession of faith." Before he could ponder the thought any longer, he found himself going forward and surrendering his life to the Lord in front of a room full of people.

The following morning, George headed back on the highway, once more hitchhiking to numerous places. During his travels he sometimes went through trials of rejection and struggles with his old lifestyle, still trying to find direction for his new life. His journey eventually led him to a mission in Flagstaff, Arizona, where for the next three years he worked and ministered to the street people who found shelter there. During this time, he had a vision to purchase a school bus and drive the highways to minister to hitchhikers. He soon found a bus and converted it into a motor home. Periodically he left the mission to pick up hitchhikers and share with them the love of God, while helping them in their time of need.

And then we met.

And the Lord God said,
"It is not good that man should be alone;
I will make him a helper comparable
to him."

Genesis 2:18

2
Meeting George

It was 1980. My friend Mabel had been given several tickets to the annual rescue mission banquet held every September for the community of supporters. Even though there wasn't much interest on my part to attend, with much persuasion I was talked into going. "Only if my friend Lynn can come," was my ultimatum. With that, we all went, not knowing what to expect since this was our first experience with rescue missions. Little did I know, my future husband would be at this event.

I remember the night so vividly. We hadn't been there for more than fifteen minutes when, from across the room, I saw him. His back was towards us. We were all seated at a large round table, talking and taking in the sounds of music and laughter.

Musing at the sight of him, I slowly leaned over to Lynn and quietly said, "Hey, Lynn, look at that man over there."

"What man?" she asked curiously. As I was trying to give her instructions on where to look, she spotted him. Her next obvious question was, "What about him?"

"Well, if he looks that good from behind, think of what he might look like from the front," I said, very intrigued. Lynn looked at me, a bit surprised. Just then, he turned around. Immediately, my heart began to pound. Some might say it was love at first sight. From a more mature standpoint, I would say it was probably infatuation at first sight. Nevertheless, I couldn't take my eyes off him. To top it off, we soon found out, as he was approaching the stage, that he was one of the speakers for the evening program. Talk about captivating! Not only was he gorgeous, now I would have a chance to get a glimpse of his character. As he spoke, I was mesmerized by every word that came out of his mouth. What especially impressed me, as he shared with the audience his stories of picking up hitchhikers, was how God would provide for his needs as he labored in the Lord by faith. All I could think of during his presentation was, "I've got to meet this man!"

When the banquet was beginning to wind down, I felt compelled to make my way over to George. What to say didn't even cross my mind. That was the least of my concerns. Approaching him was another thing.

Now standing in front of him, unexpectedly my jaw locked up. Totally speechless, a condition that is quite foreign to me, my heart began to palpitate. It was so awkward. Now was the time to say something, anything.

"Hi." My voice crackled, as I stared blankly at him.

He answered back. "Hi." It would have been to my benefit at this point if George had said something more. He didn't. In the uncomfortable silence that followed, we just stared at each other. One of us needed to say something before this moment got any more embarrassing.

"Your presentation was great tonight," was all I could come up with.

"Thank you," was his short reply.

My mind went blank. There weren't any other words to say. "Thank you," I repeated back. It seemed fitting at this moment to turn around and walk away.

I couldn't believe I had just done that, but wanting to kick myself for locking up wasn't going to help. Returning to the table where Lynn was still sitting, I told her what had happened. She thought it was funny. It wasn't a bit humorous to me. I could only hope it didn't leave George feeling as embarrassed as it did me.

The next few weeks after the banquet, I kept thinking and daydreaming about him. The funny thing was that I forgot his name. Trying to remember, all that came to mind was the name "Greg". Lynn couldn't remember his name either, so between the two of us when we talked about him, we referred to him as "Greg". I had a major crush on him, but I kept it to myself. Lynn was the only friend that knew anything about my secret infatuation.

A month and a half since my encounter with George, my thoughts and dreams about him were still active. Mabel, the friend who had invited me to the banquet in the first place, had been hospitalized, and one evening I went up to visit her. As we were chatting about all sorts of topics, her husband broke into our conversation. "Jennifer, do you remember that one speaker the night of the banquet?" he said nonchalantly.

That seemingly random question really got my attention. My ears were perked up. I wanted to make sure that the secret of my heart wasn't revealed to them, so responding with a bewildered expression, I asked, "Which one? There were several speakers."

He said, "The one with the school bus ministry."

I acted dumb for the moment, and then answered slowly, "Oh, yeah... I do remember him. Well, what about him?"

He began to tell me a story about how this person had walked away from the Lord, had started drinking and now was in a drug rehabilitation center trying to straighten his life up. I didn't buy it for one moment, and expressed my thoughts strongly to them, insisting it had to be just gossip. They could see that this tidbit of information disturbed me greatly.

Mabel's husband asserted, "Well, you better believe it because this data came from a good source."

My heart sank. How could this be? He seemed to be so in love with Jesus, and consequently sincere. His testimonies were powerful and his character seemed incredibly strong. I had a hard time believing that he'd throw away all that he had gained for the false pleasure of alcohol.

After the hospital visit, I went home feeling completely burdened. That conversation about George would not leave my mind. I still wasn't convinced it was true. Even though Mabel's husband said he heard the news from a good source, I was persuaded in my heart that it was just a false rumor.

The following day, I felt I had to find out if this story was in fact true. The rescue mission would be the source to go to. There was one slight problem. Not remembering George's name, and almost positive that his name wasn't "Greg", was a dilemma. "I know," my thoughts schemed again, "Mabel probably remembers his name. (She was released from the hospital early that morning.) If she doesn't, then maybe she has the brochure from the banquet. His name would surely be in it." I quickly called her.

I could tell by her voice on the phone that she was very tired. She didn't remember his name either. When I questioned her about the brochure, she wanted to know why I was pursuing this information. I told her that I felt so strongly that the rumor about George was untrue, that I was going to get to the bottom of it by calling the mission.

She snapped, "Well, I'm too tired to get up and get it."

Maybe it was her abruptness or the resistance in her tone that angered me. Pausing, not sure what to do or say next, and yet still angry, I finally replied, "Fine, I'll find his name out on my own," and we said our good-byes.

Now I had to come up with another plan. "I guess I'll just have to call the mission and find out his name on my own." So I did. It didn't occur to me that George himself might pick up the phone.

"Hello!"

"Hi, I'm trying to find out some information about one of your employees," I said in a businesslike manner. "Unfortunately, I don't know his name. He was one of your speakers at your banquet recently."

"Well, we had two male speakers."

"He was the one who had a bus ministry and picked up hitchhikers," I said.

"Oh," he paused. "Was he the really good-looking one?"

Without thinking, I replied, "Yes, that's the one."

"Oh, him!" he answered, "Well, that's me! I'm George."

Suddenly, the conversation felt a bit overwhelming. "Oh my goodness, what do I say?" I thought.

Into my confusion over what to do next, George broke into my thoughts. "Who is this?"

Trying to compose myself, I said, "My name is Jennifer. I had heard a crazy rumor about you, and wanted to know if it was true." Proceeding to tell him the story, I finished by saying, "I didn't believe it was true, so I called to find out."

George told me to my relief that another man had come to the mission recently who was struggling with drugs and alcohol. The mission encouraged this man to go to the rehabilitation center. It was just a mix-up in identity. How comforting to hear that it wasn't George after all, and now I finally knew his real name.

Then an uneasy quietness crept in over the phone. How should I proceed? As nervousness set in, once again I could feel myself locking up. I quickly said a few words, and then ended the conversation with a friendly good-bye. I hung up and took a deep breath. After regaining my senses, I was upset to find myself in this state again. Why hadn't I stayed on the line and gotten to know him a little better? There was nothing that could be done about it now, and surely my chances were blown. Calling him back was not an option. He would think I was neurotic. I just had to let it go.

A week went by. Lynn invited me to her church several times in the past, so this particular Sunday I decided to take her up on the invitation. Sitting in the pew together, chatting before the worship service began, Lynn leaned over to me and very quietly said, "Don't turn around, but in a little while look to see who's sitting behind us." Trying to be patient and follow her instructions, I finally did just that. Quickly, I turned back around. It was George! My heart started to pulsate. My mind was racing and at the same time I was thinking, "I have another chance! This time don't you dare blow it!"

Of course, trying to apply my heart to the message being shared that morning was nearly impossible because my heart was somewhere else. When the church service was over, I noticed George was at the back of the church as one of the greeters, shaking hands with those leaving. "Here's my chance," I thought, and gracefully moved in the line that was formed to shake his hand.

Approaching him, I said in a sweet tone of voice, "Hi, how are you?" He looked at me and delayed answering back, which immediately made my mood a bit tense.

He finally responded, "What?" I repeated myself. He just stared at me, and then turned all red with embarrassment. "I'm fine."

We both just stared at each other. Our gaze seemed like eternity. It was now past time to move on. There were others behind me trying to leave. That was it! I wanted to scream inside with frustration. "Lord, why is it so hard to meet him? I become dysfunctional every time he gets near me." I left, once more disappointed.

That didn't keep me from thinking about George, though. Throughout the next few weeks, I started to accept the fact that my chances of connecting with him and having a normal conversation were slim.

One day while working at the mall in a clothing store, I noticed that the manager was feeling a bit depressed. During my lunch break, I walked down to the card store to purchase a greeting card to cheer her up. While browsing through the cards, one jumped out at me. Pictured on the front of the card was a cat sitting on a bench, holding a bunch of balloons, with the message, "Today I was thinking of you..." Inside the card was a picture of a cat ascending in the air. It read, "...And I got carried away". It reminded me of my feelings toward George every time I saw him, so I bought it.

That evening I showed the card to Lynn. She agreed it was very cute. Jokingly, I wrote inside of the card, "Your anonymous phone caller," and then signed it, along with my phone number. We both had a good laugh.

Jesting back and forth about this whole thing, Lynn piped up. "Jennifer! You should actually mail that card to him."

"Oh, yeah, right. I already wrote in it," I responded.

She continued. "That's what I mean. I think you should send the card just like that. This is an excellent way to meet him."

"Lynn, don't be ridiculous, that is way too forward."

We went back and forth over this card business until finally she said, "Well, I believe it's the Lord's will that you and George meet, and this is the way for you to do it."

I tried to end the conversation. "Lynn, I will not put that card in the mailbox, and that's final."

She was so persistent that this was the Lord's will that it was beginning to annoy me. Thinking she would drop it if I attached some guilt and responsibility on her part, I added, "If you think it's God's will that this card is supposed to be mailed, then you pray about it and do what God tells you to do."

She agreed. She would pray about it. The discussion was over. We both went to bed.

The following evening, upon returning home from work, Lynn informed me that she was obedient to my instructions and prayed about the card. Not again, I thought. "Do we have to deal with this subject again?"

"Well," she continued, "I felt after praying that God was telling me to put it in the mailbox, so I went with my heart and did it."

I couldn't believe she really did it! "Lynn, tell me that you're joking. You really didn't do that, right?"

Coming to realize there was no joking about it, and that she really mailed it, I was not a happy camper. I started to cry. This whole thing was so embarrassing. How would I ever face him, or even talk to him for that matter, if he decided to call me? Then, contrarily, my next thought was, "What if he doesn't call me now? I'll feel so rejected." Either way was a trap for me. With all these thoughts rapidly racing through my head, there was only one possible solution. It was time to move back to Minnesota. Lynn tried to calm me down, which she did, but it still didn't change my mind. I was going back home to Minnesota. Besides, this was a good time to see my family again anyway, which gave me an excuse to go home.

Two days later as I was busy at work, Lynn called to let me know that George had responded to the card. He had called to find out who this "Jennifer" was. She admitted to him that she was behind mailing the card and explained everything. He wanted to talk with me, so she called to tell me he would be calling back that evening at six o'clock. When I got off the phone with Lynn, I was hugely excited and at the same time incredibly nervous. Getting so worked up inside thinking about it, several times during the day I found myself in the bathroom sick to my stomach.

Six o'clock in the evening finally arrived. Lynn and I were both sitting in the living room. The phone rang promptly. "Oh, Lord, help me," I was praying as Lynn picked up the phone.

"It's for you!" she said with this huge grin on her face.

I whispered to her, "Please leave while I talk to him alone." I grabbed the phone and took a deep breath. My heart felt like it was going to come right out of my chest from pounding so hard. I said in a jittery voice, "Hi."

George responded in a light, joking manner. "Hi. This is George, George of the Jungle." What an ice breaker! We both laughed. That response calmed my nerves incredibly. He jumped in the conversation again. "I remember your phone call recently about the rumor you had heard, and then I received this card from you, and now you've got my curiosity going. Who are you?"

It was the intervention of the Lord. I finally felt at ease with George. Deciding to start at the beginning, from the night I met him at the rescue mission banquet, and ending with Lynn putting the card in the mailbox, I laid it all out. Thank God, he overlooked my forwardness.

Then he asked me the question I had been dreaming of for months. "Would you like to go out with me this coming Thursday night? My church has a home fellowship that meets every week. It would be great if you joined me."

I was ecstatic! Being aware that we really didn't know each other at all, I thought it would be more comfortable if we shared a meal together before going to the fellowship. I eagerly said, "Yes, I would love to go to your fellowship with you. But, before we go, would you like to come over for dinner so we can get to know each other a little bit better?" He liked that idea too. So it was set. He would come to my house at six o'clock the next Thursday evening.

It was hard to believe I actually had a date with the man of my dreams! All because Lynn's prayers led her to do something that was, days earlier, one of the craziest things I could have imagined. It really blessed me that she cared so much to go out on a limb for me even though I had strongly opposed her opinion or tactic. Lynn was happy for me too, especially because I had changed my mind about moving back to Minnesota. All week long leading up to our date she

kept posting silly little handmade signs around our apartment; one read, "Guess who's coming to dinner?"

George showed up right on time. Our meal was a bit
awkward like all first dates can be. Neither of us ate much.
Afterwards we headed over to the fellowship at the pastor's
house. During the whole evening everyone in the group
kept staring at me. Naturally nervous at my first date with
George, now intimidation was also starting to set in with this
group of people. Later, George told me they were all staring
at me because the group had been praying God would bring
a wife into his life to help him in the ministry. They were all
wondering if I was the one they had been praying for.

From that night on, we continued to see each other almost
every day. My infatuation was turning into love, along with
a growing interest in the work he was doing at the rescue
mission. I was working at the mall in a clothing store full-
time as an assistant manager, and doing modeling on the
side. Yet, each day my desire to go to the rescue mission to
help George minister to the poor and needy became much
more interesting and intriguing.

I was just thankful he spent the time with me that he did,
knowing that the mission took up a lot of his time. There
were many nights he would get phone calls from those
whose vehicles broke down, stranding them on the highway.
He would gather his tools, and using his mechanical abilities, go out and fix their vehicles while he shared the love of
Jesus with them. There were many different aspects to the
ministry that I grew to love. I couldn't wait to finish work so
that I could go down to the mission and be part of it.

Within a short period of time, my heart's desire was to
spend the rest of my life with George. Had he felt the same
about me? Time would tell. Not willing to reveal my heart
to him, especially since I felt our relationship had begun
on a note of forwardness on my part, I felt waiting for him
seemed more proper.

We would take long walks alone in the evenings around the neighborhood and share our thoughts about many things. I could tell George wanted to open up to me on issues of love, yet he went around the subject every time it came up. Then one night on one of our evening strolls, out of the blue he began to expose his feelings of love toward me. At the time we happened to be on the side of the rescue mission building. He sat me down on the steps, told me how much he loved me and proposed to me right there and then. I had just been waiting for him to open up to me about how he truly felt about me, but perhaps not expecting a proposal from him so quickly. It came as a surprise, actually catching me off guard. Although spending the rest of my life with him was on my mind, was I really ready for this right now? Suddenly uncertainty swept over me. In my confusion, giving him an answer right then was difficult. But now it was my turn to express my feelings to him. I shared my concern about really knowing whether or not it was the Lord's will for us to be married.

This was the first time I ever "laid a fleece" out to the Lord, a way of seeking to discern the Lord's will (Judges 6:36-40). Not yet completely sure deep inside if it was the will of God for the two of us to be together, I told George it was important for me to talk to my dad about our relationship. If he was positive about the relationship between the two of us after we had a chance to talk, I would marry him. If he was negative about it, I would wait. I asked the Lord to work through my dad to give me the answer I was looking for. This may not sound like a tremendous fleece for those of you who don't know my dad, but for him to be positive about this relationship would take the hand of God. First of all, my dad is one hundred percent Catholic. Catholic fathers want their daughters to marry a Catholic man. Secondly, my father always preferred the clean-cut looking men for his daughters. He never went for the hippie, bearded type, like George was at that time. The biggest issue would be telling him that George was a missionary, living on faith for support. He would never understand how George would be able to support his daughter and grandchildren with this kind of lifestyle. God would definitely have to intervene and perform a miracle. I knew if my father gave us his blessings and consented to this relationship, God was in it.

It was Christmas Eve. George was waiting at the mission while I went home to talk with my dad alone on the phone. After the phone call, the plan was to come back and give George my answer.

It's kind of comical, looking back at the dialogue my dad and I had together that evening. Thank God, it started out well. He was in a very good mood. Then the moment came to tell him about the man whom I had met and fallen in love with.

One of the first questions he asked me was, "Does he have a beard?"

This caught me a little off guard. "Why does that matter?"

He chuckled, and then changed the subject. After talking for a while, we came back to our original conversation.

"Dad, I'm thinking about spending the rest of my life with him."

"So what does he do for a living?"

"Well," taking a deep breath, "He's a Christian missionary who works at a rescue mission. Besides working at the mission, several times a year he goes out in a school bus, picks up hitchhikers, and shares the gospel message of salvation with them."

"So, how does he get money?" was the next logical question.

"He trusts in God for his provision. What's amazing, Dad, is that the Lord enables him to do this by providing in incredible ways. Some things he has shared with me are miraculous. This has been going on for three years."

He then observed, "You like to spend money; how is that going to work for you?"

Looking back now at the question my father asked twenty-seven years ago makes me understand how much wisdom he had in seeing future complications in our marriage. Through the eyes of a young twenty-two year old, life looked quite different than it did to one with years and experience behind him.

My answer was, "Oh, Dad, money doesn't matter when you've found true love. Our love will see us through."

He changed the subject once more. After some more small talk, the time came for him to give me his advice or opinion about this marriage. We had been on the phone much too long. It was the question that would determine my future.

"George has asked me to marry him. What do you think?"

This was a moment to trust God. No matter what my father said, my faith told me God would speak through him. I must admit, feelings of nervousness had enveloped me.

In a very loving but concerned voice my dad replied, "If you really love him and feel like he's the one for you, then go with your heart."

Unbelievable as it was, he actually said the words I'd prayed he would. This was exhilarating! Over and over the words kept running through my mind, "Wow, my father actually gave me his approval. Thank You, God!"

Driving to the mission, trying to contain my excitement, I could hardly wait to give George the good news.

George was standing there looking at me as I came through the back door. Stopping right in front of him, we found ourselves looking at each other eye to eye, very soberly. From the look on my face, I could see he concluded that the answer was no, as I watched his smile turn into a frown.

Into this tension-filled moment, I said, "My dad said..." and then I paused for a second, "Yes! I will marry you!" As I jumped into his arms with great joy, he twirled me around.

*

Preparing for a wedding can be quite stressful with all the planning that goes into it, yet for me, during this time the emphasis on spiritual issues had more weight. One day during our engagement, George made a remark about the amount of money I spent on my wardrobe. Working at a clothing store at the time and receiving a good employee's discount, I begged to differ. He even went as far as suggesting that by browsing through the clothing room at the mission, there might be a chance of getting my clothes for free. Besides, soon we would both be missionaries living by faith. Talk about appalling! I couldn't believe he would suggest such a thing. We're talking used clothing here, and in my mind that meant stained and outdated. He just did not understand. Working at a mall, one needs to dress in modern, up-to-date apparel. This debate was one of the first of many we would have together. I made it very clear that his suggestion of my wearing used clothing wasn't going to happen.

Several weeks went by after this discussion. One day George and I were visiting with Ginny, the wife of the superintendent of the mission, at her home. Their house was attached to the mission building, which gave them easy access to the people they ministered to as well as the convenience of being on the grounds for situations that would arise. As we were visiting, there was a knock at the door. Ginny answered it. Standing there was a well-dressed woman with several bags by her feet. Peering out the window, we noticed a very expensive car parked in the driveway.

"May I help you?" Ginny inquired.

"I hope so," responded the woman. "I've brought some clothes I would like to donate." She had one request, however, that the clothes to be given first to the staff. "Hopefully they will fit someone who works here. If there isn't anyone working here that can wear them, then you can donate them to whomever."

As Ginny expressed her gratitude, George and I got up to help carry the several large bags inside. After the woman departed, the three of us emptied them and started going through the contents. To my surprise, much of the clothing bore designer labels; some of it was new with the price tags still attached to the garments. I was awestruck, and then I noticed that these items were not only my colors, but they were all my size! As it turned out, no one else that worked at the mission wore my size, so I was blessed with them all. It was unbelievable! Just three weeks earlier, in my arrogance I had been stamping my feet at the thought of wearing donated rescue mission clothing, and now I found myself thanking God for the generous gift of clothing I could hardly have afforded on my own. George was just beaming with joy as he watched me all the while.

My pride in this area started to crumble (of course there would be much more to be dealt with later in other areas) and soon I was making my way into the clothing room periodically to see what was in there. After we were married, that's where most of my "shopping" took place.

*

Besides dealing with some of our differences in the way we saw life during our preparation time for marriage, the Lord gave me opportunity to also get a taste of the ministry at the mission.

The cook who regularly worked there had not had a vacation for a while. She wanted to go back to the Navajo reservation to spend some time with her family. I gladly volunteered to take her place for one month. Also, the offer to live in her room at the mission while she was gone would allow me to minister to the women in the evenings by getting them ready for bed, and early in the mornings getting them up. I was thrilled at the opportunity to dive into the work and be a part of the staff. After my first night on the job, however, I wasn't sure what I had gotten myself into.

In came Marilyn. She was filthy. There was no other word for it. You could see the line of dirt from the neckline of her shirt. Without exaggeration, it looked as if she hadn't bathed in six months. She kept looking around the room with shifting, fearful eyes. She appeared completely lost. I felt so sorry for her, especially at the thought of her living on the road all by herself. Trying to strike up a conversation with her was nearly impossible. She kept completely to herself.

The mission was full of people that evening, but Marilyn happened to be the only woman that came in that night. When everyone had their fill of food, I took her up to the women's dorm and showed her the routine: the shower room, the clothes basket to put her clothes in, and clean pajamas to put on. Her clothes were so filthy that I suggested she get something clean to wear for the morning. While she showered, I went down to find some clothing for her. As I searched downstairs for the right outfit for her, suddenly from upstairs came a horrifying shrieking noise that ran right up my spine. The screaming was coming from the women's dorm. Bolting out of the room, I ran upstairs and whipped open the door. Marilyn was standing there all alone, wrapped in her towel, next to the shower where I left her.

"Are you all right?" I said worriedly.

"Yes, why wouldn't I be?" she replied.

"Well, I heard you screaming and thought something was wrong."

"I wasn't screaming," she insisted, all the while staring at me with an odd expression on her face.

I turned around and began to walk out of the room, realizing that I wasn't dealing with a normal person. I shut the door behind me and stood outside the door listening. Within a couple of minutes, she started up again.

This time, two voices were coming from the room: her normal voice, and then the voice of a man. "I'm going to kill you!" shouted the man's voice. In Marilyn's voice she was screaming and pleading for her life.

I was not prepared for this, nor was I about to go back into that room by myself. This was a time to find Ginny. When I located her, I explained everything that was going on. We decided the two of us would deal with this together. We walked upstairs, opened the door, only to find Marilyn still standing by the shower, wrapped in her towel, by herself.

"What's going on, Marilyn?" Ginny asked in a compassionate tone.

Again, she denied that anything was wrong. Just then, she turned and looked at me with a glare in her eyes that looked like the devil himself. Every hair on my body stood up at that moment. Trying to hide our nervousness, we reminded Marilyn that she needed to take a shower before retiring for the night. She informed us that she wouldn't be taking a shower.

"If you don't take a shower, you won't be able to stay here tonight," Ginny explained.

"Well, I'm not leaving, and I'm not taking a shower either!" she said abruptly. Her demonic expression continued to surface as we talked back and forth with her. At last, when it was clear that she was not going to follow the rules, Ginny calmly said, "Look, Marilyn, if you won't cooperate with us, I'll have to ask you to leave."

Marilyn continued to resist us. "Then I'll have to call the police if you won't leave peaceably," Ginny told her.

"Call the police then, because I already told you that I'm not leaving!" she said, her anger escalating.

Ginny and I looked at each other, deciding it was time to leave the room. As soon as we left, Marilyn again began to scream in different voices. The shouting continued until the police arrived within ten minutes. Of course as soon as they entered the building the screaming stopped. We explained what had been going on. They went upstairs, only to find a quiet, innocent, poor-looking woman, standing there all by herself, fully clothed. In a sweet, gentle voice she told them that she didn't understand why we would be asking her to leave. She claimed that everything we had said about her was a lie. I believe she had the officers almost convinced, just by the way they were looking at us. Once more, as they were talking with us, Marilyn turned to look at me with that piercing evil stare. I was so glad that others were in the room because there was fire dancing in her eyes. Finally the policemen escorted her out of the mission and drove away. As soon as they left, she again began to scream outside the mission. "At least she's on the other side of this door tonight," I thought.

And this was my first night on the job. Could I make it here for a whole month?

*

If ever I have met a man full of the love of God, and who had an ample amount of wisdom, it was Harry. Harry was the former superintendent of the rescue mission. Now elderly, he lived at a Christian compound located in the area. What amazed me about him was how much scripture he knew and how many people he actually brought into the kingdom of God by sharing the gospel. He had played a big part in George's life too. He helped George to understand the Bible and the basic principles of Christianity when George first surrendered his life to the Lord. Needless to say, George felt deep respect for him.

One day while I was hanging out in the kitchen of the mission, Harry slowly walked up to me, stopped, and gave me a deep penetrating stare. Then he spoke these words to me, face to face: "Jennifer, when you marry George, your life will never be the same. You are going to live a very adventurous life."

At the time, I remember thinking what a sweet, kind, and humorous thing that was for him to say to me. Now, looking back, I realize that Harry had a good deal of insight into our future. He was actually prophesying over me. The truth of those words is still being played out in my life. I have never forgotten them.

Within six months of courtship, George and I were married. That's when the adventures of living a supernatural life in faith really began.

But without faith it is impossible
to please Him,
for he who comes to God must believe
that He is,
and that He is a rewarder of those
who diligently seek Him.

Hebrews 11:6

3
The Tale of the Toilet Tissue

After George and I were married, we decided to move to Albuquerque, New Mexico. We felt that leaving everything that was familiar for one year would allow us to spend time getting to know each other better; after all, we had met and were married within a six month period! It seemed like the logical thing to do, particularly since the rescue mission consumed most of our time with the needs of others and left us very little time for ourselves.

Returning from our honeymoon, our plans were to gut out the school bus and rebuild it into a nice motor home for our trip to New Mexico. Remembering the day George started the work project is quite amusing to me now. He asked me to go away for the day so he could get as much done as possible. Imagining what our new motor home would look like filled me with blissful anticipation as I went out with one of my friends. That evening when I came home, I was so excited to see the work George had done. I hoped that he had turned the bus into a beautiful motor home with oak cabinets, nicely tiled countertops, a microwave: you know, the kind you see at the RV lots. I did realize that he wouldn't be able to complete our home in one day, that it would have to be done in phases, but as it turned out, George's idea of a comfortable motor home was quite different than mine. That evening, he was so happy to show me what he had done.

He said, "Close your eyes, and when I tell you to open them, then open them!" He led me into the bus with great enthusiasm. "All right, open your eyes!"

Opening my eyes, what was before me was a total shock. He had used four two-by-fours to construct the sink legs, cut a hole on the top of a piece of plywood and laid in a stainless steel sink. He had it plumbed, and it was all exposed. In the bedroom, a bed was constructed of a piece of plywood over four two-by-fours, with a mattress placed on top of the wood. Rustic would be a kind word for it. I stood there frozen in my shoes, not knowing how to respond. George was so proud of what he had accomplished. The moment was becoming overwhelming.

"Well, do you like it?" he finally asked.

I did what any woman would do. I started to cry.

"I take it you don't like it," was his response. Not a single word came to my mind. "Well, honey, this is just to get us started. You'll see, as time goes on, we'll make it just like you want it."

He was so sweet and gentle about it. Then when he hugged me, I was ashamed of my reaction. Listening to his reassuring words, I knew he was right. In time, we could make it look like the dream house I imagined.

Several days later we packed up our new wedding gifts and were on the highway, heading east with sixty dollars in our pocket. We were both very happy newlyweds, ready to start our lives together. In my realm of thinking, I was riding off on our white horse, with my Prince Charming, to live happily ever after. I've heard that they call that "The Cinderella Syndrome." That's exactly where I was at.

Our first few days together were really fun. We met new people and shared the gospel with those the Lord put in our path. Finding a cozy place to park our new home, we began to feel that we were settling in. After a week or so of leisurely fun, I thought that now it was time for the two of us to settle down and look for work. However, when I expressed these thoughts, my lovely Prince Charming responded in the most disturbing manner.

"What do you mean? We have a job. We work for the Lord. He'll supply all of our needs."

This kind of thinking did not compute with me. Yes, I understood he had lived with this philosophy as a single man, but now he was part of a married couple. "No, I mean we have to get a real job where money comes in through a paycheck," I explained.

"We have a real job. I've been laboring for the Lord since living a Christian life. We work among the poor and He promises to take care of us. That's what His word says, so we need to stand in faith believing He will take care of us. What do you think I've been doing all this time back in Flagstaff?"

This conversation was beginning to make me feel ill. We debated this subject through the evening until it got pretty heated. I was completely frustrated by his thinking, and likewise he was having a hard time with mine.

"Put the money in the bank and then I'll believe," was my final analysis of the topic. George's comment that I didn't have any faith really hurt. I snapped back in my anger, saying, "Well, God says that you're worse than an infidel if you don't supply the needs of your family!"

"Are your needs being met?" he asked. At this particular time, he had a point.

I admitted, "Yes, right now our needs have been met, but we can't go on like this forever."

"Why can't we?"

This discussion was just aggravating me. I was especially upset that he would tell me that I didn't have any faith. That is not what any Christian wants to hear, especially coming from her newly married husband. The more I thought about it, the more enraged I got, fuming mad that he would dare say that to me. There was nothing more to discuss. I decided to wait for an opportune time when our needs were not being met to prove my point. I was sure that time would come. Hopefully, then he would come to his senses and get a real job.

Within the next couple of weeks, that day did arrive as I had expected it would. We were driving down Interstate 25, heading south in our school bus. I needed to use the bathroom and then realized we were out of toilet paper. We were penniless. My mind began to scheme. "I got him now!" was my first thought. "Need not met!" I came to the front of the bus where he was sitting in the driver's seat and informed him that we were out of toilet paper.

"So, how are you going to meet my need of toilet paper today? We have no money to buy any, and it's now needed."

George could see exactly where I was going with all this, and he wasn't too happy with me. He turned around and said a bit sharply, "You know, if you would just stop for a moment and ask the Lord for toilet paper maybe He might give it to you."

You can imagine what was running through my mind at this point. With my hands on my hips, I sarcastically replied, "Okay, well, Lord, I need toilet paper and I need it right now because I really need to go to the bathroom!"

At that very moment, and not a minute later, a big truck loaded with furniture and other household items bungee-corded together passed us on the highway. It looked like a hillbilly family right out of the movies. What happened next was the most incredible phenomenon I had ever encountered. Two rolls of toilet paper flew off the back of the truck as it was passing us. The timing couldn't have been more perfect, as they edged around us and rolled on up the road. George pulled over immediately and stopped the bus. He jumped up out of his seat and quickly ran to get the rolls. As he stepped back into the bus, he walked straight over to me and proudly laid the toilet paper rolls in front of me on the table. He was grinning from ear to ear. There in front of me lay two rolls of toilet paper, one still wrapped in its original packaging, and the other one half gone.

"There! There's your toilet paper!" George said joyfully.

I couldn't believe my eyes. I had a better chance at winning the lottery than for this to happen at this precise moment. I stood there staring at the toilet paper, trying to process what had just happened. "You're such a blockhead!" I was finally ready to admit of myself. "The Lord has to literally throw toilet paper at me before I'll believe Him!"

It was a life-changing experience for me. Although it took faith for me to step out and believe Jesus died for my sins on a cross, and through the shedding of His blood my sins were forgiven, and received salvation by what He did for me, I hadn't quite experienced God in such a personal way as this. Having a taste of God's reality, I was just beginning to understand the one, true, holy God who hears our cries, and who really does meet our needs. This was the introduction of the many manifestations God would show me. It wasn't a religion we were involved in. This was going to be a way of life.

I slowly started to grasp the calling that God was placing on George's and my life in the ministry. It would require us to depend on Him in supernatural ways. We would need to listen for His voice and trust Him wholly for our needs. I backed off on nagging George to go out and get a "real job". But to be honest, our spiritual debates didn't stop there. Many times during our first year of marriage, feelings of culture shock swept over me. But I learned, even when things got really rough, to go back to my foundation, to the covenant that was made in marriage. I came to believe that the Lord had given George to me not only for a companion, but to teach me His ways.

I will instruct you and teach you
in the way you should go;
I will guide you with My eye.

Psalm 32:8

4
Our First Year of Marriage

Our first year of marriage was difficult, living together and adjusting to our differences. In addition to that, it was hard struggling with the idea of living out a life of faith. This was one year of many that the Lord would be teaching me in multiple ways things I had not understood before. I am so thankful for His love, mercy and patience, because in my weakness, even now I constantly have days that fail Him. I guess that's called human nature. It's a good thing that in my faithlessness, He still comes through and shows me His faithfulness.

The Lord continued to give me glimpses of His reality, even in little things and ways that don't seem to matter in the big picture, but served to help me in my faith. One such time was on a day when we borrowed a motorcycle from a friend. It was a beautiful day for riding. We invited another friend who also owned a bike to join us for the afternoon. Before leaving on our excursion, I happened to be wrapping a gift and didn't have any scotch tape. "I'll have to get that later," I thought, wanting to get on with the day. As we were traveling down the road with our friend trailing behind us, he stopped on the side of the road for some unknown reason. We stopped ahead and waited for him. While we were sitting there, I looked down, and guess what was lying by my foot? A roll of scotch tape! Obviously, it was exciting to find it. More exciting than finding the tape was experiencing the Lord's hand in my life. He had reminded me again of His realness. God's timing is phenomenal. Someone had to drop the tape at that exact spot for me to find it. If there hadn't been a need for tape this particular day, it wouldn't have been that big of a deal to find it in the first place. Everything, large and small, was in play as the Lord orchestrated it.

*

When George was single, he had met a missionary couple who lived in Arizona, close to the New Mexico state line. They were an elderly couple who labored among the Navajo Nation on the reservation. As our days and weeks went on in Albuquerque, George suggested we go to visit them. It would be good experience to glean from them their knowledge and wisdom of living on the reservation. Patrick and Ann were so kind and hospitable. I could see that they were very dedicated to the ministry. One evening they asked us if we wanted to attend the church service with them. We were happy to go and proceeded to prepare ourselves for the evening.

Back in our school bus, I opened the box that contained my dressier clothes. Pulling out a pretty cotton dress that I thought would be appropriate, I noticed it was extremely wrinkled. It had been packed tightly in a box and not opened since we were first married. Picture taking a lightweight cotton dress, getting it wet, and scrunching it into a ball to let dry. That's exactly what it looked like. As I glanced around, it was dawning on me that we had no electricity to heat the iron.

"George, what are we going to do? We don't have any electricity to iron clothes," I mentioned, somewhat concerned.

"We don't need to iron clothes while we're here. Nobody will notice. You'll look fine without it."

Of course it ruffled my feathers that he wouldn't take a matter like this more seriously. In the sarcastic mood that was now beginning to develop, I decided to put the dress on just as it was.

"What do you think?" I asked mockingly.

"You look great!" he replied, seriously.

"I look ridiculous and you know it!"

Frustration welled up inside me, especially when he began lecturing me on my vanity. Before long, we were in a big blowout fight. Just about this time Patrick and Ann started up the car and we knew it was time to leave. Still in my wrinkled dress, I threw on my panty hose and then put on one of my most expensive pairs of shoes just to make the contrast more apparent. This sight would have made for a good picture. Unfortunately, we didn't own a camera at the time.

We got into the car, both glaring at each other. While Patrick and Ann were full of the love of God and sharing with us the wonderful stories of what the Lord was doing out on the reservation, we both sat in the back seat, totally unprepared to bring honor to our Lord or our missionary friends by being the good example of Christianity we ought to have been.

Arriving at the church, I needed to use the restroom before the service began. Down the hill past the building was the outhouse. The incline was not going to be easy with high heels on, especially since it had rained earlier, making the ground quite soft. Knowing I would sink in the mud if I went any farther wasn't going to stop me. I was still perturbed with George for not being sensitive to my needs over the wrinkled dress. In my stubbornness, I looked at him, shrugged my shoulders and thought, "A little bit of mud with my wrinkled dress will look just fine." Down the path I went in my once beautiful, expensive open-toed shoes. Step after step, I began to sink down about ten inches into the thick, reddish mud. We're talking reservation mud. If you've ever been out there during rainy season, you know what to expect. And that red soil doesn't come out of clothing very easily either. Venturing to take another step, and then another, all the while sinking a little bit deeper, was a strange sensation.

By the time I got back up to the church the mud was halfway to my knees. As I made my way to the concrete sidewalk, it was very noticeable that each shoe was coated in clumps of mud. It was also obvious that my anger had not produced the righteousness of God. George looked at me, trying to hold back his laughter at my ludicrous appearance. If I hadn't looked ridiculous before, I really pulled it off now. We were definitely experiencing the differences between the genders over our earlier argument. (I felt unloved because it appeared that he didn't care about my feelings in the matter; he felt disrespected in the way I talked to him.) At that moment we both came to grips with our immaturity toward each other and made up there and then. No one else knew what had been going on in our hearts. They just saw two silly white people, one covered in mud, both laughing. There was just time to scrape off as much mud as possible before entering the church.

Once inside as I was trying to get comfortable, leaving my childish behavior outside, a man stood up and walked to the front of the congregation. He spoke in Navajo and then motioned for the men to follow him into the back room. They all got up and followed him, including George. As the door shut behind them, the only ones left, besides me and my friend Ann, were a group of Navajo women. They were positioning their chairs to form a circle, which made for a cozier atmosphere. I felt a little uncomfortable in the situation as they started sharing with one another in a different language. When the group settled down, the women took turns praying in their native Navajo tongue. My thoughts began to race. Should I pray when it comes to my turn, or just let them skip over me? My biggest concern was the state of my heart.

When it finally did come to my turn to pray, there wasn't anything special or even deep that stood out worth remembering, except for wanting to be genuine with my Lord and not be caught in hypocrisy. It was a comforting thought that George and I had made amends before my entering the circle of women.

When you can't verbally share with others because of language barriers, your body language can speak volumes. They probably could see my nervousness and feelings of discomfort. Hopefully, they hadn't interpreted my attitude earlier as being against them personally in any way. Although they probably couldn't see the real picture of what was going on in my heart, I knew perfectly well that it makes for a shallow testimony if we're not willing to give up our carnal ways and surrender to Him.

The whole day was a learning experience for me. Focused on my own behavior and not someone else's, and noticing how it affects everyone around me, I was starting to see more clearly the stubbornness and anger inside me, my unwillingness to yield. This would take some working on. My faith told me that God would work on George's heart; it wasn't up to me to change him. I had enough on my plate to deal with my own sin. What a good thing that God's grace and love continues to abound and that He shows us the importance and value of trials.

It's all worth it, even though we sometimes take losses because of our choices; in this case I ruined an expensive pair of shoes because of my anger and stubbornness.

*

After returning to Albuquerque, I found myself waking up each morning feeling a bit nauseous. This feeling didn't subside, it just got worse. Within the month, suspicions arose that I might be pregnant. We found a doctor in town who confirmed it, and we were ecstatic. George and I realized that we were going to need to make more improvements in the school bus before the baby came.

We met a family in Albuquerque who owned an RV and offered it to us to live in, free of charge, while we fixed ours up. Not only that, they owned a gas station and offered George a job. This generosity allowed us to upgrade the bus. Life was starting to make more sense to me. Through our relationship with this couple, we found a most wonderful church. We started attending with them every Sunday, and soon we fell in love with this body of believers, but I'm getting ahead of myself here.

After doing more remodeling on our bus, one day a very wise man approached George when he was all alone. He shared with him how important it was to make his wife comfortable during her pregnancy. "She needs the security of a hospital, and a place where her home is stationary." George took that advice to heart. He decided to move us to a trailer park where we would live during the rest of our time in Albuquerque. He also found full-time employment as a mechanic, and arranged for me to have the baby at a local hospital. It was a calm and relaxing time for me, other than dealing with morning sickness.

I remember the first day we moved into the trailer park. As we were pulling into our space and trying to level the bus, the neighbors from next door came over and invited us for dinner. "What a friendly couple," we thought. The invitation was especially welcome, since I wasn't in any mood to cook after putting everything back in its place from the move. Rachel, the neighbor, told me later that it wasn't like her to invite strangers over for dinner. She wasn't sure what made her do it, but we were happy she went with her first inclination. (This couple has turned out to be among our closest friends to this day, and they have played a huge part in the various ministries we have been involved with over the years.)

The rest of the year, as we anticipated the arrival of our baby, we now remember as a time when we were really broke. But we can say with all confidence that we never went without.

There was the time we only had fifty-six cents to our name. We decided to walk over to the nearby fast food restaurant and split a bag of fries between us. Those were the most appreciated fries we ever have had.

Another time, there was a little extra money for us to go out on a Friday night date. We decided to go to a local Mexican restaurant. As we were standing in line waiting (it was a buffet) we struck up a conversation with another couple in front of us. The four of us hit it off really well. When it was time to pay the cashier, they insisted that they pay for our meal. What a blessing to be touched by their kindness.

God again during our early years of Christianity was teaching us, especially me, that we can be content when we have abundance and when we have nothing (Philippians 4:12). I'm still on the learning curve with this teaching too.

As I mentioned earlier but got ahead of myself, regular attendance at our friend's church was a delight. Every week we fell more in love with the pastor, his wife, and the congregation. It was one of the friendliest churches I have ever attended. Little did we know, the congregation unanimously agreed during one of their services to minister to us as a family for a season in any way that the Lord led them. We didn't find out until years later that it was actually their goal to bless us during this time. Knowing now that we were their target for ministry, it makes sense that every Sunday there were two or three families waiting in line to invite us for lunch. At the time we just thought that they were exceptionally friendly.

One of the most cherished memories we have of this church took place during the Christmas holidays. I was now around seven months pregnant. The pastor's wife, Sarah, came up to me and explained that the church was planning a Christmas play. They thought George and I would fit the part of Joseph and Mary, seeing that I was pregnant. It was an honor that they would consider George and me for the main characters of their program, but a bit reluctantly, we had to turn it down. We explained that we had plans to travel back to Flagstaff for the holidays. Sarah didn't take "no" for an answer. She insisted we be in this play. In order to work around our schedule she was even willing to change the date. They would do the performance the week before we were to leave. We talked it over and decided that it seemed like a good idea. We would be pleased to be in the play.

"So, where's the script?" I asked. "We'll need to start working on it now since we don't have much time."

Sarah told us there wasn't going to be a script. We would need to ad lib our parts. Improvising on stage in front of the whole congregation was not my cup of tea. My qualifications didn't fit in what they were asking of us.

Sarah could sense my insecurity about the performance. She explained, "I will narrate the Christmas story. You and George don't have to say a word. We'll have you both come out on stage and sit on the two stools that we will have placed on center stage." She continued to explain the scenario. "On the right side of you, we are going to place a manger scene with a real baby, and situated around the manger will be several young children from our congregation."

After hearing her plan, it seemed more feasible to me, especially the idea that we didn't have to say a word. We were all set.

On the night of the program, in our costumes, we walked to the center of the stage and sat down. The children gathered around the manger, with the live baby placed inside the feeding trough that someone had so wonderfully constructed. The seats in the audience were all taken. We had a full house. Sarah began to tell about the Christmas story. It was going as planned. At the close of her narration, she added, "This year we've decided to give back to the Lord for all the blessings He has given us by being a blessing to others. All right, everyone, it's your turn to come up."

This part of the play hadn't been explained to us. Not knowing what we were to do next, we just sat on our stools and watched. The whole congregation stood up and one by one started lining up as they came onto the stage with presents in their hands. As they were walking in front of us, each one laid down their gift at our feet. Then they hugged us and moved on as the next person came and did the same thing. Sometimes I can be a little slow at figuring things out, and this was no exception. I was sitting there thinking, "This is so sweet, but who are we giving all these gifts to?" It didn't dawn on me until about the tenth person had walked by and hugged us that these gifts were actually for us. This happened to be a surprise baby shower! We were completely fooled! And their creativity was such a unique idea! It was overwhelming to experience their love for us when we finally realized what they had done. George was very moved by their kindness and consideration, and I just wept as each person continued to lay package after package before us. The church even gave us a crib.

At this time we were living in a school bus that only had so much room, maybe two hundred and forty square feet. The gifts filled every empty space we had. It was so much fun opening them, and most of all being so blessed by our Lord's provision for our new baby. We didn't have to buy any baby things for two years. The biggest blessing in all of this has been the prayers and love the church continued to give us over the years in ministry the Lord would be calling us into.

Finally the day came that our baby boy, Jonathon, was born. It was one of the happiest days of our lives.

Soon our one year commitment to living in Albuquerque would be up. We were planning to return to Flagstaff to begin life not only as new parents, but in the work of the ministry as well.

Blessed shall you be in the city,
and blessed shall you be in the country.

Deuteronomy 28:3

5
Our Return to Arizona

Coming back to Flagstaff was such a delight. We had missed friends and the familiar settings. Although we were happy about the decision to go to Albuquerque for our first year of marriage, reaping the blessings of new friendships we developed and allowing George and me to be able to work out some of our differences of life in a more private setting, it was nice to be back home.

One thing had changed in me during our year in Albuquerque. I was confident we were called to minister for the kingdom of God. But assurance that we would live happily ever after together was shaky. Yet God would use events over the years to enable me to understand His love, promises, provision and protection in a deeper sense. The previous year, with occurrences such as the toilet paper, scotch tape, etc., did solidify how real He was and that He had a calling on our life, but as weak as our flesh can be, there were many times that I did not trust in Him as I should have.

Harry, the former superintendent of the rescue mission, had a vision of taking men who came to the mission out into the forest to cut wood. He believed good hard work would give them a sense of worth and help him to build a closer relationship with them. Most importantly, it would give him the opportunity to share the gospel on a more personal level.

He asked George to pray about heading up the ministry. George was in total agreement; he actually loved the idea. Immediately he jumped into this ministry with joy, and ran with the vision. He gathered together tools for woodcutting and bought a big boxed truck to haul the wood into town.

Within a short period of time, we had a lot of customers purchasing wood. It was hard work, there were some setbacks, but overall it was showing fruit. All the while we continued to live in our school bus, parked on the mission property. As George stayed busy with the men and woodworking, my hands were full being a full-time wife and mom.

After a while, George suggested we take a breather from all the busyness of the ministry and move our school bus out into the woods for a week or two. This way we could camp and enjoy the great outdoors. I already thought our entire life was one big camping trip, yet the idea of being out in the pines did suit me more than hanging out in the back yard of the mission. I enthusiastically went along with his plan and we soon moved.

One evening as we were returning to the city with a truck full of wood, we stopped in the mission to see how the group was doing. One of the employees, Toby, asked if he could spend a couple days with us, knowing the fresh air and wilderness would do him some good, too. We had always enjoyed Toby's company and didn't hesitate at his request.

By the time we arrived back into the woods, the night was as black as it can be when the moon is not visible. Not only could we not see two feet in front of us, it had also rained while we were away. The soil was very soft. The truck was quite heavy and began to sink down into the mud as we tried to move forward. George didn't want to get us any more stuck than we already were, so he suggested we get out of the truck and hike to the bus. It was fairly close. Or so we thought. Getting out with Jonathon in my arms, we all trudged through the forest looking for our bus. What we thought might be a ten or twenty minute hike at the most, turned out to be an hour trek. We still couldn't see the bus. George pulled out a book of matches from one of his pockets, hoping that it would give us some light. As he lit each match, it either blew out from the night breeze or burned down to his fingers. Needless to say, the matches didn't help. Feeling pretty worn out by now, we decided to turn back and spend the night in the truck.

Somehow the forest has a way of looking all the same after a while. We wearily roamed the woods, endlessly looking for the truck. We were lost and we all knew it. The chill of the night started to set in. Feelings of panic began to sweep over me as thought of being out here all night in the cold, especially with my baby, became more of a reality. There was only one logical thing to do at this point: PRAY! Why hadn't we thought of this idea two hours earlier?

After soliciting the Lord's help to give us direction, we all suddenly realized we were only several yards away from the truck. I wished it could have been the school bus, but the truck would do. We opened the door of the back of the truck box only to find it filled with wood chips from our earlier delivery. Before crawling in, we shared the chore of cleaning it out to make a comfortable place to sleep. As the winds continued to kick up, George and Toby built a fire off the back end of our trailer box that took the cold chill off. We knew we couldn't keep the fire burning all night if we wanted to get any sleep. The only reasonable thing to do was to all cuddle tightly together to keep each other warm. Remembering the blanket in the front seat of our cab, George hastily went up front to get it. Then the four of us nestled together, covering ourselves with our cozy blanket as we set out to survive the brisk night in the mountainous outskirts of Flagstaff.

As the dawn approached, I was never so happy to see sunlight. Awaking from the hard bed, feeling a bit stiff, the first thing that came to mind was the scripture "...but joy comes in the morning" (Psalm 30:5b). With hunger setting in, we all eagerly got up and decided to go hunt for the school bus.

Funny how things look so different at night compared to the daylight. It turned out that we were only a ten minute hike away from our original campsite. Ah... home sweet home!

*

The firewood business continued, and we periodically stayed in the woods to get away from the city life. After a few months of living back and forth like this, the idea of a permanent home started to look more inviting. Realizing how expensive housing was in Flagstaff, we knew we would have to trust in the hand of God for direction and for His provision. Our only asset was the woodworking truck. We put that up for sale, knowing that our other pickup truck could be used to haul smaller loads. While we waited on the Lord for our big wood hauling truck to sell, it was used several times to help people move. From then on, I looked for a new home.

One day, our family was taking a Sunday drive and came upon a trailer park full of mobile homes. We had spotted one for sale that didn't seem particularly nice, but we got out of the truck to look at it anyway. Peeking through the cracks of the curtains hanging at the windows, we could see it needed a lot of work. That didn't scare me because I love to decorate; it would be a nice challenge. The trailer actually looked like something affordable, without our having to go into a lot of debt. Before pulling away we wrote down the phone number posted on to the sliding glass door. I started to get really excited about the thought of moving out of our small two hundred square foot abode and into a three bedroom mobile home. I prayed that the Lord wouldn't let it sell to anyone else if it was meant to be ours.

A couple of months went by. No one was biting at the sale of our wood hauling truck. We weren't making enough extra money to put aside to even make an offer to the owner of the mobile home. Unless we had something to offer, there was no sense in calling. George was feeling my frustration and came up with an idea. Maybe the owner of the mobile home would be interested in trading for our big truck. He decided to call; after all, all he could say was "no".

We learned that the owner was a young man in his late twenties. He wanted to see the truck and came down to the mission within the hour. To our surprise, he showed a lot of interest. The truck was something he could use for his business. The blessing was that the value of our truck and what he was asking for his mobile home were comparable. We all agreed to trade straight across. We went to look at the mobile home to make sure it had a solid foundation, and also to make sure it would meet our needs. It wasn't until he made the remark, "Do you know that I haven't had one bite from anyone wanting to buy this home the whole summer?" that I knew this home was meant to be ours. God had honored my prayer to hold it for us. Even though it was on property that we would have to rent, we knew this was the provision we had prayed for and God was opening the doors for us. We made the trade and moved in right away.

Shortly after we moved, reality started to set in. Ministering at the rescue mission was not bringing in enough money to allow us to fix up the mobile home. How could we live in a fixer-upper without fixing it up? This was unfathomable. Making extra money and still being a "stay at home" mom was going to be tricky. I had decided to start a small business in my home. Along with Jonathon, I watched five children (and on one day a week seven). Being able to make extra money was my motive, yet I soon discovered that spending time with children was a privilege as well as a great responsibility. They were so impressionable. Sharing the love of Jesus with these little ones was a joy. This also gave Jon opportunity to have others to play with. It worked out just as planned. The babysitting kept me rather busy that next year. Not only did our home begin to take shape, we were able to take a nice two-week vacation at the end of the year.

I was really enjoying life during that year, other than one thing that kept cropping up every few months. We had missionary friends from Mexico who came to Flagstaff frequently to visit the church we were attending. Stopping by to see us was always on their agenda too. That didn't seem bad in itself, but their mentioning to us the need for another couple to help them do a survey in Mexico always aroused George's interest. They also felt strongly that the Lord wanted us to join them.

This couple was working for a mission organization in town whose plans were to compile information on the northern parts of Mexico. This data would help other missionaries who were interested to understand more about the indigenous tribes that lived there. The survey could take up to a year, and traveling to remote parts of the Northern territory of Mexico would be safer with another family along. We got along well with them and they also had a two-year-old son. Our families were compatible.

George had met Aaron and Theresa several years before we had met. He considered Aaron one of his best friends. They all had a lot in common, especially how the three had a love to serve God in any capacity the Lord had for them. In other words, they were sold out for Jesus. A couple years before George and I had wed, they had gone to Mexico together to scope out the prospect of Aaron and Theresa working there full-time. During this trip, they bonded even closer as the Lord took them through many adventures together. Needless to say, George thought very highly of them. So whenever they came up to visit and asked us to join them on the mission field, it would stir George up.

Personally, it became an annoyance to me. That was the furthest thing from my mind; it was not what I wanted to spend my life doing. George, on the contrary, would light up and get all excited about it, wanting to make a commitment to go. It was hard on both of us to have me quench his dreams and vision. Each time for weeks after they left, I would suffer guilty feelings for not following my husband's ambitions. Then things would cool down and get back to normal. Realistically, George knew he couldn't take a resistant wife into the mission field and think that it would work. He prayed that God would change my heart.

I had my own big plans. Finishing up the redecorating of my home and thoughts of selling it to buy another one were on my agenda. "We could sell this house for more than we paid for it and buy another dumpy house, fix it up and resell it, making a profit on each one, and keep doing that until we have a home that we could pay off." This was my dream and goal, not George's.

One day, as I was laying out these plans to the Lord, He began to deal with my heart concerning Mexico. The Lord was actually giving me a choice. He showed me that if we stayed in the United States He would bless us materially with my plans to labor for the house, but going that route would not bless me spiritually. If I would yield to go to Mexico for one year with George, and work alongside Aaron and Theresa, He would bless me spiritually, yet not materially. It was hard to decide which was more important. I thought and prayed about it for three months. Mentioning to George what the Lord had shown me was not something I elected to do. If he even had a glimmer of hope about going to Mexico, he would work to influence my decision. I could see the benefits of both options. The idea of being poor in another country was hard to swallow, yet I so much wanted to grow in the

Lord. On the other hand, knowing the comforts of our own country, with its plush advantages, and being blessed materially sounded inviting too.

During a time of contemplation, I envisioned a red tool box waiting to be filled with tools. Each tool placed in the box represented something used in ministering to other people. I somehow knew the wisdom and knowledge gained on this trip would give me one of the most commonly used tools in this red box for future ministry.

My decision to go with the option of spiritual growth won out. It made more sense. We could always come back to the States and regain the materialism that was lost. The opportunity of spiritual growth from the Lord was priceless. This was the season. This was our time to go. My mind was made up. I would share my thoughts with George after church on Sunday.

Sunday morning arrived and we went to church as usual. Unbeknown to us, the director of the mission organization that Aaron and Theresa worked for was asked to be the special speaker by our pastor. His message that morning was on missions. As he began to talk, he turned his discussion to Mexico and shared what God was doing through the work our friends were involved in. He ended with an invitation to the audience.

"I believe God has put on the hearts of a couple sitting in this church service this morning the calling to go to Mexico to work with Aaron and Theresa. You know who you are. You need to be obedient to that calling, and step forward to the call," Tim spoke out in a semi-loud voice.

I don't believe he knew we were the ones he was talking about, yet he was staring right at us when he said those words. My heart started to pulsate, knowing without a doubt that George and I were that couple. I couldn't wait to get out of church and tell George all that had been going on inside my mind for the last few months.

Church had now ended and we were heading out of the parking lot, providing a good time to tell him. "George," I said excitedly, "I have something to tell you."

"What is it, honey?"

Just then our friend Debbie came running out of the church. She was waving her arms and yelling, "George, Jennifer, stop, stop, I need to talk to you!" We had always known Debbie to be a quiet, reserved, conservative woman, not moved by much emotion. By her actions, she seemed to be out of character this morning. We sensed urgency in her voice. As we stopped at the corner, she approached our truck.

"What is it, Debbie?" George asked, concerned.

"I don't know how to tell you both what I need to tell you." We could tell she was struggling for words. She continued, "Please don't get upset with me, but I need to share with you what God showed me this morning in church." She had our full attention. "When Tim started talking about a couple being called to go to Mexico with Aaron and Theresa, He showed me that it was you. Whatever you do with this information is up to you. I just wanted to be obedient to the Lord by telling you what He showed me."

George looked at me in bewilderment, finally responding, "Debbie, thank you for being bold enough to tell us this."

This was confirmation for me of what the Lord had been putting on my heart for the last three months, and I spoke out. "You see," I told George, "this is what I was just getting ready to share with you before Debbie came running up to our truck." I briefly explained my desire to go to Mexico, thinking it would be better to wait until we were alone to share with him what else the Lord showed me. Debbie began to cry, so moved that the Lord had used her to deliver His message to us. George was elated that I really wanted to go to Mexico; perhaps he was actually more stunned than elated. We all left the corner of that street that morning in a surreal state of mind, filled with the peace of God. On our way home, I explained to him in detail my thoughts during the last three months. It was important for me to make sure he knew my decision wasn't a hasty one.

The next week provided more confirmation from the Lord that we were doing the right thing. The following Friday, we were invited to a home fellowship with several friends to get together for a time of worshiping the Lord through music. George had called Aaron and Theresa to come up to Flagstaff from Southern Arizona to join us for this night of fellowship. He had mentioned that we were interested in going to Mexico with them for the next year to do the survey work. He also suggested that we not tell anyone yet of our plans before praying together as couples as we waited on the Lord. They were in agreement, and gladly came up.

The fellowship was great. Afterwards, we spent time with Aaron and Theresa praying. Before joining them, we would need to sell our home, talk to our church about going, gather support, and get approval from their mission director to come under their leadership and covering. We believed if it was the Lord's will for us to go these things would fall into place. With that settled, Aaron and Theresa went back home.

A few days later I received a phone call from Betty (the woman at whose home we were for fellowship the previous Friday). "Jennifer, I need to share something with you." There was excitement in her voice. "On Friday night, as we were all singing together, the Lord revealed to me that you and George are the couple that should be working alongside Aaron and Theresa." I chuckled as I began to share with her what the Lord had shown us earlier, and that we knew it was His will for us since last week. Her phone call was just another confirmation. She was as stirred with joy as much as I was.

The next couple of months went as we had hoped. Our home sold, our church was excited about us going (even though they could only commit to a small amount of financial support at the time), and the director of the mission compound, Tim, was totally supportive of us coming on board. "You will need to attend our two week cross-cultural training program that will be held soon if you want to go to Mexico," he told us. We were more than willing to go. This would be good training because we knew nothing of foreign missions, nor could we speak a word of Spanish.

The date was set. I was once again ready for our next adventure.

Give, and it will be given to you:
good measure, pressed down,
shaken together,
and running over will be put
into your bosom.
For with the same measure that you use,
it will be measured back to you.

Luke 6:38

6
Preparing for Mexico

Geoge and I were scheduled to meet with the other missionaries affiliated with the mission organization to attend their annual two week cross-cultural training program on the Navajo reservation northeast of Flagstaff. Instruction would begin on Monday for one week of classroom studies, followed by one week when each couple was assigned to live with a Navajo family on the reservation. It all sounded adventurous to me. I was ready to go. Of course, there was much to do before leaving. Putting together appropriate clothing was something to take into account. I had already had one bad experience with my attire on the reservation, and I wasn't going to let that happen again. More importantly, we would need to find a babysitter for Jonathon for two weeks. I felt somewhat reluctant since he had never been left that long before. It would have to be someone that Jonathon felt comfortable with, and someone we also felt comfortable with.

Before long, our friends Bob and Sheri stepped up to the plate. We hadn't known them very long, yet we loved and trusted them from the beginning. Their deep commitment to the Lord was something to be appreciated, and we enjoyed the uniqueness in their character. They weren't the kind of people that just went along with the crowd. If they saw things differently than the popular opinion, they made a statement. We could always count on them to challenge us in everyday situations that arose. We were pleased when they volunteered to care for Jon the two weeks we were gone. We also liked the idea that they had a son who was a few years older than our boy; that way Jon would have someone to play with during our absence. I remember the day we left him. Packed inside his bag of clothes was an 8x10 framed photo of George and me. This would help him not to forget who we were. Two weeks can be a long time for a two-year-old. I told him that every time he felt homesick, he could pull the picture out of his bag and look at us.

Another important accessory for this trip was a good pair of hiking shoes for the reservation. For a while, it had been my desire to own a nice pair of Nike athletic shoes. This trip gave me a good excuse for getting them now. Seeing how much they cost, it was clear that they were out of our price range, but it was still hard to bring myself to buy another brand, so the search went on in hopes that there just might be a pair out there on sale. To my relief, after some diligent seeking, I did find just what I was looking for on sale. One pair left, my size, for ten dollars! That find boosted my spirit. I was now the proud owner of the shoes I wanted. I gave thanks to the Lord for enhancing my life every time I looked at them and on the subsequent days as I wore them.

Finally, the day came for us to leave. We headed to the reservation. As we were traveling, I kept thinking about all the awesome things the Lord was going to teach us.

The first week of classes we learned about different indigenous tribes, and took tests to expose our spiritual gifts in the body of Christ. A personality profile was done for each of us, which was very interesting, to say the least. They even gave us a taste of learning another language. We had hoped for Spanish, but their choice was Navajo. The Navajo language is one of the hardest to learn, so they probably thought that after a class like that, all other languages would be a breeze. What was most difficult to comprehend was the tonal nature of the language. One can use the same word, placing another tone on it by saying it through your nose, and it will have a totally different meaning. The harder I tried to learn, the more humble I became. For some reason, the teacher thought it was a good idea to call on me during this class. Every time I opened my mouth to say something, the class had a good laugh.

Toward the end of the week, I was really missing my Jonathon and was ready to go home. Still, I knew it was important to push myself through the next week living with a Navajo family. Hopefully, they would speak English.

The big day arrived for all of us to be placed in our new homes. We all piled into the back of the director's pickup truck. Driving down the dirt roads, traveling a lot of miles, he began dropping each couple off with the families they would be staying with. George and I were the last to be let out. Apparently we would be staying in a place that was the farthest away.

As the director stopped to let us out, we noticed in front of the pickup truck a huge tent filled with at least one hundred Navajos. It was then that Tim informed us that we would be attending a big tent revival. The family we were staying with happened to be part of it. He brought us over to the woman we were to stay with and made a quick introduction, then jumped in his truck and was on his way. We both stood there, feeling a little shy because no one spoke English to us, including our hostess. The nice thing was that they were having a cookout. A few people standing around ushered us over to the food. They were probably feeling just as uncomfortable with us as we were with them.

The food was delicious. After we ate, we were hoping our hostess was about ready to go home and get us settled in. Instead, we were escorted into the tent meeting as the speaker was just beginning to share. Following the first person's talk, another person came up front, and then another and another. The music started, and for the next four hours, between the music and testimonies, all in Navajo, the meeting was getting livelier by the minute. At first it was a bit intriguing, because this was very different than what we were used to, but after four hours we were becoming weary. It was when the clock hit two a.m. that I just couldn't take it any longer. My eyes couldn't even stay open. The Navajos had definitely put me to shame when it came to worshiping the Lord. They had energy. Lying down on the bench against the tent walls was all I could do. I'd had enough for one day, let alone going into the second day. George was feeling the same, yet he continued to show attention to what was going on, even though he didn't understand a word that was said either. My repeatedly saying, "This can't go on much longer," wasn't helping it end any sooner.

When it came around to three a.m. the worshippers must have sensed our fatigue, because our hostess along with two male drivers motioned for us to get up and follow them. We didn't hesitate. We quickly jumped into the back of their pickup truck, feeling great relief to finally be going where we would be spending the next week. Away we went down the dirt road again. Although it had been dark back at the tent meeting, I hadn't really noticed the total blackness of the night until now. Suddenly it was pitch black and the atmosphere was starting to take on an eeriness. My imagination began to run wild, remembering the stories they told us back in our classroom studies of the superstitions and things that happened on the reservation. Trying to lighten my fears, I half jokingly said to George, "What would you do if they pulled the truck over right now and told us to get out?" That thought would frighten anyone. We laughed uneasily, thankful that this didn't happen.

We were happy to at last arrive at our hostess's home. Martha was kind to us right from the start. She could speak very little English, yet we could tell by her countenance that she was a humble woman, full of hospitality and love. As we entered her house, she quickly lit the lantern that was lying on the counter. Motioning for us to follow her, she led us into a nice bedroom, placed the lantern down next to the bed, said good night to us in English and immediately left us alone. We were grateful for her gesture, understanding that the language barrier was uncomfortable for all of us.

We were exhausted. Ready to collapse for the night, at the same time we had experienced so much in one day that we wanted to process a few of our thoughts before going to sleep. After a half hour of sharing our impressions of the events of the day, we were more than ready to sleep. George blew out the lantern, but as we laid our heads on the pillows, within thirty seconds we found ourselves jumping up simultaneously, startled by a coughing sound that came from several feet away from our bed. George quickly lit the lantern again. We looked around the room but saw no one. Next to the wall, positioned in the corner, we discovered a huge loom. Hanging from it was a beautiful half-done rug with gorgeous bright colors interwoven with sheep-colored wool that hadn't been dyed. We slowly moved over to the loom and looked behind it. Lo and behold, we found five little children all snuggled together under blankets, staring up at us. We were just as shocked as they were as we stared at each other. "Hi," George and I said at once. None of them answered us. They just stared. We didn't want to scare them any more than they already were, so we returned to our bed, blew out the lantern and lay down again.

Feeling a bit embarrassed, I whispered quietly, "Do you think those children understood everything we just shared with each other a little while ago?"

"I don't know," George answered, and we both wondered, finally saying our goodnights.

Our next week with this Navajo family taught us a lot. With no electricity and no running water, and having to use an outdoor toilet, that, incidentally, had no door on it and faced a well-traveled road, we were learning to be flexible.

Martha's gift of hospitality and continued love and kindness inspired me to want to bless her with something. We didn't have the money to bless her financially, so I decided giving her something I owned would be in order. Nothing I thought of seemed appropriate. I continued for the next couple days asking the Lord to show me something I could give her; something she would really like.

The day before we were ready to head back to the mission base, we had all planned a hike up into the terrain surrounding where she lived. Fifteen minutes before our departure, rain began to pour down. "Well, I guess we won't be hiking today," I observed. Not understanding a word I said, Martha continued to get ready for our hike.

"Looks like we're going on the hike anyway," George concluded. Within minutes, we were out the door. I was actually sensing a touch of freedom from my inhibitions as the water continued to pour heavily down on us. I remembered walking in the rain as a child with such enjoyment, yet as an adult I had stopped, somehow feeling inhibited about it. We were having a wonderful time hiking up the mountain with Martha and her children, as she tried to communicate with the little English she did know. She was doing quite well.

When we began to tire, we found a comfortable sheltered place to rest. The view was magnificent as we stared out over the cliffs. Suddenly she pointed to the Nike athletic shoes I was wearing.

"Me like your shoes," she said in her broken English.

"Thank you, I like them too. They are very comfortable," I replied.

Just then the Lord prompted me. I had been praying for days about giving Martha something she would like, and this would be the perfect gift. "Oh, no, not my Nikes, Lord!" I thought animatedly, appalled at the very thought of giving them up. "Anything but these! You know how badly I've wanted a pair of these, and how long it's taken me to get them." Feeling a little guilty about my selfishness and trying to justify my behavior, I piped up again. "Besides, Lord, she probably doesn't even wear my size." There was silence between the Lord and me. Out of curiosity, I turned to Martha, and asked her what size she wore. She didn't understand me, so I motioned for her to put her foot up against my foot. When I realized that her foot was the same size as mine, my heart sank. I didn't say anything more to her about the shoes, but all the way down the mountain I was mentally trying to convince the Lord that it would be better to give her something else. By the time we got back to her house, though, the Lord had convinced me that giving her the shoes would be a gift out of love and sacrifice since they meant so much to me. I had made up my mind. My generous side won out. I was going to give my Nike athletic shoes to Martha. After talking it over with George, he suggested waiting to give them to her when we were ready to leave. This way she wouldn't feel obligated to have to give us a gift back.

We were all sitting around the living room resting from our big hike when Martha disappeared to her room for a while and returned ten minutes later with a grin on her face. She walked over to me and handed me a beautiful handmade turquoise necklace. I looked up at her with a puzzled look on my face. "This is for you," she spoke in a precious soft voice. I stared at it, running my fingers across each piece of turquoise. I didn't know what to say. I could see that this necklace was valuable, with the lovely patina of age.

Nearly speechless, I said, "Thank you." Just an hour earlier I was walking down the mountain trail, battling with myself and the Lord, trying to convince us why I should keep my shoes, and now she just handed me a very beautiful piece of jewelry that had infinitely more monetary value than those shoes. Guilt and shame visited me again.

Since she had already given me a gift, I thought it was the right time to give her the shoes now, rather than waiting the next day. I jumped up and went to my room to get the shoes. Even though they were still a little damp from the hike, in my excitement I couldn't wait.

"These are for you," I said, handing them to her.

"For me?" she responded joyfully.

"Yes, I want you to have these."

She thanked me glowingly. We were both delighted, as we sat admiring and touching our exchanged gifts.

The next day our director came by to pick us up. Although we knew we would miss our new friends, we were happy that our mission adventure on the reservation was coming to an end. We only had one more night left on the compound before returning to Flagstaff to be reunited with Jonathon.

On the last evening, all the missionaries gathered in the sanctuary where we were invited to share our experiences on the reservation. As I was sitting there, listening to each story, I began to ask the Lord to show me what experience would be most edifying to share. The Lord put on my heart to share my Nike shoe experience. Even though it would be hard to reveal the honesty of my heart, it was a valuable lesson for me, not to mention humbling.

On the trip back home to Flagstaff we were so excited to be picking Jonathon up from our friend's home. It seemed forever since we had seen him. When we got there, Jonathon was in the room napping. I walked up to him and whispered his name. He turned to look at me from the crib. A great big smile popped up on his face. I picked him up and brought him out to see George. We all kissed and hugged, and then stayed a while longer to visit with our friends. When it was time to leave, Jonathon seemed to feel a little strange about leaving with us. He had gotten used to Bob and Sheri, and wasn't sure if he should leave or stay. I felt a little dejected that he was wavering over who he should be with, but we won him over and he finally consented to come home with us. It bothered me the next week, every time I thought about Jonathon adjusting that quickly to a new family in just two weeks. I came to conclude that the Lord made us in such a unique way, so that when babies lose their parents from unfortunate circumstances, they are able to adapt to new parents fairly soon.

After our experience on the reservation, the director and his wife invited us over to their home for dinner. The time alone with them would enable us to debrief a little bit more, and also give us opportunity to get to know each other better before leaving Flagstaff to work alongside Aaron and Theresa.

The evening with them was pleasant. Before we were ready to leave, Tim handed me an envelope. He asked me not to open it until we left. Once inside our truck, my curiosity got the best of me and I quickly opened it. Inside was a letter with sixty dollars attached. The letter was very precious. It explained how the Lord had laid it on their hearts to buy me another pair of Nike athletic shoes since I had given mine to Martha. (In 1984, sixty dollars for a pair of Nikes bought one of the newer styles, whereas, the pair I had purchased earlier on sale had been an end-of-the-season style.) I realized then that we cannot out-give the Lord. I gave up something that to me seemed to have a great value, and God overflowed my cup by blessing me with more than I ever expected.

The next month, we were very busy getting ready for our trip to Mexico. I was looking forward to our move, and working hard to get everything taken care of, trying not to forget anything.

After much preparation we were now ready to go. Or were we?

And this commandment we have from Him:
that he who loves God must love
his brother also.

I John 4:21

And now abide faith, hope, love, these three;
but the greatest of these is love.

I Corinthians 13:13

7
Our Year in Mexico

Memories flood my mind as I reminisce about our time in Mexico. I would never trade or change anything of what we went through in that one year, as God had taught us so much. George and I were also blessed to be able to experience this journey with our friends, Aaron and Theresa. I'm not saying it was easy, as you'll soon discover as you read on, yet in some of our most difficult trials together we developed a bond of love that is of immeasurable value to this day.

The weekend we were ready to leave, Aaron and Theresa came to help us with the move. Our plan was to move in with them until a house of our own was available. They lived in the town of Bisbee in Southern Arizona, five miles from the border of Mexico. This made it quite convenient, since traveling every other month from Mexico to the U.S. would be a regular occurrence. The fact that we both had two-year-olds who could play together with was an added bonus. This freed Theresa and me up with extra time to do other things.

Our agenda took us down to Mexico for one month at a time. Each trip consisted of visiting different missionary families living in the northern region of Mexico. The return to Arizona the following month would enable us to restock, repair vehicles, and do whatever else came up to get ready for the next trip.

Gas prices in the eighties were nothing compared to now, and yet there were still concerns about how much it was going to cost because of all the traveling required. To save on gas, the guys decided to convert our trucks into propane. It was very cheap back then. Our trucks were able to go five hundred miles on one tank, which only cost five dollars. Imagine that! We did a lot of traveling.

We found ourselves among a tribe of Native American people called the Tarahumara, or Raramuri, as they call themselves. They inhabit the northwestern parts of Mexico, mainly the Copper Canyon region, as we know it in the U.S. The Spanish originally discovered this tribal people in the state of Chihuahua back in the 1500's, but the Tarahumara, being the shy and private people that they are, retreated for the canyons scattered throughout the Sierra Madre Mountains. Today, some live in caves, under cliffs, and in small wood and stone housing in remote places. The tribe is considered Mexico's second largest native Indian group, with an average of fifty to seventy thousand people. Their lives are very simple compared to our lifestyle, and undisturbed by our modern ways. They are friendly to outsiders, but as I mentioned, shy.

Their diet consists mostly of corn and beans, yet other produce can be found in the area. (Due to the severe droughts in the past, many of the people have suffered from famine, as we saw firsthand.) Traditional clothing among them is colorful and quite beautiful. Between the handmade woven belts and brightly colored fabrics, it is a sight to see. Sandals are their choice of footwear, though plain bare feet are common too.

The Tarahumara are well known throughout the world as runners. Raramuri actually means "runners" in their native language. Good thing: this is their only means of transportation. The villages are spread out so they must travel long distances to get to and from each community. Many villages were accessible by vehicle, but four wheel drive is a "must".

To get to some missionary villages required traveling on dirt roads for days. Our vehicles were tough enough to survive the ruggedness of some of the terrain we needed to drive through. Setting up camp wherever we ended up for the night was always an adventure. Putting up our tents and situating our kitchen and the cooking supplies gave us just enough time to eat and clean up the area before the sun went down.

All of the water that would be used for our one month trip was hauled in the back of our trucks and became a rare commodity. Showers were an occasion, few and far between and much appreciated, one every five days. We would heat up water on the wood fire and pour it into a five gallon bucket that Aaron had constructed as a shower. He placed a water spigot on the side of the plastic container. The shower stall was constructed of PVC piping, with shower curtains attached with clamps to go around the walls. The assembly of our stall needed to be next to a tree so the bucket could be hung off a limb above our heads. It was quite unique, but I don't think it would have sold on the market to the standard camper, especially for those in a hurry, since it was an all-day process to put it up. I always looked forward to shower day. You can imagine, after traveling on dirt roads for five days, what our hair alone looked like. My hair is not thick, yet this was one time in my life when it was.

My most memorable shower experience took place one beautiful sunny morning shortly after arriving at a missionary home situated deep into the mountainous terrain among an indigenous tribe of people. It had taken us days to get there, going over the rocky roads and passes that were hard to cross.

It quickly came to our attention that there was no running water in the village. This meant having to set up our own shower again. Shaun and Mindy, the missionaries, showed us a nice area down the hill from their house to set up our stall. Looking below us, there was a perfect tree to hang the five gallon bucket, so the men fabricated the piping around it. We were ready to go. One by one, each of us took our turn. This time I was last in line.

Skipping down the hill singing a tune, it was obvious how much this bath time meant to me. As I entered the shower stall, the clouds were rapidly gathering together above. Just minutes earlier it seemed so nice out. "Oh, I hope it doesn't start to rain," I thought, quickly taking my clothes off. Just then a big gust of wind came up and started to blow the shower curtains in every direction. As I was trying to move as fast as possible, rearranging the clamps on the curtains, adjusting them to keep the wind from ripping our curtains apart, suddenly the branch holding the five-gallon bucket broke loose from the tree. The bucket tumbled down and landed smack on the top of my head. Feeling a bit faint and beginning to see stars, I knew I needed to stay focused, although I felt sure I was going to pass out. With no clothes on, this was not a time to do that. Just then the rain came pouring down. Standing there by myself for who knows how long, just dazed and trying to regain my composure, I realized I had to manage somehow to get dressed.

By the time I got my wet clothes back on and struggled up the hill, I looked like a drenched rat. Everyone stared at me, the wet rat standing there at the front door. "We were wondering what happened to you," George remarked. "We were just getting ready to look for you." He paused. "So, why are you so wet?" It was worth a good laugh after I told them the whole story of my predicament, but not an experience I wished to repeat.

*

After going in and out of Mexico for several months, we discovered a village among the Tarahumara tribe where a missionary family and several Christians lived. George and Aaron wanted to drop off some supplies for them, so one afternoon planned a trip down into the village. Our water supply was getting low too. Pumping water out of the river that was located in the community would replenish what was needed for the rest of the trip. It would take them a couple of hours to do all this since they had to filter the water, so they suggested that Theresa and I stay back with the children because the drive was so long and rugged. We agreed to set up camp out in the woods and let our boys get some play time in. To this day, I can't figure out what Theresa and I were thinking to let our husbands leave us alone in the wilderness of Mexico with our two-year-olds. At the time, though, it seemed like a good idea.

As the men headed down the dirt road, we started to set up camp. It was around four o'clock in the afternoon, with some daylight still left to put up the tents and set up the kitchen. The boys were having fun as they ran back and forth, playing in the dirt and chasing each other.

Dusk was approaching. It was time to wind down and relax; George and Aaron would be gone at least another hour. Starting to get comfortable, suddenly we heard what sounded like a truckload of men pull off the dirt road just a short distance from our campsite. From the sounds of their conversation and tones of their voices, it was clear that they had been drinking. It was when they turned off the engine of their vehicle that fear gripped both of us. Immediately, Theresa and I realized our vulnerability. Quickly grabbing our boys and taking them inside one of the tents, we began to whisper to them how important it was not to make a sound. Then, fervently beginning to pray, we asked God to protect us, and to put a desire in those men to get back into their truck and leave. At this point, our camp was very quiet.

Within the next ten minutes, the men all jumped into their vehicle and left. It was then we recognized that staying here alone hadn't been a good idea after all, especially when our husbands still hadn't returned after another hour. They had only planned to be gone for two hours; now it was two hours too long. As we were starting to imagine what we would do if something happened to them and they didn't return, the enemy was getting a foothold in our thoughts.

We needed to get our minds off thinking the worst, and building a fire kept us busy momentarily. Although we were hesitant about starting a fire, concerned at the possibility of attracting uninvited guests, the chill in the air told us otherwise. Sitting around the fire and telling funny stories was all we could do to keep our minds off of the absence of George and Aaron.

Our story time was cut short when we were rudely interrupted by a couple of bats that decided to ruin our fun. They kept abruptly swooping down close to our heads and then flying off again. No way were we going to stand for that. The only thing to do was to put the fire out and continue our storytelling inside the tent.

Once inside, the boys got warm and cozy as we cuddled them close to us. For some reason, our stories took a turn from funny to scary. I have to admit I started it. Within five minutes, I had us all so scared that we both decided we had better dwell on more cheerful, positive things.

Thank God, the men finally returned to our campsite within the next hour. I don't know how much longer Theresa and I could have taken it, both trying to stay confident that our husbands were all right. We slept soundly that night, knowing we were all safely together. I hoped never again to find myself and my baby in the wilderness of Mexico in such a vulnerable state.

Back on the dirt road again, Aaron wanted to make contact with another missionary he had heard about. There was just one slight problem, but nothing that couldn't be overcome. The area where we needed to travel happened to be malaria-infested. We had plenty of bug spray. All we needed to do was drench ourselves with it. It did perturb me that Aaron waited to tell us about the problem until just before entering the village, yet I let it go because there was nothing I could do about it now.

I had been suspecting for the previous weeks the possibility of being pregnant, since several times a day I had felt like vomiting. Putting chemicals on my body was not a good idea, but between the two evils, the spray won out. "I'll just spray all around you and your clothes," George said, trying to calm me down. "It doesn't need to be put directly on your skin." Not wanting to waste any time, George started to spray me first. As he was spraying, he accidentally got some of it into my mouth. I wasn't in a good mood to begin with, but when that happened, it set me off into a tizzy.

"Oh great," I said sharply. "This is not going to be good for the baby if I'm pregnant."

Stomping off, I jumped into the truck. As I sat in the vehicle fuming, Theresa and George got in and tried to cheer me up by joking with me and quieting my fears.

Meanwhile, Aaron set off on foot, looking for the house the missionary supposedly lived in while we stayed near the truck. The two boys were happily playing in the bed of the truck where our sleeping gear and supplies were neatly stored.

Within the next hour, we had attracted quite a crowd of people from the village. George and I couldn't speak Spanish, so Theresa conversed with those that made their way to the window of our vehicle. She listened to them for a while and then periodically translated to us what was being said. At one point, she seemed a little nervous. Trying to decipher what they just said, and trying to act calmly, she repeated back to us in English, "They just asked me if we were "Hallelujahs".

The last Hallelujahs that came through their village they killed." Theresa was so diplomatic. Quickly changing the subject, within minutes she had them all laughing and enjoying themselves with us *gringos*. What she had shared didn't lighten my bad mood any. I was also getting anxious because Aaron had been gone for what seemed like hours. There was no more patience left in me.

To top off this less then exciting evening, the boys started screaming and laughing at the same time. Looking back to see what they were up to, we discovered that they had gotten into the port-a-potty and were splashing urine all over our sleeping bags. That was the last straw! Angrily I went to the back of the truck and cleaned Jonathon up while Theresa cleaned Joshua. I couldn't even open my mouth for fear of exploding at any moment.

Finally Aaron came back. We got back on the road to find a good camping spot for the night. I was glad we had distanced ourselves from that village, first because of my concern that they would find out we were Hallelujahs and kill us, and secondly, I wasn't being a very good example of a Hallelujah.

My feeling ill didn't subside. Every day sickness continued to invade my body. Then when I was looking through a medical book belonging to Aaron and Theresa, my suspicions arose that I might have several of the diseases described. Having experienced three sets of symptoms described in the book, I became convinced I had all three diseases. Aaron, Theresa, and George all thought one of us was becoming a hypochondriac. Aaron decided to nip it in the bud by suggesting we all get tested for the things I complained about. After finding a clinic in the city, we were all tested. Every one of us had amebas, giardia, and worms, three of the things mentioned in the book. We bought the required medicines and were back to health soon. Incidentally, relief flooded me knowing that pregnancy wasn't in the picture after all, since the bug spray episode had me really worried.

Taking a day off work and enjoying the culture of Mexico was an occasion that I always looked forward to. We made our way down to Guadalajara on one of our trips. Aaron and Theresa had heard of a big marketplace there that had floors and floors of everything you could imagine that was sold in Mexico. Interested in seeing it, we made our way over there.

Once inside, it was just as we had hoped it to be. Jonathon was strapped on my back in a carrier. After a while he didn't want to be up on my back, because he too was intrigued with the things he was seeing. He was starting to feel a little heavy too. Pulling him forward and letting him down out of the pack, I stood him right beside me. It wasn't even one minute later that I turned around and he was gone. This is every mother's worst nightmare. We had actually lost Jonathon in the hugest marketplace we'd ever been in. My mind began to race as feelings of panic swept over me. I looked up and down the aisles, but there was no Jonathon. I quickly ran over to George and told him what had happened. Frantic, all four of us started yelling for Jonathon, going up and down the aisles for what seemed like eternity. Realistically, it was only a few minutes. Several yards in front of us stood a man holding Jonathon above his head, who was crying and calling out for us. I was never so happy than to see my son as at that moment. Two or three minutes of agonizing terror were all I could handle. The man let Jonathon down and he swiftly ran over to us and jumped into my arms. Holding him tightly, my body shaking all over, I broke down crying. I couldn't thank God enough for giving him back to me. We stayed very close to each other after that incident. It shook us all up.

Losing Jonathon in Guadalajara was one of my most difficult experiences in Mexico, but next to that was when we met Maria. Maria was a young Tarahumara mother Theresa and

I had met while hiking through the mountains. Traditionally, the women of this tribe carry their babies either on the front or back of them, usually wrapped in very colorful woven blankets that they make themselves. The day we met her she had two babies, one strapped on the front of her, and one on her back. She was sitting on a rock while breastfeeding the baby she was carrying on her front side. I couldn't speak Spanish, so Theresa did all the translation, which she so graciously did for me on a regular basis. Many Tarahumara women only speak their native tongue, but Maria could speak Spanish, so we were able to communicate with her.

Her babies were so cute. The one on her back kept staring at me with his big brown eyes. He stole my heart. Observing that these two babies looked very close in age, it sparked my curiosity. How could this woman have two babies of her own that looked only months apart? I asked Theresa to ask her how old they were. After talking back and forth with each other for a while, Theresa turned to me and explained that the baby on her back was actually the older one, although he was the one that looked younger. Matter-of-factly, the mother shared that she could only feed one of the babies because she didn't have much to eat herself. She wasn't producing enough milk for the both of them. Therefore, the baby on her back was going to die. As she was explaining this to us and Theresa was translating it all, I looked over at the doomed baby on her back. The baby was looking at me again with those big brown eyes. My mind literally could not accept what I was seeing or hearing. I knew we were able to give the family immediate help, but what were we to do about a whole nation of indigenous people in the same predicament, especially through the winter season where food is much scarcer? I stuffed those feelings deep inside me and blocked them out of my mind. I didn't know it at the time, but it's called culture shock. At the time I had never heard of it, let alone experienced it.

The next few weeks we went on with life as usual. When we returned to the States to restock and repair our vehicles, I called my mom. She shared with me how things were going back home and then turned her focus on me. "So, honey, how was your time in Mexico this last month?"

That question somehow triggered my pent-up feelings about Maria and her babies. I started to cry. My mother had no idea what was going on. The more she questioned me, the harder I sobbed. Finally, when I was able to compose myself and tell my mom the story, she started to cry too. The more I elaborated on the details, the more anger began to well up inside me. It just seemed so unfair. I ended the conversation by saying, "You know what? I'm not going back down to Mexico any more. I don't want to see starving people die when I can't do anything about it." Feelings of indignation enveloped me. "Look at us Americans up here living like we do, and hundreds of miles away there are starving people!" My mom consoled me as she always does, but it didn't change my mind. I did not want to go back to Mexico.

After I got off the phone with my mom, I gathered Aaron, Theresa, and George together to let them know of my decision about not returning to Mexico. They could not talk any sense into me. Aaron knew he needed to call Tim, our director of the mission, to let him know what was going on. When Tim heard of my determination, with his experience with missions he knew immediately that I was experiencing culture shock. He called us all up to Flagstaff for a meeting.

When we arrived, he wanted to talk to me alone in his office. I came in and sat down. Looking around his office and noticing how nice everything looked, that indignant feeling once more started to well up inside me. I was ready for a fight to prove my point about why I wasn't going back to Mexico.

"Jennifer," Tim said softly. "Explain to me what happened down in Mexico this time around." I started to tell him everything in detail. When I finished he said, "So, what's your plan? How can we change the situation down there?"

"Well, of course, we need to send food down into that village to feed everyone," I responded abruptly.

"When we feed everyone in that village, what about the one next to it?"

"We'll feed them too."

"Then the next village?"

Before long he drew such an all-encompassing picture of the reality of hunger in our world that I couldn't take it any longer. I was totally overwhelmed. I knew I couldn't take on the whole world's hunger. I started to sob. I felt so helpless.

After I had a good cry, Tim very gently and graciously explained to me that I was experiencing culture shock. This happens when the reality of a culture that is totally alien to you is standing right before your eyes and you can't take it in. He also pointed out the cruel fact that the problem of starvation existed, and that I could not solve it on my own. My solution was like taking a tiny band-aid and trying to cover a gigantic sore with it.

"Yes, I understand that you can help people in need, but the best thing you can do, Jennifer, is to do what God has called you to do, and not try to take the whole world's problems on yourself."

Suddenly, my thoughts began to readjust to normal. I felt a bit more at peace. "It makes sense," I said a lot more calmly. "If I stay focused on what the Lord is calling me to do, I'll be more useful." I sensed deep down that God wasn't calling me out of Mexico over this shocking experience. It was an intimidating arena, but I was willing to give it another try. We all returned to Bisbee to plan our next trip down.

*

The making of the "Jesus Movie", dubbed in the Tarahumara language, was quite an adventure for all of us. This internationally esteemed film, following the story of Christ as described in the Book of Luke, has been translated into many different languages, but this was the first time that the organization that had ownership of this movie gave anyone permission to translate it for a people group of less than one million monolingual speakers, and we now had the rights to do that. The Lord opened the doors for us to take on the project of going into a village and recording this movie into the language of that village, spending a good solid month in one place to accomplish this.

We were also graced to have another couple join our team during this time, Tom and Marla. They are both very talented missionaries trained in this sort of work. As they worked on the literacy end of the ministry, George and Aaron worked on the mechanical end. Theresa and I were in charge of the kitchen duties, making sure everyone was fed. We all had our assigned tasks to do and each one had its complications. Not only did we all live in the back of our pickup trucks, but we had decided to do this during the wet season, and the rains were relentless.

The wet weather created another problem we hadn't foreseen. After weeks of nonstop rain, our clothes were wet and we couldn't get them dry. We couldn't even air dry them, for lack of available space inside our vehicles in which to hang them. Needless to say, by the time we returned to the States, we had bags full of moldy throw-away clothes. That's when I realized it was better to buy used clothing to wear on our trips, because much of it would be destroyed by the time we got back.

One morning it had rained so hard that Theresa and I couldn't even get to the house where the rest of our team was conducting the recording for the movie. We hadn't foreseen that the water would rise so high in the creek that stood between us. Because of this dilemma, Tom, Marla, George, Aaron, and the other workers were without food for the entire day. At least the children were with Theresa and me, along with the food supply. We could only communicate by screaming back and forth across the deafening roar of the water between us. Fortunately, by late evening, the level subsided just enough to allow them to cross over to our side. We had one pack of hungry people to feed that night.

That evening, George came back with a funny story of an incident that had happened to him while on the other side. He and Aaron decided to put the generator they were using to do the recording in a nearby outhouse, so the sound of it wouldn't be picked up during the taping. The generator quit running, so George, being the mechanic of the group, was designated to fix it. He brought the tools he would be using into the outhouse and worked away at getting it back up and running. Before long, he discovered that one of his most liked tools had accidentally fallen into the toilet hole. He was perplexed. There was no way George even wanted to get near the hole, let alone reach into it. No one else was volunteering to bend over and reach down into the hole to get the tool either. He was on his own. After thinking it over, he decided he wouldn't do it, yet the more he thought about it, the more it ate at him to lose this particular tool, knowing that the tool couldn't be replaced until we got back to the States. What if we needed it sometime in the duration of our trip?

George came up with an idea: if he found a big sturdy stick he might be able to pull out the tool. I guess it was a sight to see, because the others were laughing for days about the sight of George stooped over into this hole with the stick, trying to fish his prized tool out. After a good amount of maneuvering the stick around in the toilet hole, being totally grossed out the whole time, he was finally able to rescue it. He was more then ready to get a shower that day.

We continued to come back to this village, spending a lot of time there. It was well worth the effort, because the finished product of "The Jesus Movie" came out sounding terrific. Little did we know the Lord would use George and me several years later to show this movie not only to the Tarahumara tribe, but in other languages as well to thousands of indigenous people.

Amidst all of our adventures in Mexico, there was a time toward the end of one year that I started to go downhill emotionally and spiritually without even realizing it. Little things that normally wouldn't bother me began to wear on me. My usual attitude of viewing life through healthy eyes changed for the worst, as I found myself criticizing just about everything, including my co-workers. Before long they just couldn't do anything right in my sight. I set up a little black book that I held in my heart and added to it daily the things that I thought were wrong with the ministry and with Aaron and Theresa. Although they certainly hadn't done anything horrific to make me that angry, it was the nitpicky, everyday little irritations I allowed to build up inside without dealing with them. It was ridiculous, but real. They were patient with me, yet there was an unhealthiness in our relationship that none of us could deny. In retrospect, I can now see that it was nothing more than spiritual warfare. At the time, that wasn't a concept I could clearly see. Now, through experience, I can see that one of the most common tactics that the enemy uses to break up the work of the Lord is to build enmity between brethren. All too often, when we look at people and our situation, we concentrate on the negative and fall right into the trap of the enemy. Instead, we should be staying focused on the Lord, confessing our own sins daily (sometimes even by the hour or moment for that matter), and not use our energy looking at what everybody else is doing wrong. It's hard enough to go through life making ourselves right, let alone trying to change everybody else. The Bible talks about putting on the armor of God, that we may be able to stand against the wiles of the devil (Ephesians 6:11). Needless to say, Biblical thinking wasn't permeating my life during this period of time.

I'm so glad the Lord didn't leave me in this state, wallowing in my pity party for long. Again, He showed Himself faithful by not leaving me or forsaking me, as He promises in His word (Hebrews 13:5b). Instead, He began to show me a way out of my sinful state of mind, and eventually to use this experience to help others that have gotten caught up with bitterness and anger in their own life. It didn't happen overnight though.

After our year of commitment was up, we decided not to recommit ourselves to another year. My anger and bitterness had taken its toll. I was unsettled inside spiritually, upset that though the Lord had told me that when I left Mexico I would have this wonderful, valuable tool that would be placed in my tool box, I felt I was leaving Mexico empty-handed. For months after our departure, I still wasn't willing to give those feelings up.

There's something about anger and bitterness, especially when we blame others for our sin, that at first makes us feel so justified. Yet after a while we feel the sting of it. That was the case with me. It left me feeling so unhappy in life.

Not able to take it any longer, I fell before the Lord one evening and cried my eyes out. "This bitterness is eating me up, Lord. Please help me to overcome my ill feelings of Mexico. I know it's wrong; forgive me for harboring these thoughts for so long."

Sleep was sweet that night. The release from the burden that I had been hanging onto for the past months had lifted. But by the next morning those same thoughts were being entertained in my mind again. Several days would pass by, and I'd begin to not only feel bad about being bitter, but also feel guilt welling up inside because I was back where I started. The sin had taken root again.

This went on for weeks, and each time my guilty feelings would get worse. I felt so defeated. Once again, repentance was in order. The Lord's forgiveness was always there, leaving me feeling great until the next day arrived. Finally, one evening after weeks of being on a spiritual roller coaster, I recognized that I didn't have any power over this sin. Addressing the Lord on this issue, I asked Him to show me what I was doing wrong. So He did.

When we continually sin for some time and then suddenly ask the Lord to heal us, we expect God to miraculously take away our sin with no work on our part. Yes, we are forgiven instantly, that does happen, but sometimes He requires us to make a conscious effort at disciplining ourselves onto Godliness. In this case, that is what He revealed to me. He showed me that when my day started out, it would be important to take my thoughts captive. On a practical level, it meant that at the very moment I found myself thinking bad thoughts, I was to stop myself and say out loud, "I will not think those thoughts." This would be my spiritual exercise for the day.

My first day of discipline was unbelievable. It was amazing how many times I said those words. It seemed like every five minutes the words were coming out of my mouth, the whole day. By the end of that first day I was exhausted.

The Lord showed me that this process was like physical exercise. When a person starts out in an aerobics program it is so tiring, but by the next month it is much easier. It would be the same for me. So the following day, I kept on with my spiritual exercise. It was still hard, and yet instead of every five minutes, it became every fifteen minutes. By the end of the week I had it down to every hour, saying, "I will not think those thoughts." After a month of saying those words only once a day, I was feeling somewhat victorious. Healing was on its way.

Just about the time I thought victory over bitterness was licked, the Lord spoke to my heart again concerning Aaron and Theresa. Not only did the Lord want me to have control over my thoughts, He also wanted me to be able to genuinely build my brother and sister up around other people. This would be my next assignment for healing. Every time I was fellowshipping with others and their name was brought up, my assignment was to say something good about them, nothing artificial, just a word about the genuinely good qualities that they truly possess. So I began to practice this part of the healing process also. It was amazing how many opportunities that came up. I believe the Lord allowed them to pop up for my sake. This part of the exercise turned out to be fairly easy compared with the "don't think these thoughts" routine.

Then the Lord prompted me again, adding a third step to my healing process. He told me that every time Aaron and Theresa came to town to visit the church, it would be good to invite them over for dinner. I could do that! This part would be a breeze! Lo and behold, the first time they accepted my invitation for dinner, I couldn't believe how many of the old feelings of anger sprang up in my heart when we were face to face with them. Feelings of defeat swept over me after they left. "This awful attitude of mine is never going to subside," I thought, yet within days I was able to take control of my negative thoughts again. Believe it or not, this whole procedure took about a year. Within that year, we had invited them over three different times, each time getting easier for me.

I remember so vividly the day the Lord wholeheartedly healed me. Aaron and Theresa had come to town for a visit. We didn't know they were in the area until one afternoon they called George and me on the phone and asked if they could come over. Of course we said yes, and we were soon together once again.

After an hour or so of a really good, healthy conversation, our topic of discussion led to believers becoming angry with one another. Since this subject was fresh on my mind, it was easy for me to readily jump into this dialogue. Knowing that Aaron and Theresa never had a clue about the extent of my anger down in Mexico, because I had never opened up to them about the depth of it, it felt safe to tell them a story about my experience with anger and bitterness towards some friends of mine at one time and how the Lord helped me to deal with it. I began to share my story about how God took me through an exercise program of healing, not giving them a hint that they were the couple that I was actually describing. As I neared the end of my story, they both looked at each other and then turned and looked at me in consternation. Was I talking about them? I had to laugh, and then confessed with sincerity that this story was in fact an illustration of what had gone on in my life and what the Lord had taken me through.

"I'm able to bring this up in my life now," I said quite confidently, "because I believe I've overcome my anger toward you." I went on to explain, "You see, all along, sin was actually reigning in me. Not willing to look at myself and my own faults, through my sinful eyes I could only see your sin and blame you for all the problems. I was not right with God." Suddenly I realized that an apology was due. It was time to ask forgiveness for my wrongdoing. I told them, "I'm sure that during our time in Mexico, with my sinful attitudes, I made your life miserable. I'm sorry!"

They both lovingly hugged me and forgave me for my behavior. At that moment, the most awesome thing occurred. I literally felt pounds of weight lifted off my shoulders; it was like I took off a heavy backpack. "You have overcome. You are fully healed." I knew these were the soft words of the Holy Spirit speaking to me. Simultaneously I was visited by the knowledge of the valuable tool that the Lord had given me, a tool called "overcoming bitterness and anger". This tool, this knowledge, is one of the most valuable tools I use in ministry. With it I am able to help others who suffer with the same problem. The enemy is out there trying to destroy us, and subtly brings discord among us so we will become defeated. If we can't love one another, how will we ever be able to talk to the world about the love of God?

From that day on Aaron, Theresa, George, and I have been developing a strong beautiful relationship. They are two of our closest friends. We regularly thank God for them. What a priceless gift from God!

Do not labor for the food which perishes,
but for the food which endures
to everlasting life,
which the Son of Man will give you…

John 6:27

…and the sheep follow Him,
for they know His voice.

John 10:4

8
Change Up

Our year commitment was up in Mexico, and it was now time to inquire of the Lord what was next for us. George wanted to stay in Mexico, but he knew my heart was not sold on being there. He always told me that he would not force me to do ministry; the Lord would have to change my heart. Unfortunately, my heart was far from wanting to make a long-term commitment in Mexico, so we returned to Flagstaff.

After weeks of seeking an open door from the Lord and nothing opening up for us there, we decided to go back to the Albuquerque area. We owned a small travel trailer we had purchased earlier, so we hauled it along and parked on our friend's property, thirty miles out of town. This time of our life was difficult, because we knew the Lord wanted to use us in the ministry, yet we needed a time out to pray, and to be still and know that God was God.

We did some part-time work in Albuquerque. I babysat for a family that had a three-year-old girl. The mother was pregnant and had complications. She was instructed by her doctor not to do any lifting. George worked for her husband doing handyman work for a business he owned. It was easy enough to keep us going financially as we sought the Lord daily for direction.

Within a couple of months, I woke up one morning not feeling well. I called in sick, expecting to be back to baby-sitting the following day. Even when I had to call in sick again the second day I wasn't too worried, but by the end of the week when I still wasn't feeling any better, I knew it was something more than a run-of-the-mill flu. George insisted we go to the doctor. At first I was resistant because that wasn't my favorite thing to do, but he persisted and won out. I couldn't even get out of bed to get into the car. He had to carry me.

George checked me in at the clinic, and as we sat waiting for my name to be called, it took every bit of strength I had to just sit in the chair. By the time they called me and placed me in an examination room, I was unable to sit. I was sprawled out on the floor when the doctor entered and was quite surprised to see me lying there. I looked up at him and said, "Sorry, but I don't have it in me to sit in the chair."

Immediately he said, "Without testing you, I can already tell you what is wrong. You have hepatitis. Your eyes are as yellow as yellow can be." I remembered George had made a remark earlier about my eyes looking yellow, but it didn't dawn on either of us that I might have hepatitis. I needed blood work done to make the diagnosis official. The doctor asked if I did babysitting. When I told him that I did, he explained that some babies are carriers of hepatitis and may never get the disease. The germ is inside the fecal matter where it is transmitted by changing diapers. I had no idea before this that babies could be carriers.

The doctor also mentioned the disease could hang on for months before it cleared up. I couldn't believe it! "How am I supposed to baby-sit, being in this condition for months, Lord?" I was so sick that even taking care of Jonathon was going to be a problem. George would either have to hire a babysitter for Jonathon or quit his job. It was beyond me to understand why the Lord would let this happen.

My emotions were at a real low over this whole mess. It was hard to see at the time, but the Lord was allowing me to have some quality prayer time with Him, since I was in bed most of the time, with very few visitors. You mention hepatitis and it has a way of chasing friends away, and I didn't blame them. Hepatitis is very contagious.

As the Lord is always in control and ready to make all things work together for good (Romans 8:28), He was right on time. A week or so after my diagnosis, I woke one beautiful sunny Saturday morning praying to God about our difficult situation. The Lord spoke as clear as day to me and said, "Jennifer, Hal (the superintendent of the rescue mission in Flagstaff) is coming to visit you and George today. He's going to ask you to come back to the rescue mission to work there again."

When the Lord spoke to my heart, I have to admit it seemed a bit farfetched, because Hal was in Flagstaff and didn't know where we lived. He knew we lived outside of Albuquerque somewhere, but surely he'd never be able to find the place, we living so far out. I rejected the idea, thinking that perhaps it wasn't God speaking to me after all, only wishful thinking on my part. "Besides, I have hepatitis and he won't want to come near us when he finds that out," I told myself.

Although we doubt God, He is still faithful when we're faithless. Within the hour of dialogue with the Lord, Hal's voice could be heard in the yard talking to George. "Lord! It really was You speaking to me!" I was filled with excitement, now believing Hal had come to offer us a position at the mission.

When he came to the door of our trailer, I advised him not to come in because the house was contaminated with hepatitis germs. "I didn't travel all this way to not come in," Hal replied. "Besides, the Lord will protect me." It really blessed me that he came inside and trusted God to protect him, just to visit us.

The land where we were staying was not an easy place to find, located thirty miles outside of Albuquerque, out in the wilderness on a dirt road. One of my first questions to him was, "How did you find us?"

"Well, I called Dave since he was out here visiting you a while back, and he drew me a map," Hal explained.

I didn't mention to Hal what the Lord had revealed to me earlier in the morning, because I wanted him to ask us just as the Lord had told me. After several hours of visiting, though, he never brought the subject up. He kept commenting about the ministry at the mission and the blessings of the Lord, adding how someone in the community had donated an apartment complex to the mission along with a house. He went on to tell us of their vision to start a new ministry by housing street people, but still he didn't come out and ask us if we would consider being a part of this new ministry. He finally said, "Well, it's time to get back on the road. Flagstaff is a ways off and I want to get back by tonight."

Before he left, I decided that I had to say something about my earlier conversation with the Lord since he had not brought it up. "Hal, this morning the Lord told me you were coming here today to see us." I added, "He also revealed to me that you had a purpose for coming here besides the visit."

He looked at me quite surprised. "Really, what did He tell you?"

"He told me you were going to offer us a position at the mission."

With a big smile plastered across his face, he sat back down at our table. He answered, "God told you right. That's exactly why I did come here. I just didn't think this was a good time to bring it up with you being sick and all."

George and I sat back down at the table with him. He began to lay out all the details about the ministry he had in mind. The ministry he was referring to concerned the apartments and the house that were recently donated. The mission would give us the house to live in and we would rent out the apartments for very little to those who were homeless or needing a cheap place to live. Our ministry would be to help people not only to get back on their feet financially, but also to teach them some basics of life, to share the love of God with them, and just to show them love like parents would to a child.

Hal wanted us to take a few days to pray about it. George and I were excited right from the beginning, yet we felt it important to spend days inquiring of the Lord to make sure this was His will for us. We asked Him to close the door by not letting this proposal go forward if this wasn't His plan for us.

Still plagued by hepatitis, we knew that I would need to receive a healing touch from God to move forward in this new ministry. So we prayed for that too. Several days later, George called Hal to tell him that we wanted the position. "Great!" he responded. "The board of directors is excited about you coming too. So, when can you come?"

"Well, as soon as Jen feels well enough to travel. We're hoping for a quick recovery."

I started regaining my strength in the days following Hal's visit. By the next week, I had reached almost full recuperation. Having a goal and purpose in life, with a new ministry on the way, probably played a part in helping to strengthen my immune system. Still, I knew that the healing power of God was upon me by how speedily I was mending.

When I was hired as the babysitter for the family in Albuquerque, I had given them my word that I would commit to staying with the job until the end of the mother's pregnancy. It was important to them that their little girl had only one caregiver during her mother's time of pregnancy. They felt strongly that going through several different people could be too stressful on her. When they found out that I had hepatitis, however, they didn't want me to come back for the sake and safety of their unborn child and their little girl. This understandably broke the contract that I had made with them. After Hal left our home and we accepted the position, I realized that if I hadn't contracted hepatitis, I would have been committed for another five months to the babysitting job and we might not have been offered the ministry. Our Lord truly had a way of working things out for our good even when our situation seemed so bleak.

*

The next week we were packed up and on our way back to Flagstaff, the hepatitis healed.

I was thrilled to be able to live in a house after being in a small nineteen-foot travel trailer for months. The house was rundown and not very pretty inside, but we made an agreement with the board of directors that we would renovate if they paid for it. I love redecorating, so I was more than willing to get started almost as soon as we moved in.

As we began the renovation process of the house, it soon became clear that my expectations and vision exceeded those of the board of directors at the mission. I was really into wallpaper in the mid-eighties and had a perfect picture of how our bedroom should be decorated. I envisioned country blue paper with burgundy roses scattered throughout the design of the paper. When I went hunting for this particular design, it wasn't difficult to find just what I was looking for, since those colors were popular that season. When I came home with the estimated cost to wallpaper our bedroom, the board of directors was not on the same page. They didn't agree to be extravagant; they agreed to renovate it; that meant paint, not wallpaper. I was crestfallen because that's what I had my heart set on. I knew I would just have to save my own money and budget it in.

A couple weeks after my wallpaper disappointment, Ginny called me. She had received a call from a local business that just bought a decorating company. They had some miscellaneous wallpaper in storage that they wanted to donate to the mission. Ginny thought I might be interested, so she gave me the number to call. I have to admit my first thought was, "I'm sure it's probably old, outdated stuff that no one would buy, left over from the previous owners." Still my curiosity got the best of me so I called the business.

The woman answering the phone was friendly enough; we shared back and forth and built a rather quick friendship. She invited me down to her store to see what she had. When I arrived, she took me down to the basement. You can imagine how blessed I was when she opened the door and in the midst of all the wallpaper rolls stood the country blue with burgundy roses printed paper. "How can this be? Here is a roll of popular paper among the dated stuff!"

That still soft voice was reminding me that Jesus loves us and even cares about the little things in life. I left there, thanking my new friend for her generous gift to me, and thanking Jesus for giving me the desires of my heart. (The Lord likes to bless me in rolls: toilet paper, scotch tape, and now wallpaper.)

You would think that after experiencing the wallpaper blessing from God, my faith would be increased. Sad to say, I found myself again doubting the provision of God.

While still in the season of decorating, I thought with the country blue scheme that country blue dishes for our kitchen would be in order. George and I never received a set of dishes for our wedding. We had a hodgepodge of dinner plates, each with a different design. There was one plate that I was partial to that stood out from all the rest. It had a country blue design printed on an off-white ceramic. George and I decided we would slowly buy pieces of this set, one by one, since they weren't cheap. It was a very popular design at the time, easily accessible at the major department stores in the mall. Now that we were settling into our home, this would be a good time to continue building our dinnerware set. When we discovered just how expensive these dishes really were, we realized it would take us a lot longer than we thought to buy the whole set.

While we were in the store looking at the dishes, I started to feel a bit discouraged, knowing I would only be able to buy two plates with the money I had on hand. George, sensing my mood, piped up. "You know, honey, the Lord can just give us this set of dishes. Let's wait for them to come into the mission."

Boy, did that set me off. "Excuse me, but these are not the kind of dishes that get donated to the mission," I said sharply, irritated with his sarcasm. It ticked me off so much that I couldn't even get into the joy of buying the couple of plates I actually had the money for. I reluctantly concluded that I would just go home and wait for a better time, when I had a little more money. Meanwhile, George was silently praying that God would prove me wrong and send that set of dishes through the mission.

About a month passed since our little debate in the mall. One day Hal and George went to pick up a donation that was called in. As they were loading boxes into the mission truck, Hal noticed a nice set of dishes. He made mention to George that maybe he would like to put them aside for the new lounge/kitchenette area they were adding onto the upstairs family room of the mission. When George looked up and saw the dishes, he almost fell over with delight. "Hal, this is an answer to prayer. Those are the exact dishes that I prayed for a month ago." Hal was staring at him a little strangely at this point. George knew he owed Hal an explanation, so he shared with him the whole story. After hearing what George had told him and how he prayed that the Lord would bring them in to prove to me God's provision, they both concluded that these dishes were meant to be mine. Hal gladly gave them up.

I wasn't home when George arrived back at our house with the dishes. He set the box of dishes in the middle of the living room so I wouldn't miss them when I walked in the door. He was in the kitchen when I entered, just waiting to see my response. I immediately noticed the box lying there on the floor. I walked over and opened it up. "Where did you get these from?" I said in shock.

"The Lord put it on someone's heart to donate these dishes to the mission. And you said 'Dishes like these don't come into the mission,'" he said, beaming with joy. I stood there looking at him in disbelief, unsure if he were really telling me the truth. George continued, "Honey, is anything too big for God?"

Shame started to knock at the door for my lack of faith, but I didn't stay in that state very long, so overjoyed was I that the Lord bestowed on me this wonderful gift. Those words, "Even in my faithlessness, He is faithful", permeated my mind.

I wish I could say at this point of my story, "I never doubted God again." God still had to show Himself to me in His supernatural ways over and over. So He continued on.

*

The rescue mission made an agreement with the donor of the apartment complex that they wouldn't evict the existing tenants. We would have to move slowly on our plans to turn the complex over to renters, agreeing to comply with the program. That doesn't sound like it would be such a difficult bargain to keep, but that the apartments had been used for many years as a place of prostitution, as well as drug and alcohol abuse.

Our house was separate from the ten apartments, yet we were located just across the alley right next door. The apartments faced the opposite way, in a horseshoe shape. Each tenant shared one big bathroom and shower area designated for women on one side and men on the other, but each had their own kitchen, living room, and bedroom.

Our first week as new directors almost was too overwhelming to deal with. A few days into our new ministry two men tried to abduct and rape a girl in the bathroom late one night. Thankfully, they were unsuccessful. She got away, leaving blood splattered all over the walls. A couple days later, a tenant tried to commit suicide, also a failure. The ambulance got there in time, thank God. The next day after these incidents, I could hear two little children screaming and crying outside in the courtyard of the apartments. I ran over to find out what was going on. Out in the snow stood a little five-year-old girl and her four-year-old brother. They had told me their mother was inside, and she had thrown them outside because she wanted to be alone. They weren't even wearing winter jackets to keep them warm.

I knocked on the door. "Leave me alone!" shouted the voice of an angry mother.

"Your children are out here in the cold without jackets," I replied. "You need to open the door and let them back in."

"I want you to go away and if you don't I'm going to kill myself," she snapped back angrily. Not what I wanted to hear.

"Come with me, children," I said gently, "we'll go to my house until your mommy lets us in. Besides, it is really cold out here."

We went back to my house. After helping the children to get comfortable and cozy, I called 911 and explained the situation to them. Before long, the police were at the mother's door. I let them know that I had a key to the apartment if they needed to get in. As I stood outside her door, I could hear her screaming at all of us that she had a knife at her wrist, and if we opened the door she would slit herself with the knife. I left the police to deal with her. I needed to get back inside with the children.

It was close to half an hour before they were able to coax her into opening the door so they could get her out of the apartment and settle her down. I found out she was a beautiful young lady who had been prostituting herself in the Flagstaff area. Needless to say, her life was full of problems.

That day it dawned on me that maybe this ministry was beyond my capabilities to cope with such a rough group of people. After encouraging words from Hal and Ginny, though, who believed if God had called us there He would also sustain us, I felt more confident to move forward with zeal. George had worked in this type of ministry much longer than I had, so he felt perfectly comfortable where we were at.

That same night, George was prodded by the Holy Spirit to go into the courtyard to pray over the complex. It was two a.m. He started praying against the evil forces that had lingered in this place for so long. He asked the Lord to cover the place with His presence and, most of all, to remove those tenants from the premises that did not belong there. Those that the Lord wanted us to minister to, he asked the Lord to keep there.

By the next week, one by one, tenants were giving us notice that they were moving out. Only two tenants out of ten stayed. These were the prostitute and the one who had tried to commit suicide the previous week. Everyone else moved out within the next week. We felt sure it was the hand of God.

Now we were able to make changes that needed to be done. We placed new locks on the bathroom and shower area for starters. The need was so great that we had no problem filling the vacant apartments right away. We then rented to a family who became our overseers, without the other tenants knowing. We couldn't see what was going on in the wee hours of the night, but they were able to inform us of any drug or alcohol activity or prostitution that might be trying to make its way back. The tenants were never able to figure out how we knew so much about what was going on with their lives. It was truly a blessing to have this family placed there to warn us before dangerous situations would arise. We were able to help many people because of this.

The young prostitute was very receptive to the help that we extended to her. She jumped right into the Bible study that we held in our home every Tuesday night, and soon surrendered her life to the Lord. She and I would take long walks in the neighborhood as we talked about the issues of life.

Even though she gave her life to the Lord, she still hadn't been convicted about wearing immodest clothing. This didn't bother me, knowing that was the Holy Spirit's job to change her. However, the disgusted looks that came from people that I knew when we would run into them on our walks were another matter; they made me sad. The facial expressions from most people could be read as, "Why are you hanging around someone like that?" Still, this didn't rile me up too much until the first time we brought my companion to Sunday night church. She already felt uncomfortable about going. This wasn't something she was accustomed to. After persuading her to go with us one evening, assuring her that she would meet some really wonderful people, I realized that it had been a big mistake. Instead of warm, loving Christians, we were received by judgmental, unloving stares. She probably could feel those glares as strongly as I did, yet I never mentioned it to her, for shame of their behavior. I wanted to rebuke them openly, reminding them that Jesus associated with tax collectors and sinners. It was an uncomfortable evening, and I learned a valuable lesson that night: Don't be like certain people in the church!

My friends would often ask me about our ministry with the mission. I would describe it as having ten rebellious teenagers. Although we saw lots of growth, the growing process varied from one day to the next.

Most of the families that had come there were from dysfunctional homes and didn't know basic principles of behavior one would expect from an adult. We held classes on various subjects, one as simple as opening a checking account at a bank and teaching them how to use it. We charged the tenants very little rent, just enough to teach them to be responsible by having monthly payments to meet. Not only were we able to help others, but George and I were also growing by dealing with all the different situations that arose. That's what's so wonderful about being a disciple of Jesus. As He uses us to help others, He helps us to overcome our weaknesses as well by allowing us to go through difficult times.

There were so many great memories of laboring in the Lord through this ministry. We didn't have much money but we had a lot of happiness. Yes, there were hard times, as I've mentioned, yet the investment in people's lives was giving us great satisfaction.

The Lord used us in unexpected ways too. One vision I had while working in the women's clothing room at the rescue mission was to have a fashion show on clothing day (the distribution of used clothing for those in need in the community), which the mission holds twice a month. I wanted to teach women how to be creative in making used clothing look modern and up-to-date. With ideas such as removing buttons from men's white shirts and replacing them with big, colorful buttons, worn with a pair of jeans with the tail tucked out, from sleeves cut off to jeans rolled up, it was a fun endeavor. I gathered together several friends, from little children to the elderly, both men and women (including George and Jonathon as two of my models). It was a blast! I was blessed to see everyone get so excited about used clothing.

During those years, our family got our clothes out of the mission too. One advantage of shopping in the mission was when I got tired of my current outfits I would just trade them out.

Then there was the time George came home and told me about an ambulance he wanted to buy. I thought he had lost his mind. A different mission in town was selling it for only four hundred dollars. George was sure we could triple our money. I thought it was such a crazy idea. When he tried to explain to me his plans for this vehicle, I stuck my two index fingers in both ears and started yelling, "La la la la la!" After a few minutes of my goofing around, George asked me to please listen to him with an open heart. I still thought it was a crazy idea. "Look, honey," he began explaining, "this ambulance is in mint condition, and it's a classic. We could buy it for four hundred dollars, drive it up to Minnesota and sell it for at least fifteen hundred to three thousand dollars. We'd be able to visit your family and come back with a profit." He added, "You have to see it. It's a beauty!"

How could I fight against that? He was as thrilled as a little boy with a new toy. "You promise if we go look at it and I don't like it, you'll back out of this idea of buying it?" I was concerned, knowing we didn't have a lot of money at the time.

"Yes," he pledged, "if we both can't be in agreement on this deal, I'll back out of it."

We drove over to look at this so called "beauty". When we arrived, I was actually surprised at how nice it looked. It was an older model, one that looked like a Suburban. In the back were two gurneys on each side. I could see Jonathon would have a lot of fun playing back there. I liked it almost as much as George did. We left there with another vehicle in our possession. The plan remained the same; it was just a matter of timing. Meanwhile, we had the pleasure of owning it. One night we took Jonathon and his cousin to a drive-in movie and let them lie on the gurneys.

Every time we drove the ambulance into a public place like a restaurant, people would move out of the way while staring at us. We almost changed our minds about selling it because we were having so much fun with it. We did need the money though, and really wanted to go back to Minnesota for a family visit. So we found ourselves traveling up there shortly after our purchase.

There was no problem selling it. The vehicle sold to the second person that looked at it. A prop man for a movie company in Minneapolis ended up buying it. He was just as excited as we were about obtaining it, and had no qualms about giving us the asking price.

We had planned to take the train back to Arizona because it was one of the cheapest ways to travel back then. As we were making plans to return, my parents offered to give us a little old yellow Honda Civic they wanted to get rid of. Those of you from Minnesota reading this will know what an old car looks like after being through many a cold snowy winter. The salty roads had turned it into a rust bucket. We knew we wouldn't use it in Arizona, but it was a good alternative to get us back home. Besides, we could use the parts to refurbish another Honda Civic George had in our backyard at the time. I can still see my dad laughing when we took off in that rusty old thing.

Well, we made it to right outside of Ames, Iowa, before we had any problems. We parked ourselves on the side of the highway. George discovered that the fuel pump had gone bad. Within a short period of time a friendly trucker came by and gave us a lift to town. His seeing that we had a young child with us probably helped us get the ride.

Our hearts were thankful as he dropped us off at the nearest gas station. Once inside, George went up to the cashier and asked who owned the motorcycle parked outside in the parking lot. "It's mine," the gas station attendant replied.

After explaining our dilemma to him, George asked with boldness, "Do you think you could lend me your bike to find a parts place around here?"

I couldn't believe he was actually being so gutsy as to ask this complete stranger to lend him his bike. When the man answered "Yes", I was even more shocked. The cashier then added, "You have to leave your family here while you're gone."

I felt pretty safe waiting in the gas station. After all, it was a busy place with people coming and going, so we agreed to his terms.

George was back within thirty minutes with the fuel pump that we needed. We were back to our car with the help of a police officer that saw us walking toward the highway. Before we knew it, we were on the road again, heading toward Arizona.

I remember that road trip as a humbling experience. Every time someone would pass us on the highway, the front fenders, which were totally rusted out and ready to fall off, would lift on both sides from the force of the wind. The passengers in those cars would pass us laughing. We kept reminding each other that at least it was getting us home.

This road trip affirmed our beliefs that the Lord would show Himself faithful again by providing for us, and delivering us from our troubles. We got home safely and ended up using that car to make one good car, which we were able to sell for a fair price. What an awesome God we serve!

*

Close to one of the weirdest experiences we had while working in the ministry happened the afternoon Ginny called. She told me that a family had just arrived at the mission who said they were old friends of George's. They wanted to know where we lived because they wanted to visit us. She didn't want to give them information until she checked with us. I called George to the phone so he could personally talk with this family. He remembered them, a husband, wife, and young daughter, from his earlier days as a new Christian. They had met at the rescue mission, but he didn't really know them very well. Inviting them over for a visit seemed to be the hospitable thing to do. As we waited for their visit, George filled me in on their time together. I looked forward to meeting them.

"Hi, I'm Jennifer," I said cordially, as I let them in. George was standing next to me as they entered and greeted them with hugs. He then introduced me as his wife.

Immediately, the mother of the teenager looked at me and then back to George and said, somewhat perturbed, "George, the reason we are here is because the Lord told us that you are to be our daughter's husband."

I looked over at the young lady, who looked to be in her early twenties, batting her eyes at George with a great big smile on her face. I couldn't believe what I had just heard. George quickly jumped into the conversation, and boldly responded, "Obviously it is not the Lord's will that she be my wife. The Lord gave me Jennifer to be my wife, and besides He has blessed us with children."

Our guests now looked a little downcast. "Come, sit down. Would you like something to drink?" I said, trying to change the mood. The tension in the air was so thick you could cut it with a butter knife.

Everyone sat down as I served them beverages. The next hour of the visit seemed to lighten up as we chatted about different things. Even though we had a strange start, I thought they seemed like nice-enough people after all, until all of a sudden it turned weird again. The husband of this family started sharing bad doctrine with us, totally against what scripture taught. After we listened to his nonsense, George spoke up. "That is not what the Bible teaches at all. I don't know where you picked up this kind of teaching, but as a Christian you need to weigh what you've heard to what the scripture says."

It was as if the man didn't hear a word George said. He continued expounding. Shortly into his outlandish train of thought, George interrupted and repeated himself. The man just got a little louder and kept on. George stood up at this point and said very authoritatively, "The Bible teaches that some will come to trouble you and want to pervert the gospel of Christ." He concluded with the scripture in Galatians 1:8, "But even if we, or an angel from heaven, preach any other gospel to you than what we have preached to you, let him be accursed". The family was staring at us very intensely when George finished. This time the wife of the family started up. She didn't even get through her first sentence when George walked over to the door and opened it. "Since you won't relent from preaching another gospel, I want you to leave my home right now." They looked stunned. I suddenly felt sick to my stomach, especially when they didn't get up. As they continued trying to get more words in, George raised his voice and emphatically told them to leave our home NOW, that they were not welcome. I quickly got up and walked over to George's side. At last they slowly stood and moved toward the door, believe it or not, still speaking their doctrine as they were walking out the door.

George slammed the door behind them. We looked at each other in bewilderment, took a deep breath, and sat down on the couch. "Well, I never had to do that before," George said, relieved that it was over.

"The nerve of them to say what they said about their daughter, that it was the Lord's will she marry you, knowing we were already married," I added, indignantly. "It's like the devil to send them full of lies."

We both agreed. It was so blatant, yet we were reminded that there are those out there that are wolves dressed in sheep's clothing that come to destroy, not to bring love and truth (Matthew 7:15-20).

*

In the midst of our ministry, the Lord put a young couple, Dan and Teri, in our lives to disciple. They attended the same church we did. It was through Ginny that we first met Teri. For weeks she would mention how much Teri and I were alike, insisting that we meet. It wasn't until she asked both Teri and me to volunteer our time for the Christmas give-away at the mission that we finally actually met each other.

We loved Dan and Teri right from the first. They were fairly new Christians, and newlyweds. Teri had two boys that were close to Jonathon's age, so that drew us even closer because our boys loved to play together.

During our time of discipleship with them, we spent almost every weekend together, camping through the summer months, and during the cold season sharing lots of meals and playing games together. Needless to say, through the course of time we became like family.

We even got pregnant close to the same time. It was an exciting nine months. I had prayed that the Lord would give me a little baby girl. Not only did I ask the Lord for a girl, but I requested that she be born on my birthday. When I found out the due date, which happened to fall on George's birthday, I was all right with that too. When she was born, the Lord blessed me with the most beautiful little girl, who just happened to come on my birthday, two weeks early! We named her Laura. She was my twenty-ninth birthday present from the Lord. (My grandmother was born on the same day too: three generations all on the same day.)

Teri delivered a precious little boy named Craig two months after Laura was born. To add to all the excitement, she found out months later that she was pregnant again. She gave birth to her fourth child, another boy.

Our two families were inseparable. What started out to be a friendship of discipleship turned us into "Best Friends". While Teri and I, along with the children, were together most of the time, George and Dan were also together during the week. Dan had worked for a local business in town owned by mutual friends, Dennis and Gloria. George and I were in need of a little extra money, so Dennis hired George on too. George and Dan became partners at work.

About two years into our friendship, George's mother became sick and passed away. We needed to go back to Illinois in the middle of February to attend her funeral. We didn't have the money to fly, so we decided to drive our motor home that we had just purchased (more about that later) to save on money. After we assured Dennis that he would be back to work within two weeks, he gave George his condolences and we were off on the road again.

It was a difficult time for all of us. Not only did we have to bury George's mother, we had a breakdown in the state of Iowa as we were heading home. Iowa again!! Our rear axle seized up right in the middle of West Des Moines on Interstate 35. It was the strangest thing. I no sooner said these words to George, "You know, honey, we don't know anyone in Des Moines, Iowa. Wouldn't it be nice to meet some people from here?" when suddenly our axle broke right there and then. It didn't help that the weather was freezing cold.

There was nothing more we could do after praying for God to help us. So we waited for the tow truck after contacting a trucker on our CB to report that we were stuck out on the interstate. When it arrived, the driver wanted to know where we wanted to be towed. We suggested a place that could repair an axle. The next thing we knew, we are parked in the back of a lot with an ample amount of old car and truck parts strewn across the grounds. It was a fairly big place, with men scurrying about doing their jobs. They had friendly faces, although they were covered with grease. While I wasn't too comfortable about our surroundings, I didn't feel threatened by any of the workers. They understood our predicament and went out of their way to make us feel at home. The owner let us stay in the motor home while they fixed our vehicle. The only problem was that they didn't have another axle to replace ours with and couldn't find one in town.

Again, we prayed to ask the Lord for direction. We decided to get the phone book out and look for a church in the vicinity that would be willing to help us. It was encouraging to find the first church we called ready to jump in to assist. They came and picked us up and drove us all over town looking through the junkyards for this particular axle. Finally there was one that would work. We called my parents to ask them if they would lend us one thousand dollars to buy it, which thankfully they did. They were able to wire the money to us immediately. George decided to put the axle in by himself. Unfortunately, it was going to take another week or so to do it. He called Dennis to let him know we would not be able to get back as planned. Dennis was sympathetic to our circumstances, which took the pressure off of us trying to get back early.

We were very pleased when the pastor of the church who helped us out in our dilemma called to invite us to his church service. Someone came to pick us up. They were all so friendly and kind to us. The pastor and his family took us out to lunch and offered to pick us up for the midweek service. Little did we know that the Lord would use us to share with the congregation on the "faithfulness of God".

The memory of what I had said to George about meeting people in Des Moines a minute before we broke down on the highway flooded my mind. The Lord actually took me up on it. Here we were with a group of Christians loving on us, when a week before we didn't know any of them. (It amazes me no matter where you go in the world you will find brothers and sisters in the Lord in the least expected circumstances.)

After a nice week of wonderful fellowship, Laura caught a flu bug. She was so sick. At this point, life was getting a bit overwhelming for me. Her temperature was high, yet through prayer and medicine we were able to keep it at bay.

It was a happy day when George finally was able to install the used axle. Before long, we were on our way back home once again. The rest of our trip was uneventful, other than blowing out two tires. We finally arrived back home one-and-a-half weeks later. Not what we had planned.

Meanwhile, back on the home front, to our surprise Dennis had hired another worker. He was in desperate need of help and his business was in demand. George was furious when he found out, especially since we had just gone into a thousand dollar debt with my parents for the axle and we needed the money. He called Dennis and let him know how he felt. Dennis felt very bad about the whole situation too, so he called a meeting that evening for all of us to meet at his home, minus the new employee. He also wanted the wives to be present, remarking that with the women there would be more peace among us.

Once we were all gathered at Dennis and Gloria's home, it was brought out that Dan was the one who talked Dennis into hiring a new worker. Several months earlier, George had confided in Dan that he was planning to leave the business and mission, as we had been praying about going back out on the mission field. When we were in Iowa, Dan mentioned to Dennis that we might be leaving. Since he was in need of another worker at the time, he felt compelled to hire another man. Yet after talking it all out between all of us, he realized it wasn't the time to let George go. Consequently, he asked George to come back to work the next day.

"What about the new guy you hired?" George asked, out of curiosity.

"I'm not sure what to do yet," Dennis replied.

"Why don't you let the new guy work the rest of this week, while you take time to figure out what to do," George said. "Besides, I have a lot of work I can do in my back yard."

It seemed like a good plan for all of us. We left on that note with a peace and understanding between us, along with hugs all around, and ended the meeting by holding hands and praying together. It went quite well.

That night, I awoke around three a.m. to a horrible feeling inside. I just couldn't shake it. Was it something that was said at our meeting that was subconsciously annoying me? Did I feel uneasy about something in my day that might have been left undone? Over and over, my mind played back the activities of the previous day, unable to figure out what was making me feel so agitated. I replayed George's dissertation that he shared with us all at the meeting about not knowing what life holds for us. "Our life can change in a twinkling of an eye," he spoke, at the same time snapping his fingers in the air.

Suddenly a great fear came over me. I found myself pleading for George's life. "Lord, you can take away my house and all of my possessions, but please don't take George away from me." I finally went back down to sleep.

The next morning thoughts of what had happened at three a.m. had vanished. The day went on as usual. Teri had called me that afternoon. She was inviting us to the surprise birthday party she was planning for Dan. Right in the middle of our conversation, she shifted her attention. "Dennis, what are you doing here?" she said. In a worried tone, she then said to me, "Jennifer, let me call you back." She quickly hung up the phone.

"I wonder what that was all about," I thought. "I guess I'll find out when she calls me back."

About fifteen minutes later the phone rang. George had just walked in the door so he picked up the phone. It was Teri on the line. When I heard George sighing, there was no doubt something was seriously wrong.

"No, no, Teri, please tell me you're joking," George cried out in anguish. "Please, Lord, no."

I was frantic. What were they talking about? "George, what's wrong?"

He hung up the phone after saying he was so sorry to hear the news. He walked into the living room and turned to me. "Dan was killed in a car wreck today while working."

I couldn't believe what I just heard. Staggered, we both started to pace the floor. Just then that horrible feeling that I had experienced at three a.m. revisited me. I fell to my knees on the kitchen floor. The fear of the Lord came upon me so heavily that I couldn't even stand. Less than twenty-four hours ago, I was pleading for my husband's life, and now Dan was gone. Thoughts that George should have been in that vehicle with him, just like he had been for all those months earlier, came to mind. What if George hadn't suggested that Dan work with the new employee the rest of the week? My whole being was numb.

A sudden death like this is so hard to process. We were both in shock and disbelief. Now what? Trying to pull my thoughts together, it suddenly dawned on me what Teri's state of mind must be. "Who's with her right now?" I exclaimed, quickly dashing to the phone to call her. She answered the phone very calmly.

"Teri," I said, trying to speak just as calmly, "George and I would like to come over right now and be with you. Is that okay?"

"Yes, please come."

I could tell she was in shock by the tone of her voice. Immediately, we grabbed the kids, jumped in the car, and headed over there. Laura was too young, but Jonathon understood fully what had just happened. We explained to him how he needed to be a support for Teri's two oldest boys.

When we arrived, Dennis and Gloria were there with her. We were relieved to find her not alone. Her boys were next door playing at the neighbors, not yet knowing what happened to their Daddy. Jonathon had no idea that Teri had not yet told them about the death of their father, so when he began telling them how sorry he was to hear about Dan, they didn't understand why he was saying that. They quickly came running home to find out what was going on.

We all just sat there together staring at the living room walls, as shock permeated the room. It wasn't until the police officer assigned to the case showed up at the door that any of us were able to focus on what to do next. He asked Teri to come down to the morgue to identify Dan's body. The children went home to our house with George, while I went with Teri.

As we went there together, I understood that this would definitely be the hardest thing for her to go through. She wanted to go inside alone, so I waited out in the car, all the while praying that the Lord would give her the supernatural ability to handle such a dreadful experience as this.

The next couple of weeks were a blur, with so many people coming and going from Teri's home to comfort her. George and I often took the children during this time, and helped clean and do what ever else was needed.

At this point, no one knew the real cause of the accident. The police report confirmed through witnesses that a woman crossed over two lanes of traffic and hit Dan's truck head on. She was also killed instantly. The only one that survived the wreck was the passenger in Dan's vehicle, who happened to be the new employee. Many of his bones were broken, but, thank God, he was going to make it. They did find antidepressant pills on the floor of the woman's car, yet there was no talk of suicide at that time.

A month or so after the wreck, George happened to be attending a class on adult children of alcoholics. During one of the sessions, a woman in the group asked for prayer. She had just lost one of her close friends the month previously in a car accident. She went on to tell the story of how her friend was very depressed and talked of suicide. She told the group that the day before her friend died, she sought medical help and counseling for her depression, expressing that she was suicidal.

George started to put two and two together. He was horrified that this woman would take her own life at the expense of another, now leaving our precious friend a widow left with four young boys to raise, and those four boys would be fatherless.

We were reluctant to tell Teri what we had heard, knowing that this tidbit of information might infuriate her, yet if she found out and knew that we withheld this from her, it might cause a bigger problem. So we told her. She was just as horrified as we were when she heard the story.

This was a very difficult time for all of us, but God's faithfulness shone through once again. The Lord provided Teri and the boys with a beautiful home she designed and had built, along with comfortable financial support from insurance policies to keep her going.

On looking back after some time had passed, Teri, George, and I recalled an evening we were all together a month before Dan had died. The four of us were sitting around their dining room table playing cards. George introduced a conversation concerning life insurance. It seemed kind of odd coming from George. It's not like him to promote insurance policies. As we discussed back and forth the pros and cons of it, George became more persistent about his point.

"Dan, you need to see the importance of this. What if something happened to you, and Teri had to raise your four boys alone? That would be a real hardship on them." George communicated his point rather strongly.

After reasoning together, he finally convinced Dan that he really needed to take out a life insurance policy. That following Monday, Dan called the insurance company and obtained coverage.

We could plainly see the provision of the Lord.

Blessed is the man whose strength is in You,
Whose heart is set on pilgrimage.
Psalm 84:5

9
New Horizons

We ministered through the mission for three and a half years. Although it had its stressful moments, we were privileged to be a part of it. I think most ministries are that way; the rewards of seeing people move in the right direction toward God and experience the blessings that take place in their lives make it all worth it.

As we approached three years of ministry there, George started feeling the prompting of the Lord that it was time to move on. He wanted to buy a motor home and go back on the highway to minister to the poor and homeless. I just couldn't see it. I was perfectly content in my home, my church family, my ministry, and with my friends. The idea of being on the road in a motor home was not appealing to me at all. As a matter of fact, every time the thought of living that life entered my mind, it left me feeling very insecure.

One evening, while attending our weekly home fellowship from the church, during prayer time George asked the group to pray for us as we were thinking about going back out on the highway. The whole group unanimously showed excitement and agreed to be praying for us. I was fuming inside. He had some nerve to bring this up when I wasn't even in agreement about going in the first place. I could hardly wait to get home to let him have it! I managed to hide my feelings from the fellowship until we got home.

That evening we went around and around all this until the late hours of the night. When we realized we weren't getting anywhere with this debate, George finally said something that made sense.

"Honey, what if the Lord really wants us to do this and you're resisting Him?"

"Well," I thought, "I've been there before." So I retorted, "What if this is just your flesh getting in the way, and we're really supposed to stay here?"

George came up with an idea. "Let's lay a fleece out to the Lord. Let's ask Him to provide a motor home for us. I'll also need a job that will allow me to come and go. That way, when we need money we would have a place to come back to. We'll also need a base to be able to come back to." He ended the fleece with, "If the Lord starts to provide these things for us, we will know it is His plan to move us out."

"Fair enough," I responded.

I knew from experience that these things would only come to pass in the supernatural, since we had no money to buy a motor home, no prospect of finding a job for George that would allow him to leave whenever he wanted, and we also had to find a piece of property suitable for us to leave and come back to. We both lifted our requests to the Lord and finally went to bed.

Within four days after our night with the fleece, George came home and told me that he found a motor home for sale. Although we didn't have the money to buy it, he thought it was a good plan to start looking. That way we would get an idea of what we wanted in a motor home. I wasn't really in the mood to drive all the way across town, but George persisted, and we found ourselves going over to look at it.

We pulled up to the house where the motor home was parked. By the outside appearance, it wasn't anything to get excited about. I didn't even want to go inside, knowing we would be wasting the owner's time.

"Come on, Jen, we drove all the way over here. Besides, you just might like it."

George coaxed me. "Don't judge a book by its cover."

"All right, but I can tell you right now that I'm not going to like it," I grumbled, getting out of our car and heading toward the motor home.

George knocked on the owner's door while I stood near the RV. The man had been waiting for us. We followed him into the motor home. It was an older model, yet suddenly I could see a vision of redecorating it. It actually had possibilities. When he told us the price, it started to look even better, although at that time we didn't have a penny to put toward it. As it turned out, the owner was also a Christian man who had been laboring in the Lord. He and his wife were just getting too old to keep up with it. We told him that we would pray about buying the RV and get back with him.

When we left, it was all either of us could talk about. It was amazing how much I now actually liked and wanted the RV, particularly since I had been so dead set against it earlier. George said that if he got the job we prayed about, it would give us the extra money we would need. He wanted us to consider applying for a loan if the job went through.

"George, do banks even give loans on old motor homes?" I asked.

"Probably not, but we could always apply for a personal loan."

We had never asked a bank to lend us money, so we were treading on unfamiliar territory. This would have to be the Lord's doing. We would wait for phase one of our plan: the job first.

Two days after our talk, George came home all excited. "Honey, guess what? You are never going to believe this, but I ran into Jerry today and he's looking for a mechanic." He continued, "I told him I wanted the job, but would need

151

to come and go so that I could do ministry on the road. He really likes the idea." He finished with, "He hired me!"

I went into prayer alone. "Now wait a minute, Lord, you're moving way too fast for me. It's only been a week." One side of me was excited, especially at the thought that the possibility of getting the motor home might become a reality, yet the other side of me was not ready to leave the mission work. Deep down, though, the Lord's will for our lives was a priority. At the same time, I couldn't understand why our lives had to be so unorthodox.

Soon we were at the bank applying for a loan. Funny, I still remember the personal banker's name: Dora. She was not the typical personal banker. She stood out because she was interested in us as people, trying to make it work even though we didn't fit the usual criteria for a loan.

After we explained to her that we wanted to buy this old motor home to live in as we ministered to the poor, she asked us the next obvious question. "So, how do you plan to pay for this monthly, especially if you are leaving the mission to take on temporary part-time work?"

"Well, you see," George began, "My wife and I work for the Lord. He is our provider. We trust that He will give us the money we need every month when the money is due."

"Do you have any assets?" she asked George, hopefully.

"I own some mechanical tools and a few appliances in our home," he said, lightheartedly. We all had to laugh. Getting back to business, Dora told us that she would get back within the next twenty-four hours to give us an answer.

In all honesty, both George and I left the bank feeling doubtful. We lifted our prayer up to the Lord and waited for His answer.

The following day, the phone rang. It was Dora calling to let us know that the bank was going to lend us the money to purchase the motor home. She wanted us to come down and fill out the papers necessary for the loan to be approved. Part of me was elated, even though I knew then that the Lord was moving us out of the rescue mission ministry.

When we arrived at the bank, Dora informed us we would need full coverage insurance on the motor home. Then the oddest thing happened. In the next breath she said, "Oh, forget it, we'll just waive that policy. It'll cost a lot for you to do that. We'll make this a personal loan." What Dora did was almost unheard of, but I knew the source where that came from: the Lord's intervention. Within hours we were the proud owners of an Aspen Motor home.

We were busy the next month doing renovations. George built bunk beds for the children, we painted and of course wallpapered. New counter tops were installed and all the curtains with replaced mini blinds. Finally, the whole place was carpeted. The finished product was just as I had imagined it.

It was not yet the time to leave the mission. We were waiting on the Lord for His perfect timing. My eyes were still fixed on the property we laid out in the fleece. Maybe that would come later. Just the manifestation of the motor home and the open doors for George's mechanic's job was enough for me to see that the Lord was in this.

Meanwhile, we took our motor home out on the road on weekends. George came up with an interesting plan of survey. He wanted to get a better understanding of the highway people we would be ministering to. We put a questionnaire together, asking what they thought about God, the present day church, and life in general. We took our questionnaire and traveled on Interstate 40 between Albuquerque and Flagstaff. We would pray that the Lord would connect us with those that needed help. This gave George the opportunity to share the love of God while he fixed people's cars. If there was a wife and children, I would invite them in for something to drink and snack on while they filled out our questionnaire.

It was incredible the people God put in our path. I remember one man we picked up hitchhiking outside of Holbrook, Arizona. He was not the typical hitchhiker you would find out on the highway: no backpack, not even a hat to cover his head. The dead giveaway was his designer clothing and dress shoes. We found out that his car had broken down on the highway and been towed into Holbrook where a mechanic was fixing it. Not having time to wait because he was a scheduled speaker at a conference in Phoenix, the man decided to hitchhike. Why a rental a car wasn't an option was beyond us. Knowing that the Lord was using us out on the highway to minister to anyone in need, for us he was no exception.

We had a couple hours together in our motor home, so I started probing about this conference he was to speak at. Sharing with us his concepts of life, thoughts such as "Looking out for Number One", "Success is money" and "Finding our own power within us" gave me a good idea where his mind was situated. Our guest was claiming to be a Bible-believing man, so I challenged him on these beliefs. I reminded him of several scriptures in the Bible that were contrary to his teaching, such as Luke 16:13, "No servant can serve two masters; for either he will hate the one and love the other, or else he will be loyal to the one and despise the other. You cannot serve God and mammon (riches)", and 1 Corinthians 2:5, "that your faith should not be in the wisdom of men but in the power of God".

As we were nearing Flagstaff, the man pulled out a book that he had written on New Age Living. When he was getting out of our vehicle, he left us with these words: "You almost have me convinced that what God says in the Bible is true and the right path to take." He is one we hope to see in heaven someday.

We continued to do our survey whenever we could get away. The final analysis was that close to eighty percent of the people we came in contact with had been churched at one time in their lives. Most were bitter toward the church for one reason or another, with many thinking the church was full of hypocrites. Yet every one was thankful for our assistance. We encouraged them, telling them that our God truly loves them and has a plan and purpose for their lives in spite of what they think of the present day church. ·

We were able to make several trips to help Aaron and Theresa build their new home during this waiting period, and also waited upon the Lord to show us when to leave the mission. God was getting us ready for what He had in store for our future.

Aaron and Theresa were still working in Mexico. They opened a medical center among the Tarahumara tribe and started a co-op. Instead of getting involved in the "give-away" which can potentially hurt a culture as it affects their self worth, they began trading things such as cloth that the people can use to make their traditional dress in exchange for the traditional crafts that they make. The crafts were then brought back to the U.S. and sold. Profits were then put back into the community by supporting medical helpers and doctors who worked in the village. Wells were also dug. Aaron and Theresa asked us if we wanted to help sell crafts in the U.S. Their plan was to use the profit to support our ministry. We liked the concept, so we took on the venture for a short time. However we discovered it was consuming more of our time on the business end than on ministry. We did not want to take our life in that direction.

The Lord visited me in a dream one night as we were waiting on His direction for our ministry. I dreamed that George and I went to our friend Teri's house. She was entertaining her friends at a party she was hosting. As we were mingling with her guests, I happened to notice her neighbor, whom I could see in his house by looking through her living room window. What caught my eye was that he was holding a cross in his hand. In his other hand, he had a long thin strip of cloth. He was wrapping the cloth around the cross where the vertical and horizontal pieces of wood met. His face was stern. There was a sense of aggression in his actions. As I fixated on what this man was doing, he suddenly became aware that I was watching him. Our eyes met as we stared at each other for a few intense seconds. He then turned from the window and walked away. Somehow from the look in his eyes I could tell he was up to no good. Within a few minutes, there was a knock at the door. It wasn't hard to guess who it might be. Looking around the room full of people, I saw that no one else was paying attention to anything that was going on. I decided to answer the door. Sure enough, it was the man from next door who had stood in the window. We both again stared at each other intently. In my dream, he spoke up. "I'm the devil and I've come to kill you."

His abruptness shocked me, yet I found myself quickly answering back. "Well, I'm of the redeemed, covered by the blood of Jesus, and you have no power over me to touch me."

When those words came out of my mouth, he fell backwards onto the ground, left powerless. Amazement came over me to see such power in the words just spoken. Instead of recognizing that the power was in Jesus, I made the mistake of focusing on myself. "Wait a minute! I can't do that," I thought. "I don't have the power to do that!"

Somehow the man claiming to be the devil saw my weakness and stood back up. This time he was a little more forceful as he repeated the words previously spoken to me. Again, I stood in the blood of Jesus, knowing this was the only thing that was going to save me. He again fell backwards as before. Repeating my same behavior and lack of faith, back and forth we went with our words. This battle was becoming more problematic for me, because every time we repeated ourselves in this scenario, he became a little more powerful as he got up off the ground. By now he had me backed up into Teri's living room, all the while no one noticing what was going on. Then, in his final words, he said, "Not only am I going to kill you, but I'm going to kill all of your friends too."

Right then, the room filled with an eerie demonic sound, almost like the sound you hear when you slow down the speed of a record (for those of you who remember the phonograph and record days). Looking down at my dress, I saw the bottom beginning to curl up. The atmosphere was quickly changing into a dark, oppressive, demonic one. Not knowing what to do, I started to scream out to the Lord. Jesus was already answering me as He heard my plea for help. "Jennifer, I've already equipped you to fight this battle. Put your armor on" (Ephesians 6:10-18).

In my dream I cried out even louder. "Lord, don't do this to me at a time like this. Make this go away!"

Jesus gently responded, "I'm calling you out to minister among my people and you are going to need to know how to use your armor to do battle."

"But Lord, this kind of stuff is scary. I just want to do my weekly ministry here and go to church on Sunday."

"I have enough pew warmers. I need soldiers who will go out and fight the battle. I'm calling you as one of my warriors," Jesus replied.

I woke up from the dream, trembling like a leaf, totally petrified. "George, George," I said, shaking him awake. "I just had a really bad dream. It seemed so real!"

"Honey, we can talk about it in the morning," he replied drowsily, as he put his arms around me.

I was able to go back to sleep, yet by morning the dream had penetrated my heart. The Lord was giving me a glimpse and speaking to me about our future ministry. He was preparing me for what was ahead.

Throughout the years of ministry I have been reminded of this dream. I can safely say, "The Lord will never leave us nor forsake us" (Hebrews 13:5). Another reminder is the scripture that follows Hebrews 13:5. "So we may boldly say, 'The Lord is my helper; I will not fear. What can man do to me?'" (Hebrews 13:6).

I had thought my life was right on track spiritually. I had a full-fledged ministry working with displaced people, I was involved with the Sunday school children's ministry at church, I baby-sat twenty or so children every Thursday morning at church for moms that needed a break from their kids, besides taking care of my own family. Now, with the possibility of going out to do the highway ministry, I had to deal with my spiritual pride. The Lord intervened because He loves me too much to let me stay in that place.

One afternoon as I was busy doing household chores, Laura, who was a year or so old at the time, decided to get into my purse and pull everything out onto the living room floor. As I went over and started putting everything back into the purse, I noticed a tract (a little pamphlet sharing the gospel) called "The Four Spiritual Laws". Many of you are familiar with this booklet as it has been a Christian classic. I hadn't read it in a while so I decided to sit down on my couch and acquaint myself with it again.

Reading through the pages, I came across a diagram of two circles with chairs placed in each one. On one chair the letter "s" is on the throne, with a symbol of the cross outside of the circle. Also inside this first circle are a number of large and small dots around the chair going in every which direction. On the other chair was the cross on the throne with the letter "s" still in the circle but not on the throne. It depicts the dots all in an orderly form inside and around the circle. The two circles are supposed to represent two different kinds of lives: one self-directed and the other Christ-directed. At the bottom of that page it leaves you with the question, "Which circle best represents your life?"

As I pondered the pamphlet, it started dawning on me that my life represented the "s" sitting on the throne: self was dictating the direction of my life, not God. My life was a life of carnality. Yes, I knew I was a Christian, yet fleshly, wanting the worldly pleasures life had to offer me. Although I was steeped in the works of the Lord, my heart was far from wanting the Lord to direct my path of life. What if the Lord wanted me to go into an area where I didn't want to go? I wanted to be in charge of my own life. I actually had myself convinced that if I could accomplish all my goals, this would bring me more happiness than doing what God wanted me to do.

At that moment I started to cry. Confession started to pour out of my mouth, as I admitted to the Lord my wrong thinking, my carnality, and living for myself. I truly asked the Lord to help me surrender my life to Him for His service. Coming to the Lord for salvation is a one-time thing, yet I have learned that throughout our walk with God we need to constantly rededicate ourselves unto Him.

God accepted my repentant heart and I was very challenged at the opportunities that began to come my way. I thank the Lord for not leaving me in a stagnant place, for growing me up in His timing. He's looking for the yielded heart.

When the time finally came to leave the mission, we didn't leave Flagstaff right away. We first moved out of our home and into our motor home full-time so we could get used to it. During our move, Jerry, the mechanic that had hired George, told him that he had second thoughts about letting him come and go at will. We took it as a closed door from the Lord. Yet it didn't change our minds about going, because now we were committed to move forward. The Lord would provide for us.

In the three-and-a-half years spent at the apartment ministry, I never realized how busy we really were. My phone rang nonstop, both because the community charity groups knew that we rented apartments, and with requests for George's free mechanical work. Now that we were in the motor home and didn't have a phone, life was a lot less stressful. I had begun home schooling Jonathon two years previously, so that remained in my schedule. It took getting used to the four of us living in such a small space, but it wasn't as hard as I had anticipated it would be. What did turn out to be one of the hardest areas to overcome was something I didn't see coming. It was the remarks and attitudes of some of the people in the church.

One night while attending a service where a missionary couple came to speak, a fairly close sister in the Lord came up to me after the service. She started questioning me on our new lifestyle. "How do you plan to feed your family, living like you do?" she said, rather unkindly.

"What do you mean by that?" I asked, somewhat confused.

"You know what I mean. Where are you going to get groceries for your kids?"

It seemed like a dumb question, but I knew what she was insinuating now. Not being in the Spirit at the moment, I sarcastically responded, "Well, we'll probably drive into the parking lot of the grocery store, park the vehicle, and go into buy groceries like everybody else does around here." We looked at each with disgust and then turned in different directions and walked away. I went home that night and cried my eyes out. "How can someone be so cruel," I thought, thinking about what my friend had said earlier. "What would she do if God asked her husband to go in faith to serve the poor? Would she be disobedient to the call or go?" I asked the Lord indignantly that night.

Shortly after that incident, an attack came from another friend in the church. One day after the church service I ran into Sandra. I hadn't seen her in quite a while, so when we saw each other we were full of hugs and excitement. I asked her what she had been up to in the last couple months. She proceeded to tell me about the new addition on their house. I was very happy for her because she had just given birth to a new baby and having the extra space was something to appreciate. After we spent time talking about their life, the conversation shifted to my life. "How's your ministry going at the mission?" she asked.

"Oh, we aren't involved in that ministry anymore. God has called us to minister to the least and the lost out on the highways and hedges of America. We bought a motor home so we could travel around, ministering to those that the Lord puts in our path."

"You are so weird," was all she said, shaking her head.

Some might take that as a compliment, since the Lord does tell us in His word that we are a peculiar people (Titus 2:14 KJV), but I didn't. It was just another blow to me. After I got home and settled down emotionally, the Lord gave me a peace about it. It didn't matter what other people thought about our life, what was important was that God was pleased with us and we were being obedient to what He asked us to do. I wonder if Abraham and Sarah had scenarios like this when God asked him to pick up and move to a foreign land.

I knew this is where I would need to put my armor on to quench the fiery darts that came our way. During those trials it was a good time of foundation building, practicing a firm stance of where and what I am in Christ through the scriptures.

Not everyone was insensitive to us, though. We had a team of people that encouraged us regularly. With their encouragement and prayers, they sent us off like the early church did in the book of Acts. Our pastor was one hundred percent behind us. I wish we could say that all the elders from our church were as well, but some weren't. They told us to go out and in one year return with a report on what the Lord had done in our lives. We believe where God guides He provides. Our faith would be challenged by going out totally dependent on our Lord for His provision.

After the loss of Dan, we decided not to depart from Flagstaff until Teri was secure enough to have us leave. That day finally did come. We left, living in a faith ministry, not knowing where the Lord would take us from day to day. The Lord put hitchhikers, street people, and Christians in our path regularly, yet our time out on the highway was short-lived due to my insecurities.

It's funny how that nesting instinct we women seem to possess starts to kick in. Within a short period of time, I was revisited by my old urge to live in an actual house. Suddenly it seemed very important to me for us to plant ourselves somewhere for a time. I asked George if we could settle down again by moving out of our motor home and renting a house. I needed normalcy in my life. I was gratified that he was willing to do that for me.

Obvious thoughts of apprehension surfaced as I leaned on my own understanding of how we would pull this off. "Well, Lord, we have fifty-six cents in our name right now, and in order for us to move into a house again, we're going to need some extra finances."

We were near Albuquerque when I started harboring the idea of moving into a house. We called up our good friends, Tyler and Rachel, who welcomed us to stay parked on their property while we waited on the Lord for His provision.

Our Lord is faithful and His timing so perfect. That evening, I had called a close friend to just chitchat. In the middle of our conversation, my friend asked us how we were doing financially. Not wanting to put a burden on her,

I nonchalantly responded, "We get by. The Lord has been providing our needs daily."

"Well, the reason I ask is that I wanted to donate one thousand dollars to the work of the Lord," she said humbly. "While praying, I asked the Lord to show me who to donate it to and He put you on my mind. The odd thing is I reminded the Lord that you always have your needs met and it should go to someone who really is in need." She went on to tell me that the Lord spoke to her heart and said, "How do you think George and Jennifer have their needs met? It is I who place on people's hearts to help others out. Give it to them, they need it right now." She paused, and then added, "So, tell me, honestly, how much money do you have right now?"

I was almost embarrassed to tell her because pride was setting in. "Fifty-six cents," I blurted out. We both started laughing.

"Okay. That confirms what the Lord showed me, so where should I send the money?"

I was so happy that she had listened to the Lord. It also strengthened my faith by knowing that the Lord had opened the doors for us to rent a house. This would at least give us a month's worth of rent and to allow George to look for temporary work while we were in Albuquerque.

We began looking for a house right away when the money arrived, and found one within days. It wasn't in the greatest neighborhood, but it was fairly nice. What I really liked about it was that we had a small well, so our water intake was limitless. I was even more pleased that it had three good-sized bedrooms, and Southwest fixtures throughout. I enjoyed the looks of the house, even down to the color of the carpet.

We were on our way to Flagstaff immediately to get our things out of storage and over to our new home. Within the next week George was able to find a job installing sprinkler systems. What was so amazing about George's job was that he found himself with a crew of men up in the Santa Fe prison putting in a sprinkler system. George was able to share the love of God with several inmates, as well as with his co-workers. One of the things I love about the Lord is that He uses us no matter where we're at. While I was struggling with my insecurities, God continued to bless George with ministry.

He worked five days a week and never complained about not going back out on the road. I have to admit, I was somewhat skeptical about his behavior in all of this, yet it didn't keep me from enjoying my new home.

Besides spending time with Jonathon and Laura, my time was also spent doing the things I enjoy: decorating, meeting the neighbors, and getting involved with our new church. Because it was a mega church, we knew it would be important to plug into some kind of group. We love home fellowships, so we joined two, one on Tuesday nights, and the other on Friday nights. For the children's sake, we also met with the home school support group so Jon and Laura would meet children their own age. We did this all in one month's time.

All seemed well until one morning I awoke and began to pray to the Lord. This overwhelming feeling of emptiness came over me. Thinking about our future, the thought of living in this house day after day and going to the same church week after week gave me a sense of stagnation. Yes, this lifestyle was all right for now, but a year from now? Surely there was something more for us as a family that God would have us do. Should we go back out on the highway?

The next several days produced the same type of conversations with the Lord, and each day feelings of discontent with my life grew stronger. I decided to discuss it with George. "Honey, I feel so empty in our lifestyle lately. I thought this house would fulfill me, and yet I'm experiencing the opposite effect. I know deep down that the Lord has something for us and it's not this."

George lit up. It was as if he knew all along that this is not the Lord's plan for us. He had wisely understood that I just needed to get the notion of a house out of my system before we jumped into the next ministry. "Jennifer, I believe it's time for us to leave," he said.

"What are we supposed to do?" I said, puzzled.

"I've been praying about this for a while now, and..." He paused. "I believe the Lord wants us to go down to Mexico to help Ron and Eva in the migrant camps in Culiacan, Sinaloa."

I looked at him blankly. Why was he bringing up Mexico to me again? I thought Mexico was behind us. My next thought was, "And why am I always so resistant to my husband's direction in life?" It didn't stop me from expressing my disapproval. "George, I don't want to go to Mexico again; anywhere but Mexico!"

"It's only for four weeks. You can endure four weeks for the Lord, can't you?" he answered back.

Well, he did have a good point. If I could do one year there, surely I could do one more month. "Okay. I'll go one month, but that's it! One month!"

The timing of God was right at our doorstep again. Within the week after our conversation about going to Mexico and making preparations to go, our landlord decided to pay us a visit. It was a peculiar visit and our conversation was odd. He actually came over to tell us that his extra refrigerator needed to be stored inside our house, preferably in our dining room because there was nowhere else to put it. Out of the clear blue, all of a sudden he finds it important to store his extra refrigerator in our dining room. As far as I was concerned, that wasn't going to happen. I spoke up, "Excuse me. I am not going to have a refrigerator in my dining room. It will have to go somewhere else because there's no room there." I tried to say it as politely as I could.

"Well, if you don't put it there, then you'll have to move out," he responded, somewhat vindictively.

"Fine, then we'll move out," I said, knowing that we were heading in that direction anyway.

"Great! When will you be moving out?" he said, as if pleased with our decision.

"We can be out by the end of our rent period." That was that. We moved out by the end of the month.

We put our things back into storage and moved into the motor home, parked on Tyler and Rachel's property once again. We knew without a shadow of doubt that the Lord's hand was involved in closing the doors on the rented house. It was important for me to see that getting a house wasn't the answer to fulfillment. (Every time the urge to get a house would crop up in me during the next few years of ministry, I was reminded that a house was not the fulfillment I was looking for.) Unfortunately, we had to go through the whole moving thing for me to find that out.

There wasn't a doubt in George's mind about going to Mexico. He knew that God wanted us to go, and felt confident that He would also give us the finances to pay for the trip. He called Ron to make arrangements. They set a departure date: December 15th. We would head to Bisbee, Arizona where Ron and Eva lived, and caravan down together.

We began to tell our friends about our plans to go work among the migrant camps. Most of my friends knew what I thought of Mexico, so I asked them to pray for me that God would get me through our time there.

As the days drew nearer to leaving, my faith was starting to falter, especially after George and I sat down one evening and figured out our budget. We would need approximately two thousand dollars to go. We lifted it up to the Lord.

Week after week, as we made preparations to leave, our home fellowship groups would question us on finances. George would always assure them that the Lord was going to give us all we needed. I remember the last week of our Tuesday night fellowship before our due date of December 15th. George was saying his good-byes to everyone and asked them to keep us in prayer. The leader of the group piped up. "So, the Lord gave you the money to go?"

"Well, no, not yet. He will by Friday though, because that's when we need to leave to meet up with our friends in Bisbee," George answered as confidently as could be. On the other hand, my faith was zilch.

When we left the fellowship, I expressed to George how embarrassed I was going to be if by next Tuesday night when the group convened again we weren't in Mexico. We had three more days for two thousand dollars to come in. George's faith wasn't wavering a bit. I knew that when he replied, "I will be totally shocked if the money doesn't come in by Friday. That's how sure I am that God wants us to go to Mexico."

The next night we received a phone call from the same friend who had given us the one thousand dollars for the house rental. She knew we were planning to go to Mexico and had been praying for us. The reason for her call was God told her to give us the money to go. She then asked, "So, how much money do you need?"

Not wanting to take advantage of the situation, I replied, "The Lord didn't tell you how much to give us?"

"No," she said slowly.

"Could you go back into your prayer closet and ask the Lord to give you an amount, since it would be very difficult for me to tell you what we need."

She agreed, "All right, I'll do that. Whatever the Lord tells me, I'll send you."

Friday, December 15th came, and we were ready and packed to go. We still hadn't received the check our friend said she'd send, so we waited that day in anticipation for the mailman. It was one o'clock when he showed up. I ran over to get the mail. The check was there. We opened it to find exactly two thousand dollars in the envelope.

We hurriedly drove to the bank to make a deposit, and paid our bills. By early afternoon, we were heading to Bisbee, Arizona to meet with Ron and Eva. The following day we were on our way to Mexico for our one-month adventure among the migrant farm workers. Going for one month was my plan. God had other plans.

A man who has friends must
show himself friendly
But there is a friend who sticks closer
than a brother.

Proverbs 18:24

10
Back in Mexico

The Lord has a way of supernaturally changing our hearts to line up with His. Our "one month trip" to Mexico turned into eleven years. After two weeks ministering in the migrant camps, the Lord gave me the desire to stay in Mexico. I say supernatural because my heart was so far from Mexico before coming that even one month was stretching it. I had a lot of friends back home praying that I would be able to handle four weeks with a joyful heart, filled with the Holy Spirit. Their prayers worked! When we came back from our extended three-month trip, what was coming out of my mouth was not the Jennifer speaking months earlier. Now, we were asking our friends to pray that God would let us go back full-time.

I attribute some of our wonderful stay to the Mexican family Ron and Eva introduced us to. Jorge and Angelica opened their home and gave us a place to park our motor homes. They had seven children, a few grown and gone. Hospitality was their gift; they treated all of us with such honor and high esteem. With an open invitation to stay as long as we wanted, they made us feel very welcome.

We were located outside of Culiacan, a large metropolitan area five hundred miles south of the Arizona border, about twenty miles northwest of the town in a small village called Los Angeles. We felt comfortable and safe tucked away in this little *hijido*. To top it off, there were lots of children in the neighborhood of Jonathon and Laura's ages. The older children in Jorge and Angelica's household treated our children like their own, protecting and watching over them. Over the years, our family grew to love them like our own flesh and blood.

But let's go back to our first visit of three months. Upon our arrival, George and I discovered a dirt road in front of the house that ran alongside a canal that went miles south of where we were staying. The opportunity to hike that road every morning before starting each day was something to take advantage of. Passing the houses and corn fields as the roosters crowed in the early hours of the morning, smelling the country breeze, was a good way to start our day. This was the only time for George and me to be by ourselves since there was no privacy otherwise. During our morning walks, sharing our feelings and perceptions of the previous day took us down the road a couple of miles. Turning around, the hike back was spent praying for the day with its activities and needs, and for those that the Lord put on our hearts. In the course of these long hikes down that canal road, I started realizing what a beautiful ministry the Lord had led us to. Within two weeks, we were asking the Lord to let us come back to Mexico full-time to work among the indigenous farm workers in the surrounding area of Culiacan. I remember thinking to myself, "Why do I like this place so much? Am I just infatuated for the moment?" Yet each day my feelings of love for Mexico grew stronger and stronger.

Although the budget only allowed a month's stay, we knew that the Lord would sustain us financially if it was His will for us to stay longer. And that is exactly what happened. One month turned into two months, and then a third. Incredible circumstances happened allowing us to stay, and seeing the hand of God at work encouraged our faith even more.

Learning about the culture was a challenge because of the language barrier, something that now needed to be addressed. We didn't have our friends to help translate like we had back in the "Aaron and Theresa" days. Even though Ron could speak Spanish, we were not with him all the time. This was a good time to learn.

The Lord has a sense of humor. I remember the first Sunday church service we attended in our little village. The service was held in the evenings instead of the morning. Walking in, we noticed the wooden benches lined up one behind the other. A few chickens that strayed in and out didn't seem to bother anyone. The little children were playing and laughing as the church started to fill up. Most of the women had the top of their heads covered with round little veils, but no one seemed bothered that I didn't have my head covered. They were all very friendly. As the congregation started to settle down and the worship music started up, I was beginning to feel a little more comfortable in this somewhat strange environment. Just when I was feeling at home, our hostess Angelica stood up, walked to the front of the stage and began to talk. Not understanding a word she said didn't seem to bother me until I had heard her mention my name. Turning to Ron, the only one in our group who could speak Spanish, I asked him what she was saying about me.

"Well, she just told the audience that you were going to get up and sing a song for us," he said with a smile on his face.

"Tell me that you're joking," I pleaded.

"No, I'm telling you the truth. Look around, everyone is waiting for you."

I quickly glanced around. To my dismay, everyone was staring at me. "Ron, why did she do that? Now what am I supposed to do?" I said, starting to feel a bit panicked.

"Get up and sing a song. You'll think of something," he assured me.

Not knowing what else to do, I stood up and made my way to the platform. All the way up there I was fervently praying, "LORD, HELP ME!" I only had seconds to figure out what I was going to sing. Immediately, a song came to mind. Years earlier, an elderly missionary woman, who had ministered in Bolivia and knew that we were planning to go to Mexico, wanted to teach me a Spanish Christian song that she loved. Since that was the only Christian Spanish song I knew, and the only one that popped into my memory, it seemed like the appropriate song to sing. Would I be able to remember it?

Stepping up on the stage, I turned to the guitar player, Tomas, who happened to be Angelica's son. He was looking at me expectantly, waiting for me to give him the cue to know what to play.

"*Solamente en Cristo*," I said, shakily, yet somewhat relieved knowing there actually was a song to sing. As he started to play the chords, I felt more relaxed. Then, without thinking, I started to clap my hands to the beat of his music. Looking out unto the congregation, I saw that I had a captive audience, although eighty percent of them were staring in bewilderment as I started to sing in Spanish. Luckily, they joined in with clapping as they sang the song with me.

It was over quickly. I could hardly believe what I just did. Making my way back to my seat, I sat back down next to George, leaned over and said, "Did that really happen?" He was smiling ear to ear. He knew how much I hated getting up in front, let alone in a foreign country singing a song in their language.

After the service, several people came up to talk with me, believing that I knew Spanish following my performance. "*No hablo espanol* (I don't speak Spanish)," I answered them, to their confusion. Even our host family was surprised that I sang a Spanish Christian song so clearly.

From that day, Angelica wanted me to get up each Sunday and sing a song at church. I assured her that was the only Spanish song I knew. Besides, singing wasn't my ministry; in a pinch maybe, but not on a regular basis. She understood, yet I believe she was somewhat let down that I didn't want to pursue the music ministry in her church.

Angelica had a persistent personality, which helped a lot to get done through her for the kingdom of God. As we went to the migrant worker camps, her family came with us. They jumped right into the ministry every night, doing whatever they could to share the gospel.

Our first week of ministry was pure infatuation. As the weeks progressed, we saw the anointing of the Lord as we labored in love, hand in hand, as the body of Christ does when each of us is functioning together with our various talents and gifts the Lord gives to every one of us. Hundreds of people a night were responding to the gospel. It was a joy inexpressible. Realizing the witnessing opportunities we had at each camp, filled with indigenous people speaking hundreds of different dialects, mostly from the southern regions of Mexico such as Guerrero, Oaxaca, and Chiapas, was phenomenal. Many came from very hard places to reach, and now we had access to thousands of them in the surrounding area of Culiacan. This is what the Apostle Paul must have felt like when he arrived in Corinth. These were people groups from all different areas of Mexico, put together to work harvesting crops during a six-month period. As we were outsiders, so was everyone else in the camps. It amazed me how different each dialect sounded from another. Even though the workers all came from Mexico, their languages were as different as German is from French.

At this point, you might be asking yourself how we were able to communicate and bring the gospel to them since they all spoke a different dialect. Most of the indigenous people speak Spanish as a second language. Although the movies we showed were in Spanish, as were the dramas, singing and sharing of the message, we thought it was vital that we give each person a gospel cassette tape in their own language.

The way it was set up was awesome. In the back of our vehicle there was a cassette duplicator, along with a set of master cassettes in over two hundred different dialects. We had maps of each area of Mexico, color coordinated for each dialect that was spoken there, which were coordinated with our system.

We visited the migrant camps in the late afternoon, just about the time the migrant farm workers would be returning home. Some of our team workers remarked that the camps looked like what one might imagine a concentration camp to be, but I don't think they were that drastic. I would agree the conditions were rough, and many of them only had the canal for their source of water, which was dirty brown. Although a few of the nicer camps had water hauled in, that wasn't the norm. Some of the houses were constructed of tarpaper while others were built with bricks. Rows and rows of dwellings attached to one another, with barbed wire running across the rows of housing, did give the camps a "rundown" look. Because most of the toddlers didn't wear diapers, feces were all over the ground. Then, of course, with the feces comes the flies. The camp inhabitants prepared their food over homemade fire pits constructed of sheets of metal over rusty barrels or bricks. (Since then, most of the camps have been upgraded to better living conditions.)

First on the agenda was going door to door and inviting each family to our program, which started around seven o'clock in the evening. This was a good opportunity for us to ask them where they were from. This information helped us to know the dialect spoken by comparing it to our mapping system. If the family wanted to receive a free cassette in their language, we pulled out our diagnostic tape and placed it into our handheld cassette player. As they listened to several dialects from their home area, it was always easy to detect when their own language came up. Their faces would light up with understanding. Each bleep, distinguished between dialects, had a code number for that particular language. Next in order was to write that number down, and then go next door and repeat the process until we accumulated enough people who spoke one dialect to make a new batch of tapes. Then we had the "runners", who would take those numbers, run back to the truck where the duplication took place and hand the information over to our duplicator. The person in charge of making cassettes would then make copies and give them to the runners, who would deliver each tape back to its new owner.

Through this process, we met people on a more personal basis. We prayed for them or helped in whatever need they had, usually sickness due to the water system and hygiene. That's where the Mexican church came in. We couldn't speak Spanish in the beginning, so our brothers and sisters from the church ministered in that capacity. As I mentioned earlier, each night many people came forward in response to the gospel. It was so refreshing to see people who really wanted to hear about Jesus.

After the first week of going into the camps, we were so on fire for more. Meanwhile, we began to notice our home front had become neglected. There was not time for much other than our work, so our laundry and dishes started to stack up. The motor home was not exactly comfortable after a week's worth of messy buildup. The reality of housework was setting in. By the weekend, George felt someone needed to deal with the home, and he made it clear that it wasn't going to be him since he wasn't the homemaker. I was furious with him. "Why should I have to stay home and do all the dirty work and you get to go out and minister doing all the fun stuff?" was my complaint. This was an issue that needed to be taken up with the Lord.

As I was complaining to the Lord about how unfair all this was, and George's reaction that I should be the one to stay home, the Lord interrupted my thoughts. "I have called you to be the homemaker, not George (Titus 2:5b). You need to build your home environment up to be pleasant, not only for your family, but for Me." That took a little while to soak in. It wasn't until the Lord showed me that we were a team and I would be receiving the same reward as George for those souls won for the kingdom that I felt peace. I saw that having a peaceful and organized home base also furthered the goals of our mission. As much as I wanted to be out there every night, I could see that realistically George wouldn't be able to go into the camps if he had to manage the household chores and the children's schooling. That was my task. Another factor was that I have a difficult time driving at night, especially in Mexico. Clearly, if I wanted to go into the camps, I needed to organize my time better.

When I discovered that washing clothes by hand was going to be part of my daily routine, I have to admit being a happy camper wasn't in the equation. But like all things, you learn to make your circumstances work. With time, it was just part of the program. If it meant bringing the gospel to the least and the lost, the sacrifice of hand washing laundry was something I could do.

That was just the beginning. Then there was learning the Spanish language and learning about the local culture. One of the first things I learned quickly was how sick a person can get by drinking the water. In Mexico we all know not to drink the water, but in the school of hard knocks, I had to experience it firsthand to really know what that meant.

One night when I was freed up to go into the camps, we were invited to a family's abode for fellowship. Feeling blessed by the invitation, we gladly went. As we sat at the table, the woman of the house served us sweet rolls and bread, along with coffee and hot chocolate. I am not a coffee drinker, so I went for the hot chocolate. The only problem was that the water wasn't very hot. It was actually lukewarm. Knowing that the water source wasn't clean, I was concerned it hadn't been boiled long enough to kill the bacteria. Trying to be polite, I put all fears aside and drank it anyway. Was that a mistake!

It didn't hit me right away. I was all right through the night and into the next day. By early the next evening, though, I knew something wasn't right. We had just picked up a group of people from church who wanted to go out into the camps. Getting ready to head out, I suggested to George that he take me home first. The thought of spending hours in the camps exhausted me. Besides, it was Jonathon's birthday the next day and this would give me time to make his cake and prepare for the party we had planned for him.

After George dropped me and the children off at home, Jonathon was eager to get started on the cake. "Honey, mommy doesn't have any energy right now. I'm going to lie down for an hour or so and then we'll make your cake," I told him, barely able to keep my eyes open. I set up a movie for the kids to watch.

It seemed like I had just laid my head down when Jonathon was waking me and reminding me it was time to make his cake. "I think one more hour of sleep will do it, sweetie. Wake me up in one more hour." I lay back down, feeling more exhausted than when I went down the first time. As each hour passed it got worse. I felt bad that I wasn't getting up to make the cake, but Jonathon could see that mom was getting sicker by the hour.

By the time George got home, I was now in the bathroom violently throwing up and suffering from diarrhea. My whole body was shaking. The entire evening I was so intensely ill that I wasn't sure I was going to make it through the night. All that came to mind was the scripture "Joy comes in the morning" (Psalm 30:5b). I knew if I could just hold on through the night that I would live. Shaking non-stop, and with frequent trips to the bathroom, by the grace of God I did make it until morning. Unfortunately, I wasn't feeling much joy. Thirst had enveloped me, yet every time I tried to drink water it came right back up.

As it was Jonathon's birthday, George would have to make the cake and put the party together. I was in no shape to even help. As he was planning for the day's events, I was making my way to the bathroom for the umpteenth time. Shutting the door behind me, my body started to shake in a convulsive way. I had no control over my nervous system. My arms were moving in all different directions as if ready to go into a seizure. Screaming for George to come to my rescue was all I could think of. When he opened the bathroom door, I remember saying to him, "George, there is something seriously wrong with me." And then I was out. I fell into George's arms like dead weight. Now imagine being in a motor home, in a three by three bathroom, holding someone who has just passed out in your arms with their pants down. Poor George! He was absolutely panicked, yet he knew he had to get my pants up and get me out of the bathroom before calling for help. Meanwhile, out in the living room area were Jonathon, Laura, and several neighbor children watching a movie.

George managed to put me together and then dragged me out unto the floor. The children turned around, horrified when they saw me lying there unconscious. "Kids, you need to go outside right now," he said as calmly as he could. As the children were leaving, George knelt down to feel my pulse. There was none. Panic gripped him, especially when my eyes rolled back. It sent him out the front door yelling for help. Ron and Eva were parked right next to us so they were the first ones on the scene. "Jennifer has passed out and I don't know what's happening to her," he said, trying not to freak out.

Eva ran into the motor home and found me just as George had described. "Should we pour water over her?" George suggested.

"No," Eva responded, more composed. "Get a damp cloth and we'll put it on her forehead."

As George laid the washcloth on my head, they began to pray over me. Suddenly, I felt this pleasant sensation on my forehead. "Oh, this feels so good," I said, awaking. I opened my eyes to discover George, Ron, and Eva with a few others staring down at me while I was lying on the floor. "What happened?" I asked.

"You passed out in the bathroom. Are you all right?" George said, with great relief.

"Yes, I'm fine. I can't believe I passed out." I got up slowly, feeling very weak.

"You had me really scared," George said. "Thank God you're all right." He grabbed me in his arms and held on to me. But the problem still existed. I wasn't feeling well and we didn't know what was wrong with me. George didn't want to take any chances. He decided to go find the American doctor we knew who was staying in the area. Ron and Eva stayed by my side while he went to Culiacan.

After questioning me and giving me an exam, the doctor diagnosed me with Salmonella poisoning. "You were dehydrated and didn't have enough electrolytes. That is why you passed out," the doctor said. She summed up, "You will need to take this medicine to hydrate yourself. Meanwhile, the germ will work its way through your system."

'Well, how long does this last?" I asked in concern, knowing that just one night of this bug almost killed me.

"It depends on each individual, how quick your body can kick the bacteria out," she responded.

The rest of the day George wouldn't allow me to be alone. Since it was Jonathon's birthday, and the local church had planned a water baptism celebration the same day, George had his hands full. He asked several of our friends to take turns staying with me throughout the day. The hard part was over. My body was so weak that the better part of the day was spent resting.

God was so gracious to me. By the next day I was feeling much better. I was praising our Lord for such a quick recovery. "I hope to never to go through that again," I thought fervently. It was a horrible experience. It's amazing how such a little germ can knock a person out. We have since named those little germs "The giants in the land" (see Numbers 13:33).

*

We need to take the bad with the good. One of those good times was when Gary, Roberta, and their children came into our lives. We had only been in Mexico two months when they arrived. They had caravanned to Mexico with a family we knew from Flagstaff to participate in a big outreach planned for the month of February. Gary and his family were new to this mission field too. He was an apprentice under another missionary who was training him to record movies and cassettes in different indigenous dialects that were in the area.

The night we met stands out clearly in my memory. Parked in a different campsite than ours, when our friend Ted from Flagstaff came by to see George, Gary came along for the ride. George was still out in the camps so I invited them inside while they waited his return. As we were conversing, Gary noticed Jonathon and Laura snuggled in their beds. "How many children do you have?" he inquired.

"We have two, a boy and a girl," I answered.

"Oh, so do my wife and I," he responded. "How old are yours?" he added.

"My son is eight, and my daughter is three," I said. "And yours?"

"My son is seven, and my daughter is three also," he replied with excitement in his tone.

"That's great! We'll have to get them together," I suggested, just as excited. "Jonathon and Laura will enjoy meeting another American family here." I was happy at the thought that they would have playmates near their own ages.

There was a twenty second pause. I was watching Gary as he was glancing around our motor home. He spoke up again. "So, do you live in this motor home full-time?"

"Yes, we do. We're not sure if we'll be living here in Mexico full-time, but we're asking the Lord to open doors for us to stay for longer periods," I answered.

"We live in a trailer full-time too. We're also praying about coming to Mexico to minister," he said enthusiastically.

We paused again before he inquired, "What church are you affiliated with?"

"We have two, a Baptist church and Calvary Chapel. And you?"

"We're out of a Calvary Chapel too!"

We both were amazed at the sudden discovery of our similarities in lifestyle. Just about this time George came home. You could say George and Gary had an instant bond of brotherly love. They visited for another half hour; by then it was getting late. Gary mentioned that he would like to bring his family over the following day so we could all get acquainted. We agreed to do it, all of us looking forward to their visit.

The next day they came as scheduled. We all still chuckle about it. As we were making introductions, George, ever a tease, looked at their son, Jacob, and asked in a confronting matter, "So, are you a Christian?" Jacob, only being seven years old, turned to Roberta and said, "Mom, what do I say?" We all started to laugh. From there on out we began to bond very closely with each other.

The Lord is so good! I can't express those words enough. He knew that our family needed their family in our lives. For the next seven years He put us together as co-laborers in the migrant camps. Eighteen years later, they are just as much a part of our lives.

We couldn't get enough of fellowship together the first month. They invited us to move to their campsite, situated a few miles outside of the city of Culiacan. We found ourselves together almost every night after our return from the camps anyway, so we decided to take them up on it.

The children were ecstatic to have other American children to play with too. Roberta and I liked it because not only did it give us leverage to get our kids to finish their schoolwork quickly, but the two of us also enjoyed the fellowship together. Like me, she stayed home to keep up with the household duties, so we had each other for company when our husbands went out to the camps.

*

Money was getting low halfway into our three-month stay. I was getting somewhat nervous, which wasn't unusual for me. I constantly tried to figure everything out logically, to no avail, and yet the trials to test my faith were always present.

Arising one early morning, George and I went out to take our daily walk. Passing by our vehicle, George noticed what looked like money lying on our dashboard. He walked over and looked in. Sure enough, it was money. What was so peculiar about this whole scenario is that the doors to our van are locked every night. How did someone get into our vehicle to put the money there? Even as George first saw the money, he noticed the doors were locked. We questioned everyone in the camp, but they all denied that they put it there. Still, this wasn't something to complain about; we were actually thrilled, because this was our ticket to stay in Mexico longer. We were completely mystified how someone got into our van. We never did find out who put the money there, and probably won't ever know, yet thanked the Lord He gave us the desire of our hearts to stay the whole three months.

Our finances continued to come in from different sources, mostly from the people who came down to help in the big outreach we were planning for the month of February. They would come to us and say, "The Lord told us to give this to you." It was always what we needed for the time. Through the Lord's provision, each day my faith was being strengthened.

Just when everything was going well, my faith being built up and feeling positive about being a full-time missionary in Mexico, the enemy was on his way to come and try to discourage and rip me apart. The enemy didn't waste any time.

During our February outreach, many Christians, about one hundred of us, gathered together to impact the camps with the gospel of Jesus Christ in the surrounding area of Culiacan. It was a big event for all of us because people would be coming from many countries.

One late morning, a group of women and I decided to go grocery shopping together. A new modern store had just opened, so we were all excited to check it out. Entering the store, we each went our separate ways with plans to meet up at the checkout counter at a certain time. I was thrilled to find items in there that I hadn't been able to get since we left the States.

As the cashier was scanning my groceries, I noticed one of the missionary women acting somewhat cold toward me. Maybe I was overreacting, I thought; it was probably all in my head, so I tried to brush it off. Unfortunately, it became quite evident that it wasn't in my head after all when she pointedly ignored me in the car. Feeling more and more uncomfortable at her continued chilliness, I finally addressed her. "I've noticed that you are acting cold toward me. Have

I offended you in some way?" I asked, trying to sound as reasonable as possible.

"Well, now that you've brought it up, yes, as a matter of fact I'm very offended at you," she answered soberly.

"What did I do?" I asked, totally mystified.

"I noticed that you bought a JAR of almonds in the grocery store, and that is just plain wrong of you," she said in all seriousness.

I was still bewildered. I wasn't getting it. "I bought a jar of almonds. Explain this to me," I said, not grasping where this conversation was going.

She retorted in a scolding manner, "People give missionaries their hard-earned money, trusting that they'll use it wisely."

I still wasn't catching on. Don't we all need to eat? I thought almonds were healthy for you, and wouldn't my supporters want me to stay healthy? "So, why am I wrong for buying almonds?" I asked, now starting to feel a bit perturbed with my attacker. "Can't missionaries eat almonds?"

She jumped back with an answer. "What I'm trying to tell you is that buying almonds in a jar is a lot more expensive than buying almonds in bulk. They had bulk almonds at that store, and you chose to spend your supporter's money on a jar you didn't need."

At this point she had me riled. My thoughts went right into the flesh. How dare she attack me like this? I cook everything from scratch, from cookies to bread, and she buys everything prepared, which is a lot more costly. Talk about hypocrisy! I was ready to pounce on her with my words. Just as I was ready to point her in the direction of her boxed cookies and canned beanie weenies, the Lord intervened and helped me to hold my tongue. Everyone else in the car kept silent, not wanting to enter our bizarre conversation, and I didn't blame them. I hadn't wanted to be involved with this conversation myself. After a few minutes of silence and a time of reflection, rather than becoming enraged, I decided to take a humble position. I spoke up again. "I'm sorry I've offended you." That's all I could say. There was very little conversation from any of us all the way back, the atmosphere heavy with feelings of discord.

By the time I entered my motor home the tears began to fall. George questioned me, seeing my obvious distress. I sat down and told him the whole story. He comforted me with his words, "You know, honey, we aren't fighting flesh and blood. It's the enemy who is really attacking you. She thinks she's doing you good by sharing that information with you. We are all different and see life at different angles. Don't let the enemy have the victory by holding a grudge against her. Try to overcome this and forgive her." I knew he was right, yet every time I thought about it I was irritated all over again. What really bugged me was that she was a seasoned missionary. I felt that she should be more mature than this. My thoughts went back into the conversation. As I was dialoguing back and forth in my mind about how she was judging me for what I bought when she could buy whatever she wanted, I was interrupted by the knock at my door. I opened the door to find the woman was standing there, holding a bag in her hand. I let her in. "I wanted to give you these extra almonds since you like almonds so much," she said in a kind voice. I could tell she felt sorry about our earlier encounter.

"Thank you, but you don't need to give me your almonds, because I don't really eat a lot of them," I said, also feeling bad about our previous meeting.

"No, really, I want you to have them."

"Well, thank you." The following silence was a bit awkward. She turned around and began to leave. I followed her out the door to say good-bye. We both looked at each other again. "Look," she said, "I know I hurt you in this whole thing and I feel bad about it. But, you know, you've hurt me too. I've tried to be a mother to you and you constantly reject me." Somehow she had a way of putting me in a state of confusion. I didn't know where to go with this new development. "Mother me?" I thought, "A person needs to gain the respect of the person they want to mother. This is not my idea of mothering." I was left speechless, but I knew I needed to bring something to the table.

"I'm sorry about you feeling rejected by me. I had no idea I was rejecting you in our friendship." By this point, we were both so wound up emotionally we began to cry and hug each other. There was still uneasiness about the moment, yet I put my feelings aside and tried to make this a time of genuine reconciliation. We said our good-byes and she left.

After she was gone, puzzled thoughts surfaced again, and they consumed me all afternoon. Later, that evening while we were visiting Gary and Roberta, they picked up on my preoccupation. Roberta happened to be one of the women present during the almond ordeal so she knew what I was struggling with. "Don't let this discourage you; it's just one of the tactics of the enemy," she said. It was the same thing George had told me earlier.

Gary pulled out a video from his collection and suggested we all watch it. Reminding us of what spiritual warfare meant, the video was perfectly appropriate for the occasion. It showed a true story about a couple who felt called to the mission field overseas. Their experience was similar to ours, except they left the field, never to return, because of anger and bitterness.

Watching the video helped me to put things into perspective. It sounds absolutely ridiculous that someone would desert their mission over a petty disagreement, thwarting the work of the Lord, and yet I recognized that the battle can get so out of control that one could actually throw in the towel because of pride and unforgiveness. I wasn't going to let a few almonds get in the way of our ministry. I laid my burdens before the Lord that evening, ready to move on. I do have to admit, though, that every once in a while we all make light of it when we're around almonds.

*

Before heading back to the U.S. after our wonderful three months in Mexico, Angelica asked if we would go up into the mountains to visit an elderly couple she knew of. They lived by themselves, mostly off the land. The couple happened to be the parents of her friend that lived down the street from her. She knew this family desperately needed the Lord in their lives, and thought that going up there to show them the "Jesus Movie" would give them the opportunity to hear the gospel.

Angelica and her neighbor planned this outing one week after we would be gone, so we had to politely decline the invitation. In her persistence, she wouldn't take "no" for an answer. "This is so important for all of us. We don't know when the Lord will take them home." She added, with urgency in her voice, "It's so great that they're willing that we even come up to show the movie to them. We've planned to make tamales and make a day of it."

How could we say no, especially after they had been so kind to us and hosted us during our stay in Mexico? Besides, she did have a good point. What's one more week when it could mean someone's salvation being at stake? We stayed that extra week as Angelica and her neighbor made plans for the visit.

Our van was pretty full the day we went up into the mountains, all packed in like a can of sardines. On arriving, the girls suggested getting started on the tamales at once since it was time-consuming to make them. I had thought they made them beforehand so they would only need to be heated up. I was wrong. Not only were they not made, but we were going to make them from scratch, and I don't mean ground up *masa* from a bag. The girls were heading out to the cornfields to pick the corn that was needed. As they handed me a bucket, making food from scratch took on a whole new meaning for me. It wasn't so bad pulling the corn from the stalks. It was when the corn grinder was pulled out that I knew I was in trouble. After the corn was cut from the cob, it was then placed inside the grinder. The girls took turns operating it. I soon found my arms were in no shape to be cranking that heavy-duty contraption. For the first five minutes it was all right, but soon it was time to put my pride aside and ask George to help me out with my share of the work. I really felt like a wimp.

It's amazing how cheap it is to make tamales from a cornfield. We were able to feed a crowd of people on hardly anything. The dinner was wonderful. After the laborious preparations of the meal, we were able to show the "Jesus Movie." The final outcome was a time of rejoicing. Mom and Dad gave their lives to the Lord that evening with sincere repentant hearts, along with their deaf son. It was all so worth it.

On the way home, as we traveled back on the mountainous roads, Angelica and her neighbor were extremely happy. They just couldn't quit talking about it. They told us that they had tried to share the gospel of Jesus with the parents for many years with no response. This day they were experiencing a miracle, seeing the power of God move upon this family.

Since then, the elderly couple has gone home to be with the Lord. We look forward to seeing them again in heaven for eternity.

.....but we also glory in tribulations,
knowing that tribulation produces
perseverance;
and perseverance, character;
and character, hope.
Now hope does not disappoint,
because the love of God
has been poured out in our hearts
by the Holy Spirit
who was given to us.

Romans 5:3-5

11
Another Round in Mexico

It was such a blessing to be back in our own country, yet surprisingly, all George and I could talk and think about was Mexico. Our friends were shocked at my change of heart. They knew something supernatural had happened to me when I expressed our desire to go back full-time. It became our daily prayer to the Lord that He would open the doors to return.

Gary and Roberta also felt the same way. They were already making plans to return that summer and were going to caravan to Oaxaca with the recorder, hoping to be trained to do more recording. Two families were planning a trip to Mexico City first, then into the mountainous terrain of Oaxaca where the recording would take place. We wanted to be part of the caravan. Instead of going to the mountains of Oaxaca, though, we thought it would be advantageous to head to Oaxaca City to spend the summer learning more Spanish. The American doctor who had treated me for Salmonella and her family lived in Oaxaca City. When we were in Culiacan, she had invited us to stay with them. When she found out that we wanted to come for the summer, she asked us if we would be willing to house-sit while her family was on a planned trip to the U.S. Their housekeeper would be the only one in the house.

We began to pray for the finances to cover our expenses that would be needed before the caravan left. This gave us about a three-month time span. Oaxaca City was much too far for us to travel by car alone because of our poor knowledge of Spanish and complete unfamiliarity with the area. We weren't sure how much money it would take to make this trip, yet by faith God would provide. So, we waited.

Meanwhile, we stayed in Albuquerque. During the waiting period, George and I decided it was time to sell our white van or trade it for a more useful vehicle for future work in Mexico. A truck seemed more appropriate. We also owned a cherry red GMC Jimmy that we were willing to sell or trade along with the van. We didn't want to haul our motor home all the way to Mexico City, especially since we would be staying at a house in Oaxaca, so getting a fairly good-sized camper shell to put behind the truck would suffice for our summer plans. Checking the car lots in the area to find what we had in mind was next on our agenda.

Cruising down Fourth Street, George drove the van as I followed behind in the Jimmy. After passing several lots, George found a blue four-door truck that caught his attention. Looking at it more closely, he realized it was just what we wanted. The car dealer was inside his office, and as we made our way over to the building, we saw tucked away behind a few other vehicles a big camper shell. In our excitement, we didn't waste any time, darting over to look at it before talking with the dealer. Then we hurried inside, hoping that the salesman was ready to make a deal. George gingerly struck up a conversation with the car dealer. After some chit-chat, he mentioned that we had our eye on the big four-door truck. "Would you be interested in trading our white van that's parked outside here for your truck?" he said boldly.

Sad to say, the man wasn't at all intrigued at this offer. He made it clear that he had no need for vans. A little despondently, George told him, "The only way we can buy the truck is if we can sell our van."

"Vans just aren't a hot item right now," the car dealer repeated. He no sooner finished his sentence when the office door opened.

Two men stood before us. "Excuse me," one of them began, "Is that white van parked in front for sale?" pointing out the door toward our van.

Simultaneously, both George and I answered, "Yes, it is!"

"How much do you want for it?" one of the men asked.

"Eighteen hundred dollars," George told him.

"We'll take it!" the man cried enthusiastically, pulling out a wad of money.

"Don't you want to take it for a test run first?" I couldn't help but ask.

"No, we trust you," was all they said.

After they handed him the full amount, George pulled the keys from his pocket and handed them to one of the men, telling him we had the title with us in the glove compartment. He went out and brought it back into the office. "Are you a Notary Public?" George asked the car dealer. He was, so the title was signed and notarized, and the two men were out the door and driving away almost as fast as a blink of an eye. The three of us stared at each other in astonishment. "Did that really just happen?" I said.

"In the forty years I've been at this business, this is the first time I've ever seen anything like what just happened," the salesman said. "This is totally uncanny." We were quite amazed ourselves, yet we knew Who the source was behind the sale.

Now that we had eighteen hundred dollars in our hand, we were ready to bargain, and expressed our desire to buy the camper shell too. Our other vehicle, the red GMC Jimmy, was also parked in the lot. We asked the man if he would be interested in trading it for the camper. He looked our car over, liked it, and didn't hesitate to make the deal. He even threw in four good used tires to fit the truck. That day we drove away in our new, used, blue four-door truck with a nice big camper shell anchored inside the back of the truck. Where vehicles were concerned, we were ready for Mexico.

Shortly after our endeavor at the car lot, a phone call came from Flagstaff. Some dear friends of ours were planning a trip to Africa without their children. They called to ask us if we would house-sit and watch their kids for two weeks so they could make the trip. Not having anything else going on at the time, it gave us something to do.

Upon arriving, they said the Lord told them to give us five thousand dollars. "We don't know what you're supposed to do with it," they added, "but it's yours to use for what you want." They knew we wanted to go to Mexico, though they stressed that it wasn't necessarily for that, but we knew it was for Mexico.

So their trip to Africa was fruitful for us, while their house was full of children, four of theirs and two of ours, playing and running nonstop. After those two weeks I had a much greater appreciation for what was involved in raising large families.

Excitement was in the air. The anointing to go back to Mexico was there. We couldn't wait to call Gary and Roberta and tell them the good news about our provision from the Lord.

As we waited with anticipation for our return to Mexico, our plans were finalized. We would all caravan down to Mexico City together and spend a week or so with another missionary family that lived there. Then George and I, along with our children, would head to Oaxaca City for our Spanish classes, while Gary and Roberta's family and the recorder's family would head to the mountains to do some recording. When summer came to an end, we planned to all meet back in Mexico City and caravan home together.

We all met in Albuquerque to start our trip, our truck packed to the brim with everything we thought we would need. Traveling south, the weather and road conditions were fairly decent until the third day. A rain storm hit that morning. By eleven a.m. the water was so high it started to seep into the floorboards of our vehicles. We lost track of where the highway actually was, but didn't want to stop for fear that we would get stuck. We were relieved that at least the water wasn't forming a raging current. We were able to inch our way through until the rain finally let up. Needless to say, we were all thankful to finally arrive at our host's home in Mexico City safely.

During our time there, we were able to catch a few sights before going to Oaxaca, one being Popocatepetl, a volcano fifty-five kilometers east of Mexico City. This well-known volcano, actually the second highest volcano in North America, ascends nearly eighteen thousand feet. We learned that "*Popocatepetl*" is the Aztec word for "Smoking Mountain", reported in historical times to have erupted about thirty times, although documentation is poor. This was only one of the many interesting and widely-held legends we learned while we were in the area. Our children enjoyed hearing the history and making the steep ascent up the mountain, although they came down fairly soon since the temperature dropped sharply the farther up they went.

On our way home from this outing, our three families piled inside our truck, with a few in the back, talking and laughing about the day's activities. Not long after leaving, though, a taxi driver, who was drunk and speeding, plowed right into the side of our truck as George made a left turn. George, not at first realizing how fast the taxi was actually going, was able to maneuver our truck out of the way, dodging between other vehicles that were at a stop. Still the taxi hit us at the back end of the truck bed. Thank God, no one was hurt. We were all shaken but there were no injuries.

As it turned out, what followed was just as stressful as being in the accident.

A crowd of people immediately surrounded us, all speaking in fast loud tones, of course in Spanish. Before we could answer, we knew it was important to find someone who could translate for us, as well as someone who understood the law. We were only blocks away from our destination, so we were able to find a Christian neighbor who was willing to help us in our predicament.

Fifteen minutes or so later, the police showed up. Once our lady translator came on the scene, she and the police began their dialogue. What a mess! We could tell that she was trying to be as diplomatic as possible; unfortunately, that didn't help. With defeat plastered across her face, she informed us that in Mexico when there is an accident, the two parties involved will have their cars impounded if they can't come up with a reasonable resolution between the two of them. In this case, although she explained to the officer that we made a left turn on a green, being totally legal, and the taxi driver had been speeding as well as drinking, the police were determined to take George and the taxi driver down to the station anyway, along with both vehicles.

We were disappointed with this decision, but there was nothing else to do but follow directions. At the police department, it looked at first as if we were going to win the dispute when the officer handed George the taxi driver's license, which means victory. That lasted until several other taxi drivers showed up and began to fight for their rights. They wanted us to pay them one thousand dollars for the repairs of the vehicle.

Knowing that we wouldn't be able to get our truck back for some time otherwise, we agreed to give them the thousand dollars. Taking the monetary loss seemed easier to deal with than the Mexican police department. It would have been one thing if we had been able to personally talk with them, but everything had to be done through a translator. To top it off, we still needed to pay to get our own back axle fixed.

After hunting around the city, we found a repair shop with the parts we needed. George would be able to fix the axle himself, but the body work was going to cost another six hundred dollars. The grim realization of not being able to afford a language tutor once we arrived in Oaxaca was setting in.

At the thought of that, I moped around the next few days, at times finding myself crying over the loss of our Spanish lessons. After a few days of this, I knew it was time to snap out of it and adopt a more mature outlook. I always find it helpful to start thanking the Lord for what I do have during times like this. We really did have so much to be thankful for. We had been able to pay for the accident and repairs of our vehicle, and most importantly, no one was hurt in the wreck. Despite the circumstances, we knew that God would work everything out for good, and He would show us another way to learn Spanish that summer.

(Gary captured this whole episode on video and likes to pull out the family videos of Mexico when we're visiting. Whenever he comes to this part of the footage, I cringe inside as I remember the chaos of that afternoon in Mexico City.)

The Lord's hand was upon us during our dilemma. Despite the language barrier, George hit it off quite well with the mechanic at the body shop, who turned out to be a Christian pastor in a small barrio near the shop. After hearing that George ministered to the homeless, the pastor asked him if he would be the guest speaker at his church on Sunday. George was delighted.

Exhilarating as it would be to share at the church, George did not want to heed our advice to wear a necktie. He argued that he didn't want to put on airs with his audience, believing the church would have a "down home" atmosphere. Our friends reminded him that in Mexico, especially as a speaker, you must wear a tie. Reluctantly, he gave in after we all concurred that he needed to be respectful.

I still chuckle when I think about the moment we walked into church. George was absolutely right thinking this was a "down home" kind of church. Even the pastor was dressed in laid-back attire. George looked completely overdressed for the occasion. We all sheepishly returned his look.

Necktie or not, he did a fabulous job. We had a wonderful translator named Sharon. She had a meek, gentle spirit about her, able to set the mood with reverence to the Word. We didn't see any fruit come forth that evening, yet the Bible says that God's word does not come back void (Isaiah 55:11). His word is living and powerful, and sharper than any two-edged sword, piercing even to the division of soul and spirit, and of joints and marrow, and is a discerner of the thoughts and intents of the heart (Hebrews 4:12). Little did we know until years later, He was touching the heart of a young eight-year-old girl sitting in the audience that evening. Ten years later, while shopping in a home improvement store in Culiacan, Sinaloa (note that these two places are far apart from each other, being in different states of Mexico), a young woman approached us in the aisle. "Excuse me," she said somewhat shyly, "Is your name George?"

"Yes, it is," George replied, as we looked at her with curiosity.

"My name is Maria," she said. "You probably don't remember me because the last time you saw me I was around eight years old." She went on to say that she grew up in Mexico City and was in the audience the night George shared the gospel. "I surrendered my life to the Lord that night and have walked with the Lord all these years." She added, "I always remembered your name and your looks."

We were completely amazed, not only by what she just said, but that the Lord would put this young woman into our lives again after all these years. It certainly encouraged us to keep on keeping on.

*

After finishing the truck repairs, it was time to move on down the road to Oaxaca. We all traveled together until we arrived in a small indigenous village called Huajuapan de Leon. There we parted company.

During our stay in this village, we were introduced to a young woman and her four children. I'll never forget what I saw; it impacted me so greatly. Juanita was a beautiful, slender girl who looked to be in her late twenties. As we entered her home, I could tell that her life was one of poverty. The only thing in the first room of her home was a two-burner camping stove on the dirt floor. On top of the stove was a cast iron pan. That was everything in the entire room. No wall hangings, no dishes, nothing! As we walked into the second of the two rooms, we saw her lying there on a straw mat on the dirt floor, covered with a thin wool-looking blanket. What stuck out in my mind was the big smile she wore as we came in to meet her. Soon she began to share her story through our interpreter. We listened intently as she told us that a year earlier she was hit with a disease that left her paralyzed. After finding out that this condition was permanent, her husband deserted her for another woman, leaving her with four young children to care for on her own. Cautiously, I asked her how she was able to do that. Of course her friends and neighbors pitched in with their services, but she explained that her eldest son, around six years old, sold *chicles* (gum) to the locals to earn money. As the interpreter translated for us in English, as a side note the missionary of the village told her that this young lady borrowed a wheel chair weekly to go to the church service, at least a mile from where she lived. Faithfully, she attended every week, never missing a service. It took everything I had not to weep at her difficult situation, and yet one could see the joy of the Lord permeate her whole being. In the natural, how could anyone be so joyful at such a hopeless-seeming situation? Only through the Lord is it possible. (When we told this story to a group of believers in the States, a ministry that helps paraplegics donated a wheel chair to her. It was sent down to the missionary that ministers in the village.)

Leaving Huajuapan de Leon, we spent a comfortable time driving through the beautiful landscape as we headed to Oaxaca. We did feel a little out of our element now that we were alone without our caravan, yet we knew the Lord was with us. We were ready to meet our next challenge, finding a way to learn Spanish without the money to pay for it. God would give us direction.

Mercedes met us at the door when we arrived. She was the nanny for our friends Don and Melissa, who had offered their home to us while they were in the States. She seemed pleasant, and I could tell by her countenance that we would get along just fine. We immediately discovered that she was not bilingual either. Between our few Spanish words and her few English words, I could see that this was going to be an interesting summer.

The house was large, and it didn't take us long to spread out and enjoy ourselves after the four of us being cooped up in the camper. We were more than ready to unpack and get on with business. What impressed us was the outside brick wall surrounding the property. All around the top of the wall were pieces of broken glass bottles embedded in the dried concrete. This was to protect them from "would-be" intruders. I noticed that a lot of other Mexican people had the same idea for safety. It is a fairly common practice to landscape in this way.

Within the first couple of days together, Mercedes and I decided it would be advantageous to help each other learn the other's language. We made flash cards with an English word on one side and Spanish on the other side. When we visited the school our friends earlier recommended, we found we still were able to afford to hire a private tutor for two or three days a week. It was settled that I would take the lessons, and then teach George everything I learned that day. It wasn't as effective as if we both could go together, but it was better than nothing.

Oaxaca was beautiful. Not only were we surrounded by lush landscaping, but the Mexican people were friendly and hospitable. In the marketplace strangers would come up to us and strike up a conversation. In spite of the language barriers, they had the patience to work it out with us, which helped us considerably with our language practice. There weren't many other Americans around to speak English with, so we really had to learn to communicate in Spanish. The food was fabulous too. We took turns cooking meals with Mercedes. I think she enjoyed trying the American food just as much as we did the Mexican cuisine.

One day, enjoying another gorgeous afternoon at the house, we heard a knock at the door. We answered it, wondering who it could be. Opening the door, there stood an American family. "Hi. Are Don and Melissa here?" the man asked.

"No, sorry, they went back to the United States for the summer," George answered, wondering who they were. He added, "We are here for the summer house-sitting for them."

"We are friends of Don and Melissa. We are also missionaries in the state of Oaxaca and we've traveled three hours to see them." (This was before cell phone days.)

Sensing that they were waiting for an invitation, we were more than happy to welcome them in for a visit. Besides, we were overjoyed by the fact that they were Americans and could speak English with us.

They were so fun. We spent the afternoon sharing stories and laughing. As we were becoming more acquainted with our guests, we shared where we originally came from. When I shared that I was from Minnesota, our guests remarked that one of their co-workers was from Minnesota too. "So, what's your co-worker's name?" I asked out of curiosity.

"Terry O'Brien," he replied.

At the mention of the name, immediately thoughts of my childhood surfaced. Surely it couldn't be the Terry O'Brien I knew from grade school, I thought. I let the subject go as we conversed about other things, but within minutes that thought popped back up in my mind. "You know what? I know a Terry O'Brien that lives in St. Paul, Minnesota," I said, as they looked at me with surprise. I reasoned, "How many Terry O'Brien's live in Minnesota though?" I dropped the subject once more, yet somehow I felt the need to probe further. "Does he have red hair and freckles?" I asked. They laughed at my persistence.

"Yes, he does," the couple unanimously said. Well, how many O'Brien families have red hair, was my next thought. I had one more question before I finally dropped the subject. "What high school did he go to?"

"We don't know," they said.

We moved on to different topics, losing track of the time. At dusk, after a good three-hour visit, they needed to be on their way, since they had a long drive ahead of them. Just before they were ready to leave, I just couldn't help asking one more question about Terry. "Ask your co-worker if he ever lived on 1835 Brandon Street." They assured me they would pass the message on.

After they departed, I explained to George that when I was about ten years old, we lived in a duplex next to the O'Brien family. I was friends with the older sister. It had been twenty-two years since I last saw them. What if it was really the same Terry I knew that lived here in Oaxaca as a missionary? I left it at that.

Just three days after our visit with the missionary family, there was a knock at the door. Another missionary we previously met in Culiacan, who lived in Oaxaca City, was standing at the entrance as we welcomed him in. "I have a mutual friend that I would like to reacquaint you with," he said, as he stepped out of the way. Standing behind him stood a tall, slender red haired, freckle-faced man. He walked inside, shaking my hand. "Hi, I'm Terry O'Brien from 1835 Brandon Street," he said confidently. He didn't even look familiar. I would have never guessed it.

"Oh, my goodness, it's little Terry O'Brien, all grown up!" I said without realizing what I had just said. "Do you even remember who I am?"

"Well, actually, I don't remember you. That's why I'm here, so I could meet you," he replied.

I told my story of living on Brandon Street for about three years when I was a little girl, and how I played Barbie dolls with his sister on our front porch almost every day. His memory was coming back as he recollected the dolls and the porch. As we talked, he began to remember our family living on the other side of the duplex. We had a great time reminiscing about the different activities that went on in the neighborhood. Once he brought up the McNeil family who lived across the street, we were on familiar ground. Both of us remembered them. "How could anyone forget them," I remarked. It was hard to forget a family with ten active children. "Do you remember when one of the kids started their house on fire?" I asked. "My dad took pictures of it and for years we would have to go through the slides of the fire." We both laughed. That was also etched in his memory bank. More interesting yet, he told me three out of the ten McNeil children became Christians, and happened to be on the mission field also. Suddenly, we both looked at each other wide-eyed. What were the chances of five children on one block, including Terry and me, all becoming missionaries? We concluded that there must have been an elderly Christian living on the same block who knew those wild and crazy kids all needed the intervention of the Lord and prayed fervently for our salvation and future. Never underestimate the power of prayer!

Terry stayed and visited for several hours but at last needed to get on his way. It was such a blessing to meet up with a childhood friend so far from home after twenty-two years, and to discover he was a missionary too.

(A side note: It is a small world. When we returned to the U.S. that fall, George and I were invited to a Christian home fellowship in Flagstaff to share our experiences in Mexico. When I brought up this story, suddenly a man in the group said excitedly, "You lived on 1835 Brandon Street? That's the neighborhood I grew up in also." How remarkable is that? We didn't know each other, but discovered that we all went to the same grade school together.)

As the days in Oaxaca turned into weeks and then months, we were actually beginning to speak some Spanish. Mercedes and I continued to use our flash cards along with conversing back and forth with the new words and sentences we learned. The private tutoring lessons were going well, and I was passing this on to George. Our time spent in Oaxaca was a very good cultural experience all the way up until we were ready to leave, when we had an unsettling encounter with, well, to this day, we don't know exactly what it was. You be the judge.

One night as we were preparing to go to bed, I remembered something that I wanted to know the Spanish word for. Although Mercedes had just gone in her room for the night, I was sure there was still time to ask her one more question. She responded to my knock at her door in her half broken English and Spanish, "Just a minute, I'll be right out." While

I was waiting, I went over to the front door of the house to make sure it was securely locked. Being the "door locker of the house" that I am, I reminded myself that I had already checked the door earlier to make sure it was locked. Now for sure the door was locked! Soon Mercedes came out of her room and gave me the word I was looking for. We both said our "good-nights" and went to our rooms.

The house was designed in such a way that when you walked through the front door, an oversized, heavy wooden door, you entered the living room. If you proceeded to walk forward through the living room, you would climb a couple of stairs. Then, to your left again was a bedroom, which Mercedes resided in. Situated to the right of the living room was the dining room. To get to the guest bedroom where the four of us stayed, you took a right through the dining room into the kitchen, and then a left down a small hallway that led up to our room. It was tucked away from the main rooms, by itself.

This night was no different from the rest until about three o'clock in the morning. George and I were jolted from our sleep when we heard the heavy front door swing open and bang against the wall forcibly. We stared at each other in bewilderment. Just as suddenly, the door slammed shut, as forcibly as it had opened. Less than a minute later, the door whipped open again, hitting the dining room wall. My first thoughts were, "What on earth is Mercedes doing out there?" But as the door continued to slam shut and then open again, fear started to grip every part of me. Thoughts of people with machine guns breaking in entered my mind. I was convinced someone had come to kill us. In the midst of this craziness with the door, George lay back down in the bed, as peaceful as he could be. "What are you doing?" I whispered, not wanting the intruders to know we were tucked away in the back bedroom. "What if there is someone out there with machine guns ready to kill us?"

Still completely calm, George responded, "Our life is in God's hands. If they have come to kill us, then it's our time to go." He turned on his side, ready to go back to sleep. I couldn't believe he just said that to me. Here I was, my heart racing a mile a minute, full of anxiety. Looking over at the children, I saw they were sound asleep. I did what any smart Christian would do at a time like this: I started to fervently pray! "In the name of Jesus, I ask You, Lord, to bind the enemy from touching my family and Mercedes. If this is an act of evil, change their mind and make them go away!"

Instantly, the noise stopped. We had never heard any footsteps or any sign of someone entering the house, only the manifestation of the door whipping open and slamming shut. When the racket ceased, I wasn't about to get up and go look, nor get George up to go look either. To be honest, I was shaking in my boots, or I should say pajamas. And there lay George, fast asleep.

In the morning as we all gathered around the dining room table for breakfast, Mercedes looked at us with an expression of concern on her face. She spoke up hesitatingly, "What you do with the door last night?"

Realizing she had also been awakened and was as concerned as I was, I told her, "Mercedes, that was not us last night. I was hoping you had an explanation for us." She stared at us and we could see her mind was reeling. The children had no idea what we were talking about. Mercedes told us that after the noise stopped, she actually got up and peeked out her bedroom door. She said that she saw nothing. The door was standing open and the big German shepherd dog that belonged to Don and Melissa was walking around the dining room table. She spoke up again, firmly. "The door was lock last night. I lock it." I jumped in with my affirmation that the door was definitely locked. What could we say? It was a mystery to all of us. One might suspect it was the wind that blew the door open. Except it wasn't a windy night. The door, as big and heavy as it was, would require a lot of wind to open it and slam it that hard. At this point, I was just glad our stay was almost over, and that it was time to go back to the U.S.

A few weeks after being back in Albuquerque, a close friend of ours, Greg, invited us over for a wonderful spaghetti dinner. During the visit, he asked us the most peculiar question. "Did anything really unusual happen to you all in the middle of the night in Mexico a month or so ago?" I was stunned because we hadn't shared the story of that unnerving night with anyone yet.

"As a matter of fact, yes. Something very strange happened to us about three o'clock in the morning a month ago," I said, my eyes wide open. "Why do you ask?"

"I was in a dead sleep one night when the Lord woke me up and told me to start praying for you all. He said you were in trouble." At this point, every hair on my body stood up.

When we told him the story of what happened, he was just as stunned as we were. "Thank you for being obedient to the Lord and praying for us," we told him in sincerity and gratitude.

Since then, when the Lord puts it on my heart to pray for someone, I take it quite seriously.

HAPPY HONEYMOONERS

**OUR FIRST HOME SITUATED IN
ALBUQUERQUE, NEW MEXICO**

**OUR LITTLE TOE HEAD, JONATHON, ENJOYING
A REST ON THE ROCKS WITH A GROUP OF
TARAHUMARAS**

A REGULAR OCCURANCE OF MECHANICAL BREAKDOWNS

GEORGE HELPING BUILD A CHURCH

**GEORGE TEACHING A GROUP OF MEXICAN
BELIEVERS HOW TO DIAGNOSE AND
DISTRIBUTE CASSETTE TAPES FOR THE
MIGRANT CAMPS**

**ENTERTAINING CHILDREN WITH PUPPETS
IN A MIGRANT CAMP**

**JENNIFER TEACHING ENGLISH CLASSES TO
HER FIVE EAGER STUDENTS**

**A GROUP OF CHILDREN IN A MIGRANT CAMP
EXCITED TO GET STARTED IN MAKING CRAFTS**

SINGING AND SHARING THE GOSPEL

**OUR FIFTH WHEEL GIVEN TO US FROM THE
AMERICAN CHURCH**

**MY NEW LITTLE FRIEND FROM
UGANDA, AFRICA**

THE PLEASURES OF MINISTERING OVERSEAS

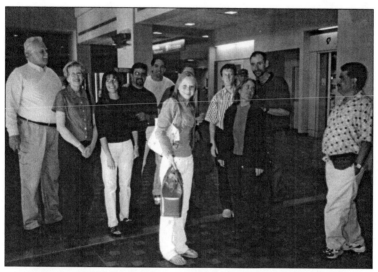

OUR CARE GROUP; THE GROUP OF PEOPLE
WHO HAVE PRAYED FOR US, SUPPORTED,
ENCOURAGED, COUNSELED, AND LOVED US
THROUGH OUR MANY YEARS OF MINISTRY AND
TRAVELING. THEY ARE THE BACKBONE OF OUR
MINISTRY

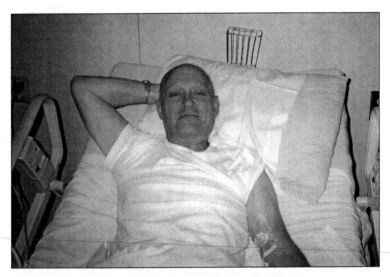

**GEORGE IN THE HOSPITAL AFTER BEING
DIAGNOSED WITH CANCER**

For the eyes of the Lord run to and fro
throughout the whole earth,
to show Himself strong
on behalf of those whose heart
is loyal to Him.

2 Chronicles 16:9

12
Open Doors for Ministry

Now more than ever, after our summer in Oaxaca, we were biting at the bit to return to Culiacan. With the autumn upon us, we knew migrant workers were making their way north from the southern states of Mexico to pick our winter produce. We still had a little money left from the summer, but not enough to sustain us for another six-month trip. Other resources would have to come in to make it possible to go again. Feeling a sense of faith, we were sure that God would provide if this was His will for us, and if He had other plans for us, we were ready to accept that too.

Provision was on its way. Visiting our church in Albuquerque, we had ample opportunity to share with friends at two different home fellowships we attended. Tyler and Rachel, who also attended the same congregation, suggested we share with the leaders of the church what we were involved in down in Mexico. It was such an enormous-sized congregation that we didn't think they had time for us. When Tyler realized that we weren't going to take the initiative to approach them on the subject of finances, he decided to talk to the pastor personally. One evening after the service he did just that. Pastor Paul took interest in the ministry immediately. He advised Tyler to have us go meet with the mission's pastor. We did feel somewhat shy about it, yet reason told us that is what we needed to do.

Kent, the mission's pastor, was a humble, meek man. His enthusiasm in what we had to share gave us hope that the church would consider supporting us financially. After a time together, he expressed his confidence in us, believing God had called us to the field. He wanted to facilitate our going, and equally to invest in the work of the indigenous farm workers; therefore, he agreed to get behind us.

Our spirits were high as we left the office. It was a breath of fresh air to finally have a body of believers who took the work of the ministry in our lives seriously, enough to get behind us financially, as well as to have the kind of prayer support we would receive from this large church.

Learning Spanish was still up front where priorities were concerned. We needed to address the issue once again since our plans of hiring a tutor full-time had fallen through during the last summer. Considering the options, it seemed beneficial to leave for Mexico as soon as possible to get a head start on the language before the group of Americans made their way down for the outreach planned again for February. We would be forced to use our Spanish if we were the only English-speaking family around. Our strategy was to drive down in our motor home, towing our truck behind, and park on property of the family who invited the group to stay during our outreach time. To save money, we planned to hire someone from the local church to tutor both George and me a few hours a day. This would also give us more time to spend with Jonathon and Laura, other than just their home schooling time. With the encouragement and prayers of our supporters, we followed this plan and found ourselves in Culiacan once more.

Our idea went as planned. In no time, we met Ana. She was a young single woman in her mid-twenties, fun loving, energetic and jolly, and she spoke fluent English. Ana agreed to meet us at the church five days a week for two hours a day. When she vowed not to speak a word of English to us during class, we knew that was not realistic. We were not quite ready for that yet, and she soon found herself going against her plan just so we could move ahead with understanding. She created a vibrant and exciting atmosphere. We actually looked forward to our lessons.

The family hosting us attended the same church as Ana. They decided to help us along with our language learning too. Every Saturday, they invited at least twenty or more people from the congregation to a potluck meal held in their yard. Their property was huge, so they had the room to accommodate them all. There was no escaping the all-day Saturday event. Don't get me wrong, I love potlucks, but when you have a whole group of people talking to you all day in a language you don't know well, it is somewhat exhausting. By midday my head would be spinning.

Each weekend morning as people gathered in the yard for fellowship, coming to have a good time, I was inside my home fervently asking the Lord to please get me through what was ahead for the day. Sometimes I would get so worked up over it that I felt physically ill. The thought of standing outside, mingling with one person after another for six hours or so, understanding hardly anything that was said to me, was nearly more than I could handle.

Our gatherings never became completely comfortable for me, yet with each passing week the language barriers were becoming less and less intimidating as we gradually gained the confidence needed. I would never advise others to learn another language this way if they're looking for an easy method, but it is an excellent way to learn quickly and affordably if they don't mind being intimidated.

During this time we met some wonderful friends. One family was the Riveras. They lived in Navolato, a town about twenty miles away from Culiacan. Marcos was the pastor of the sister church of the one in Culiacan that we had been attending. These two churches met together regularly for special occasions. The Rivera children were the same ages as Jonathon and Laura, so our families began to gravitate to each other as the days and weeks went by. Before long they invited us over for dinner. We found ourselves together quite often as our friendship began to grow.

One afternoon while visiting at their home, Marcos and his wife Bianca, knowing that we had come to Mexico earlier than the rest of our group to learn the language, suggested we move in with them for a month or so. They thought that, by our living with them, we would not only learn to speak Spanish more quickly, but learn the culture too. The whole time Marcos was expressing why he thought it was such a good idea, I was thinking, "Absolutely not! There is no way I'm going to immerse myself like this." We Americans like our privacy, and I was no exception. George told him that we would pray about it.

As were driving home in the truck, I looked over at George and said, "Can you imagine what it would be like if we really actually moved in with them?" His response was one that I wasn't expecting.

"Yeah, I think it's an excellent idea!" He continued, "We would eat with them, pray with them every morning at their prayer meeting with the church, and best of all, talk Spanish 24/7."

Although it made sense, everything in me said no. "Well, I'm just not going to do that. I know my limits and that will push me right over the edge," I retorted. Right after I said that, the Lord brought to memory what I had just prayed the day before. My prayer went something like this: "Lord, I want to be a willing vessel for you here in Mexico. Help me to walk through those open doors, and help me to be teach-able, bringing You honor." And yet my flesh was so against going to live with another family. They were nice-enough people; it was the privacy part that was getting to me.

The Spirit of God inside me was starting to move. Not wanting to resist that small, quiet voice, I yielded myself to the calling. "If I were willing to go live with them, would you want to take them up on their offer?" I asked George, hoping after all that he would say no.

On the contrary, he immediately said, "Of course I would go. What do you think, kids?" I turned around, waiting for a response, but Jon and Laura both seemed willing to go. I could see that I was outnumbered.

By the next day, conviction was heavy on my heart. I had strong feelings that we were to accept their invitation. I knew we had better do it soon before the flesh stepped in.

We packed some of our belongings and left our home parked on our host's property. Our hostess seemed excited for us too. Everyone thought it was a good idea. Once we made the decision to go, we moved quickly. We became Navalato residents for the duration.

I remember the first week of our stay. Because Marcos pastored the church, the prayer meeting was held in his living room every morning at five a.m., five days a week. Every day we got up and prayed together, George and I praying in English. Everyone was so gracious to us, they really put us to shame. Pulling myself up out of bed at that hour took everything in me, knowing that we would have an hour or so to be totally surrounded by the Spanish language. Then when it was over, guilt would come over me for thinking and acting so carnally. The least we could do is get up and be part of their lives. It was a good time of discipline for us and the Lord knew we needed it.

The food was no problem. Bianca was an excellent cook. After a time of great hospitality on their part, I also wanted to bless them with a good home-cooked American meal. I decided to make a traditional Thanksgiving dinner. Turkey, dressing, mashed potatoes: the whole works. It took some effort trying to hunt down some of the ingredients, but we were successful. The meal was a bit foreign to them. Marcos loved it, Bianca was neutral, but their children were struggling to get it down. They were trying to be polite; still, this was supposed to be a blessing, not a curse. Knowing what it's like to be in that kind of situation, we assured them that it was all right if they didn't eat it. I'm sure they appreciated our understanding.

*

Sometimes learning to speak another language can get one into predicaments that one really wishes could have been avoided. This was one of those times, definitely a case of misunderstanding.

Bianca was attending a local community college, learning how to be a hairstylist. She was nearing the end of her schooling and would be graduating the middle of December. After returning from school one day, she began to share with me what took place before graduation. Every year the school put on a big outdoor program for the community. Each graduating student needed to perform or present their new learned skill to the audience. She and her classmates would need several volunteers to go out onstage to show off the student's talent at "hairdos". She was asking me if I, as well as Laura, would consider being one of the models. It sounded like fun. We agreed to do it. She then went on to tell us that the school was going to hire a modeling teacher to teach the models how to walk the runway in a more professional fashion. The opportunity to have a professional modeling instructor made me even more excited about participating. In my broken Spanish, I relayed to her how I went through modeling school when I was sixteen years old. I wanted to let her know that my runway experience early in life, though long ago, would help me, and it would be exciting to model again. She said some more things about the program that I found hard to understand, but it didn't seem to be important so I let it go. I assured her that Laura and I would love to be models, and asked her to let me know when we needed to come to the school to practice with the modeling teacher.

A week or so had passed after our conversation when Bianca came to me and said something like this: "Jennifer, tomorrow you need to come to the school with me, but Laura doesn't need to come yet." I couldn't understand why Laura didn't need to come with us.

I replied, "Are we going to do the modeling today?" Her response didn't make any sense to me either. She kept trying to explain what we were going to do, going round and round with words, yet I couldn't figure out what she was saying.

"Just come and you'll see," she said, trying to be patient with me.

The next day at school, she introduced me to her class-mates and teachers. She seemed proud to acquaint me with each of her friends as we went from person to person. Explaining to me how important it was to meet the director of the school, she grabbed my arm and we hurriedly made our way to his office. Once inside, she made her introductions. Before she could finish, the director started rattling away a mile a minute in high level Spanish. Not understanding a word he was saying to me, my heart began to palpitate from anxiety. My biggest concern was to be tactful, so without interrupting him, I tried to listen patiently. He must have read the expression on my face. Within minutes, I heard him say, "You didn't understand a word I said, did you?" It wasn't a question that I really wanted to answer.

"No, I didn't," I responded in embarrassment.

"Well, I don't have time to repeat myself because it's time to go inside the auditorium," he replied politely. With that, we all headed toward the huge room down the hall.

The room was filled with at least one hundred people. Amidst the commotion of people talking and laughing, we found seats in chairs that had been placed in a large circle completely around the room. It was beyond me what all this was about, but I hoped it would all make sense as the program progressed. Then the photographer walked in, getting everyone's attention. How could one miss him with the gigantic camera equipment he and his assistants were carrying around? I noticed the different groups of people they were asked to stand and be positioned just right for the pictures they were taking. This continued for at least half an hour. Suddenly, from across the room, they turned our direction, making their way over toward Bianca and me. My first thought was, "Why would they want a picture of me? They don't even know me." As they neared us, I reasoned, "Maybe it's because I'm the only American in this entire room and they want a picture of an American."

The photographer reached for my hand and placed me with several other people he had with him. They snapped a couple of pictures and then thanked us, going on to the next group of people. I still didn't get it.

As the picture taking was winding down, a distinguished-looking man walked up to the podium that was placed inside the circle. He spoke for another half hour, with applause frequently interrupting his speech. Of course I still didn't understand what was being said or what was going on. Then the meeting was over. I tried to ask Bianca on the way home what that whole thing meant. Her explanation didn't make any sense either. To this day I'm still not certain what that afternoon had to do with our modeling class.

A few days more passed. Bianca came to me with excitement. "Tomorrow we will start the modeling class," she said.

I was actually looking forward to this event. I wondered what our modeling teacher would be like. "I wonder if she'll be really modern and up-to-date in her techniques, or if it will be sort of nerdy?" I thought, as Bianca, her daughters, Laura and I headed to the school on foot. "Maybe she'll just have the same moves that I knew back in the seventies," I chuckled.

Rather than feeling stressed, I was surprisingly exhilarated about meeting our new teacher. Girls were coming in the room, one by one, modeling hairstyles for the students. There were a variety of models, mostly young adult women with beautiful long hair. As we stood around staring at one another, Bianca's teacher walked over to me. In a very pleasant voice she said, "So, do you want fast music or slow music?"

"What?" I said, taken aback by her question. She repeated herself.

"I don't understand your question," I responded politely. She answered again, this time communicating very slowly.

"I understand your words," I said, "I just don't understand your question." Now we were both confused. She walked away toward Bianca. Bianca turned around and came over to me, asking me the same thing her teacher had asked me. "Do you want fast music or slow music?"

"Bianca, I'm trying to say that I understand the words you are saying to me, I just don't understand why you are asking me if I want fast music or slow music." She was now staring at me as well, just as confused as the teacher was. Right then, Geraldo, the English teacher, walked through the door.

"Let's get Geraldo to translate for us," piped up one of the students who stood nearby, listening to the dialogue we were having. "Geraldo," she called, "Could you come over here and help us to translate?"

I had known Geraldo before since he was one of the members at Marcos and Bianca's church. He and his wife Teresa were a dear couple that our family immediately took a liking to when we met them. In addition to teaching English classes at the community college, he and his wife also owned the local yogurt shop in town, and had been very generous to us. I'll never forget the surprise birthday party they threw for Laura and me one year at their house that was attached to the shop. It was quite the party! I wasn't surprised that he immediately agreed to help us out in our translation.

As we greeted one another, everyone in the room gathered around us. "So what seems to be the problem?" he asked. Bianca began to explain to him what was going on, Geraldo translating for me into English. As we conversed back and forth, we had the crowd's full attention.

I started to explain. "Geraldo, I know what they are saying to me in Spanish, but they keep asking me if I want slow music or fast music. I don't get why they're asking me that question." Just as I was finishing my sentence, the wrenching thought entered my mind that they might be expecting me to be the teacher. Feeling myself turn pale from the fear that suddenly came over me, I looked at him soberly. In the calmest voice I could muster, I said, "Geraldo, please don't have a shocked expression as I ask you this question because I don't want the rest of the group to get alarmed, but..." I paused. "Please, just tell me that I am not the modeling teacher." He tried to keep a straight face, though I could tell he was confused too.

"Jennifer, you told the school that you would teach a modeling class here. All the other teachers know that you volunteered to teach," he said seriously. "Being a Christian, you need to let your 'yes' be 'yes' to be a good example of Christianity." I was mortified. Looking at the crowd around us, I knew I needed to say something, anything. They were all looking at us, waiting for Geraldo to tell them what was going on.

"All right, tell the teacher I want slow music," I said softly. I turned around, looked up to the ceiling and said silently, "Oh, God, get me through this!" Turning back around, looking at the teacher with false confidence, while deep inside ready to have a heart attack, I said, "In what room will I be teaching my class?"

She guided me and my students outdoors, pointing to the stadium. "Oh, great, not only am I going to be teaching a modeling class in Spanish, which I can hardly speak, but I'll be doing it outside where everyone can see us," I thought in dismay. Could it get any worse? I felt sick to my stomach as we made our way to the class. All the while my complaints to the Lord were loud and clear, silently demanding to know how the Lord would allow such a thing to happen to me. As my words were spewing out to the Lord, questioning Him how on earth I was going to teach a class, especially when the last modeling class I attended was back in the seventies, I could almost picture the Lord up in Heaven smiling over all of this.

When we arrived at the stadium, it was explained to the students that they would need to have lots of patience with me since my Spanish was poor. They all were smiling, eager to see how this was going to be done. It occurred to me that they now probably all had the same thoughts that I had earlier, wondering about what the modeling teacher was going to be like. The joke was on me: modern or nerdy?

Thankfully, they were a group of people that had a lot of grace for me. Most of the class session consisted of the group following the movements that I showed to each individual student. A problem arose when the music began to play. It drew in passersby, and we soon found ourselves with quite a gathering. The students began to feel just as intimidated as I did. Within a short time I knew having our class exposed to the public wasn't going to work out. I had to request a change up for sake of privacy.

The whole situation became even more ludicrous when I found myself making up moves. I just couldn't remember all that much of what I had learned back in the days of modeling school. I hoped that no one knew but the Lord and me that I was "winging" it.

Showtime finally arrived. It seemed to me that an exceedingly large number of people arrived on the grounds of the school. Feelings of nervousness over how well the models would perform threatened to overwhelm me, and not only that, Laura and I would also be modeling.

Before the hairstyling performance began, Geraldo stood next to me in one of the aisles in the middle section of the audience. Presently performing was the sewing class, each student making her way to the stage to show off the beautiful outfits. Geraldo remarked, "You can tell this class hasn't been professionally trained like your class is." That comment stressed me to the max. When my class came out, was I going to be scrutinized as well by all the other teachers here?

I began to pray silently. "Lord, please let this modeling experience be glorifying to You. Let the school be satisfied with my labor." Just about that time, the slow music I had chosen for the models began. The first model came out, a very pretty girl with long black shiny hair. One of the stylists had curled her hair in a way that made her look exceptionally beautiful. As she started across the stage, she went into a flamboyant dance, turning her head one way and then another as she twirled around. If anyone was watching me, they could have read what was going on in my mind. It was amazing! I did not teach her that; she did it on her own. Then the next girl came out. She was just as flamboyant as the first. One by one, they each came out and gave it their all. They were really good! I wanted to cry. Each student was performing above and beyond what they had been taught. Even Laura and Delia (Bianca's daughter) did a terrific job. When the audience gave a great hand of applause, I couldn't thank the Lord enough for answering my prayer. That afternoon the Lord had intervened again to supernaturally give those girls the ability to perform as well as they did. I did not teach them how to walk and dance on the stage so professionally. Some of them turned out to be downright big hams, but I wasn't complaining. I was applauding them. When Geraldo complimented me on how well they were trained, I quickly answered, "Believe me, it wasn't me, it was the Lord's doing." I was so proud of my students for putting their all into it.

Once, in sharing this story to a friend after returning to the States, his reply was, "Why would the Lord have you go through something so secular? How did that bring glory for the Kingdom? Did anyone get saved through all of that?" His remark caught me off guard.

Thinking about his statement, the Lord revealed to me His purpose in it all. You see, after the program for the community ended, the teachers were all invited to a private party later in the day. As I was one of the teachers, I was also invited. It was awkward to attend, with my Spanish not up to par, but after Bianca prodded me I reluctantly went, feeling like a fish out of water.

Entering the fairly good-sized room, I saw a beautifully set-up buffet full of a variety of Mexican food in the middle of the room. Following the crowd, I made my way to the food line. After filling my plate, I felt more at ease to go out on the patio where several people were trying to break a piñata. Watching others make fools of themselves as they tried to hit the *pâpiér mache* blindfolded would be more entertaining than trying to hold an intelligent conversation in another language. As I sat on one of the lined-up chairs, a young girl in her late teens sit down next to me. "*Hola*," I said, trying to show myself friendly. She returned the greeting. She seemed out of place to me, as if she didn't belong at this party. Maybe it was her informal apparel that I noticed, or just the look on her face. I was even more convinced when she spoke up and told me she was hungry.

"Who are you?" I asked, surprised at her remark. She told me that her family lived in the next village down from Navolato. She went on to say that her nephew was extremely sick so they had brought him to the hospital to get medical attention. Pointing behind us, she told me the hospital was located in back of the school. The noise of the party had drawn her in. She was now asking me for food. My heart went out to her. Observing that everyone around us seemed to be in their own world, I decided that it wouldn't hurt to go inside and get this young lady a plate of food.

As I was making my way back over to the buffet, Veronica, another woman from Marcos and Bianca's church, intercepted me. All the time we were making small talk back and forth, I was feeling anxious about getting a plate of food to the young woman out on the patio. I finally brought the subject up to Veronica, telling her about this girl's hunger. She felt just as much compassion for the girl as I did, so she assisted me in getting the food and coming with me to meet her.

My newfound friend seemed very gratified as I handed her the full plate. As she began to eat, Veronica dug deeper for information about the girl's nephew in the hospital. Then she told her, "You know, Jennifer is a Christian missionary here in Mexico. We both believe that God can heal your nephew from his sickness. Do you want us to go over there after you're done eating and pray for him?" She looked at me for approval. I was game if she was. I knew nobody would miss us at the party anyway.

"I would like that very much," the girl responded gratefully, wolfing down her food.

We slipped out through the patio and crossed the street to where the hospital was located. As we approached the front door, the young girl's mother was standing there as if waiting for her return. The two of them said a few quick words to each other and then the mother's attention swiftly turned to us. Veronica spoke up and explained to her that we had met her daughter over at the college. She went on to tell her that we were Christians, pointing out that I was a missionary, and that we had come to pray for the nephew. The mother's expression grew cold the minute that Veronica mentioned Christianity. She made it perfectly clear that she did not approve of us and would not accept our service of prayer; that we were not allowed to get near her grandchild's room. The mother and Veronica were talking much more quickly than I could interpret, but I could tell by this mother's attitude that she wanted nothing to do with us. I prayed silently as the two of them conversed. Finally, Veronica ended the exchange with these words: "You know, we don't need to be present in this child's room to pray. We serve a very powerful God who loves him and wants to see him healed. We can pray right here and now, can't we, Jennifer?"

I agreed, and addressed the woman in a conciliatory tone, "If you don't mind, we'll just pray for him here." She was hesitant, but consented for us to pray as long as we didn't go inside. At that point Veronica and I bowed our heads and asked the Lord to bring healing to this little sick two-year-old boy. When we finished, we shook their hands and politely said good-bye. We headed back to the party, wondering all the while why this lady was so hostile toward Christianity. We could only conclude that she must have had a bad experience with Christians in the past. We turned our thoughts over to the Lord on this one, and went about finishing up our time at the party.

A week had passed by since that incident. I was shopping in the marketplace with George one late morning when we were startled by yelling from across the street. We looked over and, lo and behold, it was the girl I had met at the party. She was running toward us. "*Señora, Señora,* I need to talk to you," she hollered. We walked toward her. When she caught up with us, she was trying to catch her breath and talk to us at the same time. I could see she was happy about something;

she was smiling ear to ear. "Remember when you and your friend prayed for my nephew the other night?" she said, still trying to catch her breath. How could I forget?

"Yes, I do," I responded, anticipating what she had to say next.

"Well, guess what? God healed my nephew that very hour. We went up to the room after you left and the fluid that had been filling up in his lungs suddenly started going down. The doctors were amazed. But best of all, my mom knew it was God who healed him, and... and... now she wants to invite you over to our house. It is so wonderful that I saw you down here because we didn't know how to contact you."

This was indeed fantastic news. We were exhilarated the Lord had healed this little boy and that his grandmother was able to see the hand of God in his healing. The young lady added, "My mom wants you to come to our house to share with us all about the God you serve."

George suggested that we go over to their neighborhood and show the "Jesus Movie." I wasn't sure if her mother would want us to come to their village and put on a show, so we left it up to the girl. "We will be able to come on Monday night. We can show you a movie on the life of Jesus. If your neighbors want to come we can show it to everyone, and if your mom just wants us to show it to your family we can do that too," George explained. The girl was thrilled that we were willing to come. They would look forward to our visit on Monday night. Meanwhile, we talked to Marcos and a few members from the church about coming with us, since our Spanish was still not good enough to answer questions they might have about the Lord. We all were excited about being part of this evangelistic endeavor. My prayer was that the mother would be as receptive to us as the young daughter portrayed her to be.

When Monday night arrived, God did answer that prayer. As a matter of fact, mom was quite joyful to meet Marcos,

Bianca, and the rest of the group. She was more than willing to have us go around the neighborhood and invite others to watch the movie as well.

About fifty people showed up. One person that stands out in my memory was a Mexican man in his forties. I think I remember him more than the others because of the way he presented himself. Strutting into the yard where we were showing the movie, dressed in a black leather jacket, cowboy hat, boots, and tight blue jeans, hands in his coat pocket, you could tell he thought he was much too "cool" for this event. Yet, the movie and ambience were drawing him in. He stood toward the back of the group, probably hoping that none of his friends would spot him being a part of this whole experience.

I was sitting in the back of our camper shell observing him from inside. The Lord pressed on my heart to start praying for him. Throughout the rest of the movie I followed that tug, and kept praying that the Lord would soften his heart and give this man insight to see the truth about Jesus. My prayer was that at the end of the movie God would give him the faith to believe in and surrender his life to Him.

I don't know why Christians act so surprised when we pray in faith for something or someone and the Lord answers it. That's how I responded when Marcos gave an altar call at the end of the film and the "macho man" raised his hand. He was the most unlikely person in the whole group to come forward. Eight other people that night surrendered their lives to the Lord, and two of them were the daughter and mom. Another was an elderly man in his late eighties. That isn't something you see every day. It was a great night for all of us.

Marcos was able to teach the new believers the concepts of the Bible on a regular basis. And to think it all started with modeling. It just shows you that God can take something that seems as secular as modeling, and use it to direct us to the people He wants us to touch.

The Lord will also be a refuge
for the oppressed,
a refuge in times of trouble. And those
who know Your name will put
their trust in You;
For You, Lord, have not forsaken
those who seek You.

Psalm 9:9,10

13
Taking the Good with the Bad

W hen there's victory in lost souls who have found Jesus, inevitably there's going to be spiritual attacks. And that is just what happened once again.

We were all enjoying the open doors of ministry the Lord was giving us throughout the neighboring villages of Navolato. On one occasion, Bianca's brother invited the team to come to his village and show the "Jesus Movie". They made up a big meal, inviting other members of Bianca's family to come. Lots of children Jonathon and Laura's age were present, so the kids had a blast. It wasn't until the fiesta ended and we had left that evening when the trouble began.

We were traveling back to Marcos's house after ten or eleven o'clock p.m. The dirt road was no different than most we had traveled, with its dust and potholes forcing us to wind back and forth to avoid the big holes. Up ahead we could see headlights from an oncoming vehicle. As the car got closer, it was all over the road, from their lane to ours and then back to theirs. George started to slow down and moved to the extreme right side of the road. Still observing the car swerving back and forth from lane to lane, he decided to come to a complete stop until they passed, pulling over as far as he could without hitting the fence that paralleled us. Just as the car neared us, the driver turned right into our truck and hit us head on. Because we were at a complete stop when they hit us, nobody in our truck was injured. We just had time to brace ourselves.

As soon as they crashed into us, we jumped out of the car to make sure no one was injured. We noticed that none of the three in the vehicle seemed to be in their right minds. They were all high on some kind of drug. One was bleeding from his mouth, but the other two didn't have any signs of injury. Marcos engaged in conversation with two of them, while the one who was bleeding opened the trunk of their car and started chucking packages, all the same size, over the fence on the side of the road. When he finished emptying the trunk, he jumped over the fence, ran through the field and disappeared. Meanwhile, Marcos and the other two continued to dialogue about the accident. Within ten minutes, another pickup truck showed up. A couple of men got out and started loading the brown packages into their pickup bed. Then they were off: just that quick.

The first two were unwilling to accept responsibility for what they had done in smashing the left side of our pickup, causing a lot of damage. We had no other choice but to call the police. Remember Mexican law from our previous story in Mexico City? If the two parties can't come up with a solution they impound both vehicles? You guessed it. The police confiscated their car and our truck. They were kind enough to let us drive it back to Marcos's home to unload our equipment, but from there, they took it and told us it would be parked at a storage facility until later notice.

By the next day, the implications of this state of affairs began to set in. If we didn't have our truck, we would be stopped from doing the ministry. This whole situation seemed so absurd. Drug dealers hit us and we were being punished. Our next concern was how long the police would keep our truck. George wasn't about to sit around and wonder about it. He went down to the police station that next day to find out what he needed to do to get our vehicle back. He asked Marcos to go with him to help interpret.

When they arrived at the station, it didn't go as they had hoped. One of the officers told them that a court date would be set, at which time they would decide what to do. The hearing would be the next week. Waiting a whole week seemed unnecessarily lengthy, but we knew we could trust God in this mess. The two of them came home, George feeling somewhat defeated.

The next day our lives got even more dramatic. Marcos and Bianca received an anonymous phone call from a man who threatened their lives if they helped the Americans in any way. We all knew we were dealing with local drug dealers, but how dangerous they really were, none of us knew. We didn't want to put the Rivera family in danger, so we told them to stay out of it. We would handle it ourselves.

The following day, George was fidgety and felt he couldn't just sit around and wait. He decided to go down to the police station again and see if he could get them to relinquish his truck. The police department told him the only thing we could do was wait for the court date, which had now been moved to two weeks later, not one. Talk about depressing. We had no alternative at this point but to wait. So, as we waited, we prayed, along with the church, that the Lord would work everything out for good. We could all plainly see that this was a direct attack from the enemy. We were not able to go into the camps; at least not for now.

The court date finally arrived. George went to the station anticipating the release of our truck. To his dismay, the driver of the car that hit us did not show up for court. The judge set another date, telling George he would have to wait until then. Not only did this seem utterly ridiculous, it was completely unfair. All of us suspected that the drug dealer was not even near Navolato; he was probably on his way to another place. Pretty unlikely he would sit around and go to court over the accident, and, in reality, his car was a piece of junk, not worth fighting for. Everything on the car that had any value had already been stripped.

After much prayer and contemplation, George decided to go back down to the station and talk to the judge one more time. Maybe if the judge had more information about our story, he might have more compassion and give us our truck back. Not having much confidence in George's ability to speak Spanish fluently, Marcos insisted on going back with him. I don't think George believed his vocabulary was strong enough to deal with the problem either.

After listening to the whole story, thank God, the judge was willing to give us back our truck, under the condition that we pay for all court costs, paperwork involved in the accident, and storage fees for both vehicles. As crazy as it seems, and as unjust that it was that we should have to pay the other party's fees, we were willing to take the loss, knowing that the Lord would replenish our bank account. The judge did offer to give us the other vehicle that hit us, but it would have been more of a burden for us than a blessing. George decided to let them keep the blessing instead.

What was even more discouraging was what we found when we went to get our truck. The storage keepers had siphoned half the gas out of our tank, and, even as we approached, were in the process of stripping a couple of truck parts. George admonished the owners of the business that, since we were paying them for storage, they should at least have had the courtesy to take care of the truck by leaving it alone. They seemed somewhat embarrassed at his rebuke, talking very quickly to justifying their behavior and shift the blame onto others. We were just happy to get our truck back, out of the hands of the professionals.

What a blessing it was to see how the neighborhood jumped in to help fix our truck. They pulled out the huge dent left from the accident. When we bought used parts to replace the hood and fender, they helped with that too. For days several men helped to get it back to somewhat normal condition.

Our plan had been to enlighten ourselves about the culture, and that we did. We were growing by leaps and bounds during our stay in Navolato with the Rivera family. Looking back, we're so thankful that Marcos and Bianca opened their home and lives up to us. It's a treasure of memories we'll never forget. Our hearts were sold on becoming missionaries for the kingdom of God. This was a good training ground for growing us up and developing our character.

*

I always love hearing missionary stories where they go into a village and share the gospel, and have the whole village come to a saving knowledge of Him. Well, that's what happened outside of Navolato, just on a much smaller scale.

Traveling along a dirt road took us through a fishing village one beautiful Sunday afternoon. Juan, the worship leader from Marcos's church, who happened to be taking the drive with us, suggested we show the "Jesus Movie" to that village. He thought that fishermen would really relate, since some of Jesus' disciples were fishermen. We concurred that his idea was a good one, so we made plans to come back the following Sunday with our equipment.

The village was small, so we didn't bring many people with us, not wanting to overwhelm the locals. Juan with a few others and our family participated. As we knocked on door after door inviting people to come to our movie, we discovered some really friendly people. Many of them seemed lonely and were more than happy to come. One family welcomed us in for lunch before the movie started. They had plenty of fish to feed us.

Setting our equipment up on the beach seemed a bit odd. This wasn't our usual mode of operation, but the weather was perfect for it. We were excited when twenty-eight people showed up. Actually, that was the whole village, all fishermen and their families.

After showing the movie, Juan and the few others joined in playing several worship songs, followed by an invitation to receive Jesus as their Savior. Immediately, everyone raised their hands in unison. They were more than ready to surrender their lives to the Lord. What stuck out in my mind about this group of fishermen was how intently they absorbed each scene of the movie.

On the way home, we couldn't quit talking about how everyone was so ready and willing to receive the words of God. We kept praising Him for giving us the privilege of leading this small village of people to Him, and giving Juan the insight to show the movie there in the first place.

I can imagine what it is going to be like in heaven for eternity. People coming up and saying, "Remember when you shared the gospel to us when we were... ?" What a joyous privilege and reward we have, as God uses each of us, if we're willing, to lead His people into His kingdom.

Juan and one of his friends talked about continuing to go back to carry on a fellowship and Bible study.

*

Our Lord is always on time. When we pray for things, we usually want it now, yet this is not always the way the Lord works. He is pleased when we believe in Him. Waiting, with peace, is the outcome of our belief.

Although we always had enough for the day, we had really hoped for more financial security. Of course, this would be pleasing to us in the natural, but we were depending on God in the supernatural.

This was another one of those days we were feeling quite stretched in our faith. George was getting ready to drive to the Culiacan church, about ten miles from where we were staying, to pick up a team of people to work in the camps. A hundred or so of us gathered together during the month of February, from all parts of the globe. The church liked what we were doing so they opened their doors to us, and provided the group of laborers meals and sleeping accommodations. We had close to ten vehicles a night that would meet at the church, pick up the team, and drive them to a particular camp. At the end of the evening, we all met back at the church where we dropped each team off for the night. George was one of the designated drivers for one of the teams.

One of the driver's responsibilities was to pay for the gasoline. Living from day to day on faith, financially we could not set aside an allotted amount for the week. This had to come from the Lord. One day it was one of those times where our gas tank was almost empty, and we had no extra money to fill it. George suggested we walk around the house and look for loose change. That idea didn't pan out; we only found a nickel and a penny. Circumstances looking pretty grim, George's face fell. Approaching the Lord in prayer, he reminded the Lord that there was only enough gas to get to the church. Maybe if we were lucky, we could get to a nearby camp. He felt ashamed that he didn't have the resources to carry out the ministry. "Please, Lord, give me an answer today. I'm going to leave for the church, but You're going to need to intervene here," he pleaded.

He got ready as usual. I could feel his despondency. Doubts flooded my mind too, anxiously wondering whether I would even see him that evening if he ran out of gas. Oh, me, of little faith!

I was happy to see him return home that evening. I was even more excited when he walked in the door bubbling over with joy. He could hardly wait to share with me how

God had answered his prayer. "You'll never believe what happened this afternoon," he began. "One of the leaders of the outreach came to me and gave me an assignment. They wanted to know how many gallons of gas each of the ten vehicles would hold. Some benefactor paid for everyone's gas for the week." I was as elated as George as he went into more detail. "Not only did he want to pay for our gas for the rest of the week, he has also offered to fill each person's gas tank once a week, for the rest of the outreach." I was amazed! He continued, "He didn't want any of us drivers to know who gave them the gas." We both thanked God for this man's generosity.

Once again, our Lord came through. Even though we are faithless, He continues to show Himself faithful. Our worries were put to rest concerning gas. He promises that He will always take care of us, so why can't we relax and take Him at His word?

*

God continued to help us learn Spanish. After moving from the Rivera's, we took every opportunity to keep up with our studies. We would pay a church member to tutor us wherever we went. It was easier for me to study on my own, so we concentrated on George getting help from the tutor. We also continued to show the "Jesus Movie" and other Christian movies to the Mexican community on weekends, and focused on the indigenous camps during the weekdays.

The ministry in the Culiacan area was seasonal, from September until April. By May, many of the laborers went back to their homes in southern Mexico, while others migrated to Baja to work in the camps there, so we would return back to the United States for the summer months. For the first couple of years, when we came back, we were busy going to our church family to give a report on the Lord's work. After the first three years, we started to look for other ministries during those hot months. Gary, now recording on his own and working in Baja (below California) through the summer season, suggested our working in those camps during the summer months. The climate there was also much milder during this time. It seemed logical to follow the workers, so this was the area we concentrated on for the next five years.

Within a short time, the Lord opened doors for us to work with youth groups from the U.S. These groups would come down for two weeks at a time. As one group left, we welcomed the next. Our children especially liked this, because they were able to enjoy American youth as well as their Mexican friends. Most of the groups were older than Jonathon and Laura, yet they treated them like their own brother and sister.

Working with each group expanded our vision for ministry. We were able to emulate many of their ideas when they left, one of which inspired me to get involved with a puppet ministry. Puppets were used to put on a show for children illustrating biblical stories in an entertaining way. I was sure George could devise a common stage for us to use, but I knew the investment for puppets was going to be pricey. It was important to pray and seek the Lord's direction. I loved the way God answered my petition, and quickly.

Hours after asking the Lord's permission to move forward with the puppet ministry, I was invited to a home of one of the missionaries who had lived in Baja doing a women and children's ministry. Before we knew it, Gina and I were talking all about the work of the Lord. Fresh on my mind was the puppet ministry, so I shared with her my vision. Gina suddenly lit up. "You need to come with me in the other room," she said, getting up. I followed her. She handed me a big box and asked me to open it. To my surprise, there lay a Muppet-sized puppet inside. I could tell that it wasn't a cheaply made puppet; the fabric and size was a dead give-away. Not sure why she was showing me this puppet, I asked if she was using it. "A friend once gave this to me in hopes that I would get a lot of use out of it," she went on to explain. "I just don't use it enough to justify keeping it." She shared with me that just that morning she had been praying about giving it to someone who would use it, and had asked the Lord to reveal to her who she should give it to. The timing couldn't have been more perfect for the both of us. She knew immediately that God wanted her to give it to me, and I knew that the Lord was giving me the permission I was looking for to go forward in the puppet ministry.

It was even more exciting to see the provision of the Lord when we came back to the States and shared with the church and friends our desire to move ahead with the puppets.

We wanted to buy four more puppets and a few props to use in our show before returning to Culiacan. After an evening with friends, they expressed their desire to help us with expenses.

Several weeks later, on our way to Colorado to purchase the puppets, a young man whom we have know most of his life jumped in with excitement over the ministry, and also made a donation toward the puppets. We had no idea what the total cost would be for everything we wanted. We found a store that had what we needed, and when they rang up the items we wanted to purchase, it came to the exact amount we were given, with sixty-three cents left over. We were amazed that, between the two donors, the cost was almost precisely what the Lord had given us.

The puppet ministry turned out to be very fruitful over the years. We have lots of fond memories and much video footage of the fun times we had with them. They were a great addition to the movie ministry. Not only did the children love seeing them, the adults enjoyed them just as much.

*

We met some of the most wonderful families in the camps. One such family that stands out is Alfredo and Celina. We usually entered the camps by dusk during the week, but this particular day we decided to share the gospel on a Saturday afternoon. Tyler and Rachel, our friends from Albuquerque who were visiting Baja for their summer vacation, wanted to get a taste for the ministry.

After a time of singing and sharing the gospel with the crowd, we gave an invitation to receive Jesus as their Savior, asking for a show of hands. Rachel and I noticed a young couple who had their hands raised, standing toward the rear of the audience. We made our way over to this couple and shared in more detail the salvation message. To our delight, Alfredo and Celina accepted Jesus into their lives. We also invited them to come to our puppet show the next day at a nearby church. We all agreed their three children would really enjoy it.

The following day we were happy to see the couple in the audience. Rachel asked Alfredo and Celina if she could take a picture of their family, assuming that this would be the last time she would see them, since it wasn't common to meet the same family again in subsequent seasons. They gladly posed for it. When Rachel and Tyler returned to the States, she posted that picture on her refrigerator and committed to pray for them regularly.

Before we knew it, a year had passed. Tyler and Rachel were excited to come back again to minister with us in the camps. This time they wanted to experience mainland Mexico, so they came to Culiacan.

One beautiful afternoon we all piled in our vehicle for a day of sightseeing. On the way, George suddenly remembered that he needed to talk with a Christian friend in one of the camps we had just passed. Making a U-turn, he pulled into the parking lot outside the camp. "I'll be right back," he assured us, getting out of the truck and making his way through the gate.

As we were waiting for him to return, Rachel looked at me with an astonished expression on her face. "Look! There's Alfredo!" she said, pointing to an indigenous man who was leaning on the huge tree by the gate, next to several other men.

"Who's Alfredo?" I asked, not remembering him from the summer before.

"You know, that young couple with the three little kids we met last year in Baja that we prayed to receive Jesus," she answered.

"Rachel, you might think he looks like him, but that was in Baja and we're in Culiacan, quite a distance apart. The chance of that being the same person is pretty slim." I added, "Besides, how do you remember what he looked like?"

"I know that's him," she insisted. "I took a picture last year and taped it to my refrigerator. I tell you, that's Alfredo!"

"All right, let's see if he looks over at us when I call his name," I suggested. I stuck my head out the window and called his name. To my amazement, he turned around and looked our way. I motioned with my hand for him to come over to us. When he came over to the truck, I asked him if he knew who we were. He didn't remember us, and quite frankly, he didn't look familiar to me either. "Were you in Baja last summer working in the camps?" I asked him.

"Yes, I was," he replied.

"Did you give your life to Jesus last year too?" I inquired.

"Yes, I did," he responded, smiling widely.

"Well, we're the women that prayed for you when you asked Jesus into your heart," I told him. I went on to tell him about the photo Rachel had taken of his family, how she had taped it on her refrigerator and had been praying for them during the year. He was so pleased to hear that and began to tell us what the Lord had been doing in his life since we saw him last.

He said he labored in the fields during the day, and in the evenings he shared the gospel from camp to camp to his own people group, in the Tlapaneco language. As his story went on, he told us that after he left Baja that summer we met him, he went back home to share the gospel with his neighbors. Because of his zeal, many of the people in his village surrendered their lives to the Lord. This upset the local authorities, because now part of the village wouldn't participate in their pagan traditions and holidays. With their lives being threatened, Alfredo and Celina were forced to leave the village. They formed a church with fifteen other families, and made their way to Culiacan to work in the fields to support themselves.

Tyler, Rachel, and I sat there mesmerized as he shared his story. All of this in one year! Wow! Talk about the hand of God and the power of prayer! He asked us to continue to pray for him and his church. Just about this time George came back to the truck. After some introductions and a few more minutes of fellowship, it was time for us to go. We invited Alfredo and his family to a Christmas program Jonathon and our host's daughter had put together. He gladly accepted our invitation. We really looked forward to our next visit.

Alfredo and his family found the village where we were staying and showed up at the church for the program. We saw that they had an addition to their family since we had last seen them in Baja. Rachel had her camera ready and took another picture of them. When we came back to the States and saw the two pictures side by side on their refrigerator, there was an amazing transformation from the first to the second picture. In the first photo, they all looked very somber and somewhat fearful, whereas in the second they were all beaming happily, with glowing expressions.

Periodically our host family and Ron and Eva, the missionaries we worked alongside in the camps, would run into Alfredo. They reported to us how God was using him in incredible ways. The last time we heard, Alfredo is still sharing his faith in Mexico and has won many people to the Lord. He is now training his own people group to go out as missionaries to the other tribes in North America. Subsequently, the people in the village that Alfredo once was forced to leave because of the threats toward his family have all become born again Christians, as are those from the neighboring village. I know the success of Alfredo's labors is partly due to the faithful prayers of Rachel.

This is what led us to start our picture-taking ministry in the camps. We took photos, with the permission of each person who gave their lives to the Lord, to bring back to the U.S. church for anyone who wanted to pray for individuals and families. Many people on both ends liked the idea. That was an added ministry we kept up for a while. Only the Lord knows the fruit that came out of the prayer ministry.

Along with the highs, of course came the lows. Before leaving Baja, we planned a get-together with friends for a farewell meal at a local area restaurant. The restaurant seemed clean enough (other than the cockroach our friend found in her salad) that evening. Early the next morning, I woke up, sicker than a dog. Because I had numerous incidences of food poisoning in the past, we knew what I was dealing with. This would be another time that I would just have to ride it out. With me not really wanting to travel that day yet anxious to get back to the States, George made a comfortable bed in the back seat to allow me to sleep, while the kids rode in the front with him.

The trip went fairly well, considering the circumstances, until we neared the border in Tijuana. The transmission in our truck started to make a really strange sound each time George shifted into another gear. By the time we arrived at the steep incline known as the "Tijuana Hill", a couple of the gears had already gone out. We knew that it was going to be risky trying to make the hill while pulling our trailer, but we had no other choice than to try to Banzai it up in hopes of making it to the top. George punched it, trying to pick up momentum, only to find himself halfway up when the truck wouldn't go any farther. Now in a worse situation than before, we found ourselves slowly backing the truck down the road, hoping to try again and be able to pick up more speed the second time around. Once more our efforts were of no avail, and we were stranded. Again, we called on God to bail us out of our predicament.

George suggested that we unhook the trailer and leave it parked on the side of the highway. He would then look for help from someone who had a vehicle big enough to get us over the top of the hill. We could coast our way with our two remaining gears to the border and get help on the other side. Thankfully, we had friends in the San Diego area that could help us.

Leaving our trailer was not an option that I even wanted to consider, yet staying with the trailer without him while he went and looked for help wasn't any better. What would I do if someone stopped and wanted to rob us? It didn't help that I was still battling food poisoning. Thoughts of someone coming by in a truck, pulling up to the trailer and stealing everything we owned, including our house, had me really stressed. This is one more of those times that I needed to trust God.

George began to block up the trailer and detach it from our truck, while I prayed that the Lord would keep His angels' guard over our belongings. We were thankful when our truck at last made it over the hill. Now we were in a desperate search for help with the trailer.

The road took us into the downtown Tijuana area. Crowds of people filled the streets as they busied themselves with Sunday afternoon activities. Anxiety was gripping me as I tried not to let the noise and smells get to me. As George and I were driving up and down each street, considering where we should go, suddenly, there in the midst of a block full of cantinas, we found a church. This wasn't the typical place you would see a church, yet we both thought, "What a great location to reach the lost for Christ." We looked at each other in amazement. It was Sunday afternoon and there was a service just underway.

We drove around the block a few times before realizing that we weren't going to find a parking spot in this congested area. "I'm going to drop you off at the corner of this street, Jennifer," George decided. "You'll need to go to the church and find someone in there that can help us."

Still not feeling well, I definitely did not want to do that, particularly when I looked down the street full of bars and drunken men standing on the sidewalk. "I just can't do this. The stress is too much for me right now," I moaned.

"It's our only option that looks good," George replied. "We know there are people in that church, and we might not be able to find another one where they're holding a service right now." George tried to assure me, "Besides, the Lord can protect you." I took a deep breath as he pulled over to let me out, telling me he would circle the block and be back.

Standing at the corner, looking down the street I was about to encounter, my heart pounded. The 23rd Psalm came to mind and I began to recite it to myself. "Yea, though I walk through the valley of the shadow of death, I will fear no evil, for you are with me, Lord," I continued saying over and over as I made my way past several drunken men.

By the time I got to the stairs of the church, my faith was stretched to the limit. Yet not one of those drunken men looked at me or said a word to me. It was as if the Lord had made me invisible or distracted them from seeing me.

I walked up the stairs to the church feeling a little shaky. The man at the door handed me a brochure, welcoming me in. At this point, I was on emotional overload. I looked at him and started to cry. "I need help," was all I could say. A perplexed look came over his face as he stared at me, not knowing what to make of it. I knew I had to find a way to explain our problem. "My husband and I are missionaries. We were traveling back to the States when our transmission started to act up. We need someone who owns a truck to help us pull our trailer over the Tijuana hill. We left our trailer on the side of the highway, so it's important that we find someone soon," I said, trying very hard to use the proper words to clearly explain our situation.

The man motioned over another man sitting in the back of the church. He got up and came over to us quickly. As they conversed back and forth in rapid Spanish, I was beginning to feel a lot more comfortable with our situation. They then turned to reassure me that they could help. This man happened to have a truck parked down the street with a hitch that could pull our trailer. He would meet me in front of the church while I found George. I was overjoyed that everything had lined up so quickly.

Waiting in front of the church for George to drive by, I jumped into our vehicle as soon as he pulled up. Going around the block one more time, I explained to him what the plan was. When we came back around, the man was already waiting for us. Unfortunately, I realized that I should have thought to ask him what kind of vehicle he had when we saw him sitting in a small Toyota pickup truck. "Honey," George stated emphatically, "that truck is not going to pull our trailer over the Tijuana hill."

"Well, if it doesn't work, then maybe they will know someone else who has a bigger truck to help us," I responded in desperation. George shrugged his shoulders and went along with the plan.

When we arrived back at our trailer, I was elated to see it still there and untouched. George and the gentleman with the Toyota both got out of their vehicles and introduced themselves. As they were getting acquainted, George expressed his doubts about the Toyota being able to pull the trailer up the hill. The man seemed confident that it would do the job. It was now a matter of watching and waiting to see what would happen. We were all praying that his little truck could do its job.

Sure enough, without any bit of a stall, that little vehicle pulled our heavy trailer right over the hill with no problems. We were in awe. (This scene would have made a good commercial for the Toyota Company.)

We couldn't thank him enough. As we all stood on the other side of the Tijuana hill, the man told us that he was the only one in his church who owned a truck. What amazed us, more than the fact of his truck pulling our trailer over the hill, was the fact that he was the first person the man at the door asked to help. We all agreed that God's timing is perfect, and so are His ways. We thanked him again, ready for our next phase of the trial. Could we actually get to the other side of the border, with only two gears, pulling our trailer?

Back in the Nineties, the border crossing consisted of a maze that you had to drive through, weaving back and forth between cement slabs to get to the other side. It had been set up that way so it wouldn't be easy to run the border. We had thankfully made it up to those slabs and were going back and forth through the maze when we discovered our rig was too long. The border guards wanted us to back up so we could make one of the turns properly. The problem was that our reverse gear also went out, so there was no backing up. They either had to manually move the big cement slabs or we weren't going anywhere. They were quite unhappy with us, but they had no other choice but to move the slabs.

We finally got through, thinking that we were almost to the end of our trials. We called our friends to get permission to have our vehicle towed to their house. It was a blessing they answered the phone. They suggested, with the pastor's consent, towing the truck to their church parking lot where there would be more room to work on it. I was never so happy to lay my head down on my pillow for the night, knowing I would feel much better the next day.

To my delight, as our transmission was being worked on, our friend Bob mentioned that there was a mall nearby to keep the kids and me occupied. We liked his suggestion, so they dropped us off, planning to meet up in a few hours.

As I walked inside, I noticed at once how everyone seemed so well dressed. Just coming from Mexico, working among the poorest of the poor, it started to hit me how wealthy our country really is. I began to experience what is called "reverse culture shock". It might not have hit me so strongly had I been in a normal mall, but the ambience of this upscale mall was beginning to overwhelm me. The feelings I had experienced previously with the little Tarahumara baby who was starving to death because the mother was unable to supply food came rushing back. I remember looking down from the second floor as several people stood around a jewelry case, trying on diamond rings and other jewelry. Looking up, I noticed an enormous, beautiful chandelier hanging from the ceiling. Suddenly I realized that I needed to get out of the mall, because thoughts of the contrasts of the cultures were more than I could take. The children didn't share my feelings and emotions. They wanted to shop, and besides, the men wouldn't be back to pick us up for some time. I would just have to grin and bear it.

As we continued to walk around the mall, my silent prayers reached the Lord. He doesn't give us more than we can handle. Suddenly in popped George and Bob. They explained that the parts they needed would take several days to get. George didn't want to wait. His next option had been to call Gary, who lived two-and-a-half hours away, and ask him if he could tow us up to Phelan. Gary agreed to come and bring Dale, another friend, to help tow the trailer. This would give George more time to rebuild the transmission and possibly find cheaper parts. I was happy to second his idea, just glad we were leaving the mall.

Bob laughed when I told him about my mall experience. "I forgot how nice people dress here in the United States," I added. When he explained that this mall was one of the most expensive malls in the San Diego area, it made more sense that I would respond so critically. I've learned it's not a good idea to come from a poverty-stricken area after an extended time, and then go into an affluent location right away. It does something to the brain. Don't get me wrong. I'm not against the niceties of our country. I believe the Lord has blessed us greatly, and I enjoy the comforts our country has to offer. It's the contrast that can be difficult, suddenly going from one extreme to the other.

Gary and Dale arrived within three hours of the phone call. What a blessing it is to have friends in different parts of the country. We were hooked up and on the road in no time.

Within a week they located a used transmission. We ended up buying a complete used pickup truck together. Gary knew he could sell parts off the truck and make a little extra money, and we saved by getting another transmission that would have cost a lot more if we bought a rebuilt one. It worked out for both of our families.

After a nice long visit, and the needed truck repairs, we were on the road again. We headed back to Bisbee, Arizona, where we were home ported. We had learned that being close to the border was a much easier transition than driving to Albuquerque each time we came out of Mexico. We spent the time preparing for our autumn trip to Culiacan.

*

George and I were beginning to realize the trailer was getting too small for our growing family. We needed something roomier. George suggested one morning that we drive to Huachuca City, a town close to Bisbee, to look at fifth wheels. It didn't matter that we didn't have any money to purchase one; it was free to just look. I felt somewhat reluctant, but after a bit of persuasion and reasoning from George, I agreed to go. "Why tempt ourselves?" was my thought. His idea was that we could get some ideas on price and layouts.

One of the first fifth wheels we looked at seemed to be a good fit for our family. It was used and the previous owners had trashed it out. A lot of things needed to be replaced, yet we were both on the same page about fixing it up ourselves and thus getting it for a better price.

When the dealer came in to talk with us, he was only willing to go down to ten thousand dollars. He had dropped it seven thousand dollars already, so that was his lowest price. We thought someone would have to be out of their minds to pay seventeen thousand for this trailer, but ten thousand seemed workable. After all, it did have a solid frame, no leaks, and it was only a few years old. We told the dealer we needed time to think about it, and we would get back with him. Besides, we didn't have the money.

After leaving, we couldn't quit talking about it. Not that we were enamored with this one particular fifth wheel, yet it did have the space we needed and seemed more attainable price-wise. So, we prayed and asked God to guide us.

Sometimes when we pray, circumstances can happen that look as if they are the Lord's will, but in reality they are not. That's what happened this time. Within hours after our petition to the Lord, I was chatting with a friend about our desire to get another trailer, sharing with her that we had found a fixer-upper priced at ten thousand dollars. Immediately she volunteered to let us use her credit card to purchase it, with a plan to make monthly payments. Her generosity overwhelmed me, as well as her trust in us to pay her back. Showing my appreciation, I knew I still needed to discuss it with George and pray about it. We weren't used to being in debt, especially making monthly payments that would take us years to pay off.

When I brought the idea up to George, he responded the same way I did: excited at the prospect of actually being able to get the fifth wheel, but uneasy at the payments and the thought of going into debt. We prayed about it for several days, neither of us receiving any peace about moving forward with the plans. One morning upon awaking, George informed me that he was leaving for a few hours, possibly the whole day, to go to find wisdom. "In the multitude of counselors, there is safety," he quoted to me from the Bible (Proverbs 11:14). "Today I'm going to visit several different friends in hope that the Lord will give me wisdom through one of them." His idea sounded good to me, even if it meant taking up a whole day.

He returned sooner than planned, within three hours, excited to share with me what the Lord had showed him through our friends, Paul and Tammy. They were also missionaries, then building up support to go into Mexico full-time, so we had the privilege of seeing them periodically in Bisbee. What I love about this couple is that they will tell you what they think even if it's not what you want to hear. When George laid out our circumstances, Paul was immediately against it. He expressed that God is a jealous God. If it is His will that we have a bigger trailer, He will give it to us. He went on to say that when we live our lives to serve Him, depending on Him for all of our needs, He also says in His word that if we ask, if it's His will, He'll give it to us (John 14:14). Going into debt and stressing over it month by month would be much too hard.

Both of us felt so much peace. It made sense. If we were trusting in Him for our daily needs now, why wouldn't we trust Him for this? Our minds were made up. We weren't going to use our friend's credit card. We would trust God.

One of the lessons I have learned over the years is that when we ask our Lord for something, He gives us more than we ask for. We had our mind set on the trashed-out ten thousand dollar trailer that needed to be fixed up. He had something bigger in mind.

It was again that time of year to make a report to the churches and supporters of our ministry. We scheduled visits, and in between planned to look for a trailer. Before leaving on our trip, I asked God for a specific trailer. "Lord, you know my desire to have a bigger place for my family, and I believe You will meet that need if it's Your will. Is it a lot to ask You to give me a certain type?" I began to go into specifics. "Because I do a lot of cooking for guests, it's hard to have a kitchen in the middle where people walk back and forth. If it's in the back of the trailer, I'll feel a lot more comfortable. I would also like a closet in the kitchen with washer and dryer space." Diving into the details, I continued to ask the Lord for the other things that seemed important, like a slide out for more room, a hide-a-way bed for more bed space, a bathroom on one side that wasn't split in the middle, and a back bedroom where one could stand up without bending over to get in bed. I ended my prayer with, "Lord, could this fifth wheel also be carpeted with a dark burgundy color, so it won't show up the dirt?"

Throughout my walk with the Lord I have noticed that we serve a very detailed God. I first became aware of it when I read through one of the Old Testament books when God gave the Israelite people instructions to build the tabernacle. It was extremely detailed, down to the tassels on the curtains. If you have never read the book of Exodus in that light, read it some time to see what I mean. He's the same God today as He was back then.

Our first stop was in Flagstaff. We looked during the week or so we spent there, but we found nothing in the newspaper or car lots. Our second stop was Albuquerque. We found a fifth wheel on a lot that George thought was fantastic, but it wasn't to my liking at all. Besides, I thought the price was much too high for what it had to offer. Then, while visiting our supporters, something wonderful happened. Years ago, Terry, a friend of ours, asked us to pray for his boss who was not a Christian. Terry had such a burden for him that he set out to pray for him regularly. We also prayed for him. Hearing that we were in Albuquerque, Terry called us to tell us the good news. His boss received Jesus into his life. We rejoiced with him in the good news. He invited us to lunch to meet him. It was a treat to finally meet Terry's boss Mark after all these years.

Mark showed a lot of interest in missions. He wanted to hear all about Mexico. After sharing with him, he was quite excited to hear about our work. Later in the day, he told Terry he wanted to donate five thousand dollars toward our work. The timing and the amount of the five thousand dollars was awesome. Just days before our luncheon, the director of our mission called us from Flagstaff and told us someone, who wanted to stay anonymous, put up a matching fund up to five thousand dollars toward our trailer endeavor. For every dollar that came in for us, they would match it. Overnight we had ten thousand dollars!

Our next visit was to Boulder, Colorado. We looked in the Denver area and didn't find what we wanted, which still didn't stop us from plugging away with our search for just the right one. We had plenty of time and opportunity to look at more places because we would be heading up into the Midwest to visit our families.

During our stay in Boulder, while visiting George's brother, John, George picked up a newspaper that happened to be lying on the coffee table. Skimming through it, he noticed an ad of a fifth wheel trailer for sale. He made arrangements with the owner to meet the following day on our way out of town.

Driving along on our way to see this trailer, I started to ask George about details. "Does it have a slide out? What year is it? How much do they want for it?" I inquired.

"I don't know any more than you do," he responded. "I only know that it's thirty-six feet long. We'll see it when we get there."

As we arrived, an elderly couple came out of their home to greet us. They led us around to the back of their yard to a fairly good-sized Quonset hut that had been used to store the trailer. Once inside, I noticed at once how clean it had been kept, even still having the smell of newness. They told us that it was seven years old, and they had only used it three times. Immediately, I assumed that they were going to want an arm and a leg for it.

Standing in the entryway of the trailer that led into the kitchen, I opened the closet door to see what was inside and found a space for a washer and dryer. "This is a perfect layout for a kitchen," I thought. Moving into the living room, it was just as exciting to discover the slide out wall with an entertainment center placed exactly as I had pictured when I was imagining what I wanted. By the time we got to the bathroom, which just happened to be on one side of the trailer, I realized that this was the exact trailer that I had been praying for. Quickly moving to the back of the trailer to see if I could stand up in the bedroom, my heart was leaping with joy. Looking down, I turned to George and said, "Do you realize this carpet is burgundy?" He looked at me a bit strangely. He had no idea that I had prayed to the Lord for the specific details of this trailer. Trying to conceal my excitement lest they raise the price, I struggled to contain my emotions. George and the owner moved outdoors so he could show him all the goodies attached to the outside. Meanwhile, I slowly walked around outside of the trailer, laying my hands on the siding as I prayed. "Lord, this is the exact trailer I asked You for. If it's Your will for us, please let it be this one."

When they told us that they wanted seventeen thousand five hundred dollars for it, we both fervently prayed for this trailer not to sell until we had all the money we needed. We were only seven thousand five hundred dollars short of having the whole amount. We knew the trailer was well worth the price they were asking, so we didn't even try to talk them down. We had looked at many trailers already, and this one was definitely one of the nicest we had seen.

George explained to the owners that we were on our way up to Minnesota and didn't have the full amount. By the time we came back this way, if it was still available and we had all the money, we would purchase it. He went on to explain that we believed if it was the Lord's will, He would give us the balance of seven thousand dollars on our return. The looks on their faces were priceless. I wish I had a camera so I could have captured the moment. They were actually looking at us like we were from outer space. "Okay," was all they said, and shook our hands as we jumped in our truck and left.

Pulling away, George and I chuckled at their response toward us. "They think we're crazy," I said. "If the Lord gives us the money to buy their trailer on our way back, we're really going to blow them out of the water."

Thoughts of the trailer being exactly like the one I had prayed for continued to run through my mind. It convinced me that if we were going to get a trailer, this one would be it. We seemed so close and yet so far away from attaining it. In spite of our enthusiasm, we just had to wait and see what the Lord had for us.

We also knew that if we purchased it, we would still need extra money to buy a trailer hitch, since we didn't own one for that type of pull. This would now take a stretch of faith on our part. "Honey," George said, "before we go any further, we need to take three hundred and fifty dollars from our account to buy the hitch so I have time to install it. This way when we're in Colorado we'll be ready to hook right up."

My logic said, "What if we use the money for the hitch and then have to wait to buy the trailer because there won't be enough money, and then it sells to someone else?" That just shows how faithless I can be. If I prayed over the trailer that God wouldn't sell it out from under us, and would save it for us, then I needed to trust Him, which in turn would give me peace. Again, I thank the Lord for my husband. His faith has always been much stronger than mine. He reassured me everything would work out.

As the days progressed, so did our bank account. Each day we called the bank, getting more excited about the reality of actually being able to purchase it. Our week of vacation came to an end and it was now time to head back the way we came. We had twelve thousand, five hundred and fifty dollars in our account, and we found out that the five thousand dollars that was promised to us from our friend's boss in Albuquerque still was to be deposited. We were more excited than words could express. This meant that we would have exactly the amount they were asking for the trailer.

Arriving outside of Denver near the home of the owners of the trailer, we checked into a hotel. We had a little extra money in the account that we knew would pay for a one night's stay. We had twelve dollars to eat on for the evening. Discovering a fast food hamburger restaurant next door to the hotel, we were getting ready to head down there after freshening up. We planned to wait for the five thousand dollars to come in, all the while praying the Lord would put it on Terry's boss to make a deposit into our account.

Before leaving for dinner, George wanted to make a phone call to an old friend that lived in the Denver area. We had our camper shell on the back of our truck. It needed to be put somewhere while we picked up the trailer. Maybe our friend Ken would let us store it in his yard until we picked up the fifth wheel. Once the trailer was hooked up, we could put the camper shell on the top of it until we got home.

George called Ken, who was very happy to hear from us. It had been a while. As they conversed back and forth, he wanted to know where we were staying. George explained our situation, telling him how we were waiting in the hotel for the five thousand dollars to come in. As generous as he has always been to us, Ken gladly gave us permission to put our camper shell in his yard. Not only did he bless us with his yard, he told George that he wanted to pay for our hotel room. "Even if it takes you a week to receive the money, don't worry about it. It's on me," he said.

Those words released so much stress from me. This also meant that we didn't have to skimp on our dinner and go to get fast food hamburgers. We had the money to eat next door at the Chinese restaurant instead.

The funniest memory I have during this whole time happened when George called the owners of the trailer that evening to let them know we had returned to Colorado to buy their fifth wheel. "We have checked into a hotel while we wait for five thousand dollars more to come into our account. Hopefully it will be in the bank tomorrow," George said. There was silence on the other end. "Are you still there?" George asked.

"Yes... Okay... give us a call when you have the money," the elderly man responded. You can imagine what he was thinking.

In the faithfulness of the Lord, His timing always being exactly on time, the five thousand dollars was deposited the next morning. We actually had all the money to pay the couple, including the three hundred and fifty dollars we (I should say, I) wasn't sure would come in.

Making the phone call to the owners was such a delight. "We have all the money. We're ready to buy your trailer," George said happily. Again there was silence on the other end.

The elderly man spoke up. "All right, meet me at such and such bank at this time and we'll transfer the money into our account."

When we met him and his wife at the bank, they were still staring at us with that look like we were from outer space. They didn't have much to say to us, just the looks. Suddenly, they got up and left the room. Meanwhile, we sat and waited for the money to transfer into their account.

The banker who was dealing with the transaction spoke up. "You are getting a killer deal on this fifth wheel," he said. "They bought this for forty thousand dollars and have only used it a few times," he added. We assured him that we knew we were getting a good deal on it, feeling quite blessed with our purchase.

We followed the couple back to their home to pick up our newly bought trailer. I kept pinching myself to make sure I wasn't dreaming. Reality was starting to hit me when we were pulling out of their driveway with the trailer attached to our truck. Joy is an understatement for the way we all felt. We couldn't thank our Lord enough for the wonderful gift he had given us.

As we made our way back home, our friends and family were very happy to see what the Lord had blessed us with. Everyone that knows us knew we couldn't obtain a trailer like this on our own, debt-free. It was the hand of God. Our Lord was glorified over and over through that trailer. Just like Paul, our friend in Bisbee, had prophesied!

They shall fear You as long as the sun
and moon endure,
throughout all generations.
He shall come down like rain
upon the grass before
mowing, like showers
that water the earth.

Psalm 72:5,6

14
More Blessings and Trials

As if the Lord hadn't blessed us enough, He was ready to do it again. After the season of receiving our beautiful fifth wheel and enjoying it to the fullest in Mexico, in addition to having a fruitful season of ministry, we returned once again to the U.S. for our yearly turnaround. We were now preparing for the summer in Baja in hopes of having an equally fruitful time there.

To our dismay, upon arriving back to Bisbee, we found out our close friend's cabinet shop had burned to the ground. Our friends were devastated, to say the least. We immediately jumped in to help in any way we could. Next to the rubble and ashes, a little building that had been attached to the shop was still standing, but sadly the fire had left the items inside with smoke damage. They had used this small building for storage. Now they were cleaning what was salvageable and throwing out what had been hopelessly damaged. Day after day, throughout the week, we helped with the mess.

During this time our minivan also started to act up. They truly say when it rains, it pours. George didn't have time to work on it like he normally would, so we left it parked in our yard, planning to fix it later.

Toward the end of the first week of cleaning and scrubbing the damaged items, I found my thoughts dwelling on my minivan again, complaining to the Lord about it constantly breaking down. I felt a little guilty to be griping about my small petty trial compared to my friend's huge crisis and what they were going through, and tried to put my personal concerns in perspective. Still, near the end of the day I felt the need to address the issue once more. "Lord, I know my car is broke, and I feel bad about bringing it up to you at a time like this, but could You please give me a good running car that we can depend on? This other car has lots of miles and it's getting old." That was the extent of my prayer. Then I continued to clean the smoke damaged building with my friend.

Returning home that evening, we were exhausted. Before retiring for the night, I opened my e-mail and was excited to see a letter from our friend Ken in Colorado. It read something like this:

"Knowing that you are in need of another car, my friend and I have decided to help you get another one. Call me."

It took me totally by surprise. George and I had not disclosed that we were looking for another vehicle. What did he mean by this letter? Did he find us a good deal, and we need to come up with the finances to purchase it? Or did he want to bless us by giving it to us? The only way to find out was to call him.

Accordingly, the following day George called to get the details. Ken shared that he had a friend who owned a minivan and wanted to trade it in for a newer model. The dealership wouldn't give him a fair enough trade-in so he put it up for sale. Then he and his friend thought about us and decided they wanted to bless us by giving it to us. He ended the conversation by saying, "We'd like to deliver it to you in the next couple days. If you're going to be in Bisbee, we'll be there."

They were right on time. Within the day or so, they were calling and telling us to meet them at the end of our dirt road.

"Come and get your new car! We don't want to drive our car up your road, so we'll wait for you here."

We quickly jumped in the car, excited to see our new minivan. We hadn't asked about the condition or any details so we weren't sure what to expect, yet coming from Ken we knew it would be decent.

We pulled up, first gratefully greeting him and his friend. He had the keys in his hands. "Well, there's your van; it's all yours!" he said, pointing to it, and then handed me the keys.

Walking over to the van, I could see that it was fairly new; at least newer than what I had expected. I got in and started it up. It was so nice! I couldn't believe that it was really ours. Emotions welled up inside me as the tears started to fall. I was so overwhelmed by the love and consideration our friends had for us. Then, remembering my prayer to the Lord just days earlier, it hit me. Here we were sitting in this beautiful van the Lord decided to bless us with.

Ken came over to the window. "So, what do you think?" he said, smiling. He could see that I was crying.

"I don't know what to say," I said, humbly. "Thank you doesn't express enough how I really feel, but... all I can say is... thank you!"

We got out of the van and hugged them both. They suggested we go to register it in our name right then, even wanting to pay for our insurance and registration. But they had blessed us enough by giving the van to us, not to mention driving all the way from Colorado in two vehicles to deliver it to us, so we felt the least we could do is pay for the insurance and registration.

That minivan was such a blessing. We ended up taking it to Mexico on several occasions, using it to easily fit plenty of people in it as we took them to the camps. Our friends also loved the comfort of it. Not breaking down was an added bonus.

We're so glad we serve such an awesome God! He tells us in the Bible that if we delight ourselves in the Lord, He will give us the desires of our hearts (Psalm 37:4).

Note to the reader:

Our friends whose shop burned down have since rebuilt. This happened approximately ten years ago. As I was writing this story, my friend called me today and told me their shop burned down again.

*

It was time again to prepare for our summer Baja trip. Our plans were to drive to Gary and Roberta's place, and then caravan to Mexico. This would be our first trip into Baja with the new fifth wheel. From Bisbee to Phelan, California, the journey took us through the Mojave Desert during the hot season. We didn't think much about it. With everything packed, we were ready for another adventure, and taking the new minivan (gas prices were much cheaper back then) seemed like a good idea. Having a vehicle to get around in while we were in California without having to unhook the big rig would be much easier. Jonathon and I traveled in the car, while Laura and George enjoyed pulling the trailer in the big truck.

The day started out beautifully. By mid afternoon when we hit the hot desert, it was getting a little uncomfortable. As Jonathon and I were following behind our big rig, we became concerned when we noticed what looked like a cloud of white smoke coming out from under our fifth wheel. Thankfully we had CBs in each vehicle for communication. "George, did you just drive over a box of powder?" I asked. When he responded that he hadn't, we knew something wasn't right and both quickly pulled over.

Stopping the truck, George realized that the engine was on fire. "The truck is on fire!" he yelled through the CB radio.

He was trying to wake Laura, who had fallen asleep, yanking on the seat belt to pull her out of the truck, and grabbing for the fire extinguisher at the same time. You never saw two people move as fast as we did. While George was occupied with Laura and the fire extinguisher, I was running to the fifth wheel. I unlocked the door, grabbed our five gallon water container (normally I can't lift it on my own) and had it to the front of the truck in a minute's time. George stopped me as I was getting ready to pour it over the engine. He had successfully put out the flames, even though the engine was still cherry red hot.

Talk about an adrenaline rush! I was just shaking. All I could picture was our home, vehicle, and all we owned gone up in flames. When we all settled down, we thanked God for His protection, not only for our possessions, but for all of us as well. George said that Laura was in a dead sleep and would not wake up to his screaming. He had to carry her out as he was trying to put out the flames. It was when we were talking about the amazing abilities we possess when adrenaline kicks in that we realized that I had carried the five gallon container, full of water, to the front of the truck with no problem, in record time.

We were also thanking the Lord for protecting the truck engine. George couldn't see any damage done mechanically. We were able to continue on our trip to Gary and Roberta's home, driving slowly and with caution. Every so often we would stop our vehicles on the side of the highway to cool down the transmission and check to make sure the exhaust manifolds weren't red hot once again. We decided that our load was a bit too heavy for our transmission to pull in that kind of heat.

On certain trips we take, it seems we run into one trial after another. This one was starting to look that way. We always concluded though that those were the times we were in for a fruitful time on the mission field.

Once we arrived at Gary and Roberta's house, Gary's truck started acting up. We weren't even one mile out of town when the guys were pulling out their tools and work clothes to find out what the problem was. If George wasn't a mechanic by trade, I don't know what we would have done all these years. I can't even tell you how many times the enemy came against our vehicles. (Those that received our newsletters regularly were constantly praying for our vehicles.)

After an hour or so of laboring to get Gary's truck running, we were on the road again. It did throw us off our schedule somewhat, ending up in Tijuana in the late afternoon. Tackling the "Tijuana Hill" again was not something we looked forward to. Sure enough, creeping up at a slow pace, just about to top it, George realized we weren't going to make it. He slowly pulled over to the side of the highway, holding his foot on the brake the whole time. There was no way he could get out of the vehicle without the possibility of our rig rolling backwards. He called Gary, who had already crested the hill, on the CB. Being on a one-way road, it wasn't going to be easy to do a turnaround. Our only option was for Gary to unhook his trailer, come back around, and hook up our fifth wheel to get us over the hill.

Meanwhile, as we were waiting, George asked me to get out and look for a big enough rock to put behind our tire to block it up. Again, in the midst of the emergency, I ran outside and found a big rock, normally too heavy for me to lift, but because of the anxiety of the trial I did it anyway. I was able to get it behind the truck just right; the job was accomplished.

Our plans worked well. Gary's truck had no problem pulling us over to the other side of the hill. We were on our way again, now really off schedule. We would have to drive into the night, which we never liked to do in Mexico.

We were only back on the road for about an hour when I felt a sharp pain run from my hip down my leg. Within ten minutes of that initial jolt of pain, my left leg started to tingle and then went numb. I kept moving back and forth, trying to find a comfortable position, shifting my weight, but to no avail. The pain continued to get more intense. Trying to ignore it wasn't working, but I was concerned about our schedule, not wanting to stop the caravan again. When I couldn't take it any longer, George pulled over. I thought getting out of the truck and stretching would probably do me a world of good, but when I stood up outside, the pain was excruciating. I had never experienced such severe pain in my leg before. Fear set in as we tried to figure out what was wrong. George got back on the CB to tell Gary what was going on. We would need to find a rest area or business where we could pull in for the night to rest.

Ten minutes down the road, we found a gas station with plenty of parking space. There was one slight problem. In the parking lot there happened to be a drunken party going on. They were all hoopin' and hollerin', carrying on as loud as could be. We started to reconsider our options at this point. Should we stay at the gas station with the drunkards, or drive down the road hoping to find another business and possibly not finding one, thus being forced to stay the night on the side of the highway. The lesser of the two evils was to stay. At least the gas station was lit up.

By this time I was in great pain. All I was able to do was lie on the living room floor and pray and cry. Everyone gathered together around me. We were in desperate need of a healing, recognizing that we had been under a spiritual attack all day. After several of us took turns praying, Gary guessed I was having sciatica pain, and that possibly one of my nerves was being pinched. He suffered from that regularly, so he was quite familiar with its symptoms.

Meanwhile, the drunkards were still carrying on outside. Besides praying for my healing, we asked the Lord to give the men a desire to leave this location. It was phenomenal.

Right as we finished with our petition to God, all the men immediately jumped into their vehicles and left. Suddenly there was blessed quietness outside. We all looked at each other, amazed, and then started to give God praise for such a quick answer to prayer. I took a pain reliever and went to bed.

By the next morning, I felt great! Being able to sleep soundly all night helped. As fantastic as I felt, I knew I never wanted to experience that pain again, even if it meant no more heavy lifting. And I've never had another one of those sciatica attacks, thank God!

In spite of the numerous trials on our first day, that summer trip was fruitful. The manifestation of the power of God permeated the camps.

One particular afternoon, as we were setting up our equipment for the showing of the Jesus Movie and tape distribution, a middle-aged woman came up to us. She did not look at all well, with very little color. She was extremely pale. "I need your help," she said, struggling to talk. She explained that she contracted some sickness weeks earlier. She had been to several doctors, each giving her a prescription, to no avail. "Do you think your God can heal me?" she asked.

"Of course we believe our Lord can heal you. We serve a powerful God!" George answered confidently. He quickly called over the group of young teenagers who were with us. They were with a youth group from a Presbyterian church in Denver on a two week, short-term mission. "We're all going to hold hands and place you in the middle of us," George instructed. He then placed a chair in the circle and had the woman sit on it. Requesting that we all start to pray in unison, we asked the Lord out loud to please bring healing to this woman. As we were finishing, she leaped up from the chair, jumping up and down. "I feel good! I feel good!" she kept repeating. We were all looking at her and at each other. "I haven't felt this great in so long!" Her sudden dramatic response shocked us all. Yet we could all see that even her coloring was returning to normal.

"Thank you, thank you, thank you," she continued to say. One by one we were telling her not to thank us, but the Lord. It wasn't we that healed her; it was God. We were giving Him all the glory where glory is due.

Within the hour, a huge crowd gathered around us to pray for the sick. Having lived together in the same camp with this very sickly lady, the people saw the power of God. Members from the Denver church who had prayed for her were just as astounded. They had never experienced a true healing right in front of their eyes. For many of them, it was the highlight of their mission trip. Little did we know, the Lord would continue to bring miraculous healings to the camps that summer as we offered up prayers for the sick.

Another night, a sobbing woman came to us, holding in her arms her gravely ill baby girl. The baby was listless, barely moving. "Can you help me?" she pleaded. "My baby is dying. The doctors tell me there's nothing they can do for her. She won't eat, nor drink any milk, and has terrible diarrhea." George told her that we would come to her home. She needed to get her baby inside, away from the crowd of people.

George and I went to her home while the team stayed with the crowd. George took the frail body in his arms. I could see that he was moved with emotion, close to tears. We both cried out to the Lord at once, asking for His mercy on this poor little helpless baby girl. We shared the love of the Father with the child's mother and her family. We would now have to wait upon Him for healing to come. I have to admit, we both left her home knowing that if the Lord didn't intervene, the little girl might die. Every time we thought about her circumstances our eyes would fill with tears.

We didn't see that family again until two years later. One night as we were showing a movie in a camp, a woman approached us. "Do you remember me?" she said with great excitement.

"Actually, we meet so many people each night in the camps that it's hard to remember everybody," George said, apologetically.

The woman told us that we had met two years previously in a camp when she brought her baby girl to us, barely alive. She went on to tell us about the healing power of God. "After you left that night, my baby began to drink little bits of milk, and within days she began to drink more and more, until now." She pointed over to her precious little toddler who was running around with the other children. "There she is, God's miracle baby!" We were overjoyed to experience this miracle. Not only were we thrilled to see this cherished little girl, but also excited at the opportunity of meeting with this family again to witness God's healing power.

*

Our summers in Baja always seemed to go by rapidly. It was now time to return to the States to get ready for our turn around trip to mainland Mexico.

A lot of people can only see the fun and exciting part of living on the road, but there are negative sides too. I don't know how many times I've heard these words: "It must be nice traveling like you do." One previous RV owner once said, "The happiest day in a RV owner's life is the day he buys one, and the day he sells it." (I've heard that said about boats too.)

Pulling our fifth wheel to Mexico on some of the bumpiest roads had proved to be some of those negative times. Just about the time you take your eyes off the road because of some distraction, you will inevitably hit a pothole, which we always seemed to manage to do. Still adjusting to our new trailer, we learned to periodically make it a point to stop and look at the load, inside and out. Stopping at a grocery store to take a break one day, I opened the door to our house, only to be welcomed by a gallon of honey. It had fallen from the top shelf onto the kitchen floor. The floor was linoleum, that could be cleaned fairly easily, but unfortunately one quarter of the gallon had oozed over onto the carpet. What a mess! I wondered how one gets honey out of carpet. I began to scrape the top layer over onto the linoleum, heated up some water to boiling, pouring it into the carpet, and then scraped the liquid onto the floor. Pour, scrape, pour, scrape; that is what I did for the next half hour. All the while, I was trying not to complain, and not being very successful at it. What really upset me was the fact that I would now have very little honey for the next six months in Mexico.

I am often reminded during these crucial moments of the scripture in the book of James, Chapter one, verse two, "Consider it all joy when you encounter various trials, knowing that the testing of your faith produces patience." How could I consider things like this a joy? Then to top it off, once we arrived in Culiacan, a jug of apple juice on the side of our refrigerator door flew out when the door opened. It spilled into the carpet in the exact place the honey had fallen. I was at it again, pouring hot water over the carpet and sucking up the liquid from the juice. Nevertheless, I'll take carpet trials over mechanical trials any day! The pattern of nonstop trials continued coming, back to back, so we were gearing up for a good season for ministry. And that it was.

We already spent several years in the Culiacan area, and now were ready to spread our wings and explore other migrant camps. The Lord led us to Guasave, a city located approximately one hundred miles north of Culiacan. Ron and Eva knew of a Christian family there that showed interest in migrant work. He gave us the family's name. That was all we had to go on. Gary and Roberta were also feeling led to expand their horizons in ministry and agreed to travel there with us. Driving there on faith, we were leaning on the Lord to direct every step of the way.

When we arrived, it didn't take us long to locate the cabinet shop where several family members worked. It was a family-owned business. George and Gary went inside while we all waited in our vehicles parked right outside. After they shared the vision of laboring in the migrant camps, Miguel, one of the brothers, invited us over to the midweek Bible study held at their church. "I would really love to have you meet the pastor of our church. He's very missions-minded," he told them. "I'm sure he'll want to get involved in the work you are doing." He handed them directions to the church.

That evening we drew some attention when we pulled up in our rigs. It wasn't difficult for everyone to notice the new guests. They all were friendly to us right from the start. We were doubly blessed that we found the pastor's favor. After the service, he invited us over to his house that happened to be above the church. Needing a place to park our trailers, Miguel's brother and sister promptly offered us their vacant lot.

This property was the future site of a home that they planned to build. They liked the idea of us being there to keep guard. We liked it because it was close to the outskirts of town, somewhat isolated.

After spending time with the pastor, who loved the idea of working in the camps among the different indigenous groups from Mexico, he was more than enthusiastic about presenting the ministry to his church congregation. We were pleased to see how fast the Lord opened doors for us in Guasave. Now we hoped the camp managers would be just as receptive to our visits.

We grew very close to Miguel and his family from the very beginning of our stay in Guasave. Angela, the matriarch of the family, had married a German man in her younger days, taking on the German name, though the entire family grew up in Mexico. Most of them loved the Lord, taking on the traits of their mother, who had a very gentle and kind demeanor. She was quite the prayer warrior too, and always ready to lift anyone up in prayer at the drop of a hat. Needless to say, they made us feel right at home. Each of us looked forward to coming back each season to have a love feast with them.

Every day, Carlos (Miguel's brother) and his lovely wife Adiana, along with their sister Ana and her husband Jose, came by to visit us and make sure we were comfortable. They would often bring food with them. On weekends, they invited church members to come out to play volleyball. The big veranda with a woven straw roof next to the volleyball court was usually full of people and food. It didn't take us long to discover that the Wilhelm family were the socialites of the church. They had the gift of hospitality and functioned in this gift quite well.

Before long, Roberta and I noticed that we weren't getting much home schooling done because we were spending each day with our friends in fellowship. We finally had to explain to them that we really needed to do schooling, and our visits would have to be reserved for the weekends. Cristina treated us like her own and invited us over for family gatherings. Even Carlos's wife Adiana and her family treated us wonderfully.

Adiana's family lived in the mountains outside of Guasave. One day her mother invited us all to her house for a big Saturday meal. Because the drive was so long, we left early so we could have time to visit. The roads in the mountain area can be dangerous at night, they warned us, so we would also have to leave early enough to get back before nightfall. When we arrived, Adiana's mother honored us by butchering one of her pigs for a feast.

All of us were intrigued by their lifestyle up in the mountains. They taught our children how to get honey from the honeybee's honeycomb. The old-fashioned well, including a bucket tied to a rope just like we see in old movies, was very picturesque. Butchering the pig, well, that was not exactly something I wanted to be part of, but it was educational for those that wanted to be in on watching how it was done. Now, eating it was another thing. It was a joyous day; we enjoyed it to the fullest. Gary and Roberta's family and ours still talk about that day when we get together. Maybe because of what happened the following day.

For some unknown reason, every one of us, except for Laura and Jacob (Gary and Roberta's son), became terribly sick. We were so sick none of us even dared get out of bed. Whether this came about because our systems couldn't handle the well water, or we ate too much pork, or maybe both, we didn't know. When we all got better, the thought of eating pork was repulsive for a long time, although while living in Mexico, not eating pork can be hard on your social life because it is one their mainstays.

But this uncomfortable episode was soon over, and I give thanks to God for our time with them. It's a special gift from our Lord when He blesses us with friendships like the Wilhelm family.

*

The pastor from Guasave eventually relocated to Obregon, north of Culiacan, to pastor a church there. He had asked us if we would come and visit his church whenever we were in the area, so we took him up on his invitation.

While visiting, we were asked by another church in the area that had a burden to reach the Yaqui people from the Indian reservation to help them in their ministry. We thought the Yaqui children would love the puppets. Afterwards, they could join in with songs and a teaching. We felt honored that they asked us to be part of their team.

On a beautiful sunny afternoon, we drove up to the reservation, ten miles north of Obregon, to meet the team and set up for the program. The team was pleasant enough, and everything went quite well. The children were in awe of the puppets, and everyone seemed to love the singing and hearing a message afterwards. I especially enjoyed Manuel, one of the singers on the team, who had a strong, powerful voice, obviously well-practiced.

After our mini outreach, the pastor asked us if we would be interested in showing the "Jesus Movie" to his congregation at the midweek service. As George began to set up the equipment that day, the pastor came to me and asked if I sang. "Do you mean do I sing publicly, or just sing when I'm by myself?" I asked, somewhat puzzled.

"I mean do you sing publicly?" He answered.

"Well, actually, I don't usually sing publicly," I started to say, but as those words were coming out of my mouth, the Holy Spirit was nudging my heart to offer to sing in the service. Before my flesh could get in the way, I quickly blurted out, "Why? Do you want me to sing tonight?"

"Yes, I would appreciate it."

"All right, I will," I answered in confidence, yet as soon as he walked away, I felt sick to my stomach. "Lord, I can't believe I told him I would do this. I'm not that good, and besides, he has way better singers than me," I complained. Just then, I got this great idea. I would ask Manuel to sing with me. He had a beautiful voice. We could do it together.

Knowing he was somewhere around the church, I began to look for him and found him standing near the front door. I swiftly made my way over to him and asked him to be part of my song. As soon as he agreed to do it, that frantic feeling disappeared. We didn't have more than fifteen minutes before the service started so I had to plan fast. "What song do you have in mind?" Manuel asked, smiling.

"Do you know the song 'People Need the Lord?'" I asked, hoping that he knew it.

"No, but you sing it to me and I'll follow along," he responded. I quickly ran to get my sound track on cassette, and to jot down the words.

By the time I got inside and plugged in the cassette player, it was just about time to begin. We were standing off to the side where no one could hear us. Once the tape began to play, we only had time to go through it once, very quickly, before the service began. "Well, we'll just wing it," we agreed.

It seemed like before I could blink an eye that the two of us were on stage and ready to sing. George pushed the button on the cassette player, and we began. To my dismay, Manuel was singing in a different key than I was. He realized it at the same time, so we simultaneously changed our pitch to match the other's. Having done that, we were both still off key. We went back and forth throughout the whole song, trying and failing to sing in tune with each other. The final result: it was horrible! It was one of those incredibly humbling moments. We totally bombed it, but the audience was still gracious enough to clap their hands out of courtesy.

As we left the stage in humiliation, the movie began. I went back to my seat, embarrassment flooding my mind. I wanted to crawl in a hole. "Jennifer, just get over it. It's not that big of a deal," I kept telling myself, trying to ease the pain.

During my time of self-absorption, the movie ended. The pastor had asked George if he would share a few words. Two chairs had been placed on the side of the platform. "Come, sit up there with me," George prodded us. By the time we reached the chairs, I began to pray for George that his Spanish would be clear, and others would understand him.

The pastor thanked us for our willingness to come and show the movie to his congregation. Facing us, he asked

George if he would like to share a few words with the church. Suddenly, for no apparent reason, George said, "No."

Stunned by his answer, the pastor then turned to me and said, "Jennifer, do you have anything you would like to share with the congregation.?"

Just as flabbergasted as the pastor over George's response, now with all eyes on me, I couldn't think fast enough. The silence was becoming awkward, so I jumped up and said, "Yes."

As I was walking to center stage, I had no idea what I was going to say. My mind went totally blank. At this point in time, I could speak Spanish well enough to get by day to day, but to share a message in front of a good-size audience was another thing. "Oh, God," I called out once again. "It's time to intervene here!"

I grabbed the mike and looked out into the audience. I could almost envision myself fainting, but I didn't because the Lord's presence took over. He was sustaining me. Finally opening my mouth, I began to speak. "Just because I'm a missionary doesn't mean that I am full of faith," I heard myself say. I continued, "but without faith it is impossible to please Him."

Those were the last words I remember saying. From there on, as I continued to speak, I had no idea what I was saying. This went on for five to ten minutes before I returned to my seat next to George. The audience applauded. I turned to George and said, "What did I just share?"

He responded, "I have no idea."

I was beside myself. I wanted to cry. As the pastor got up and ended the service with a few last words, I was beyond embarrassment. Not only had I sung totally out of key, I shared a message that didn't make any sense. I said silently to the Lord, "I never want to come back to this church again. I'm so mortified at my performance tonight." But just then, as we were exiting the stage, an elderly woman came up to me. She had to have been in her late eighties or early nineties. Standing inches from me, she leaned in and said these words: "What you spoke tonight meant everything in the world to me. Thank you very much for sharing your heart." Her voice and tone was so sincere. If the evening went south, this moment made up for it. Even if I made sense to no one else, the Lord had opened her ears to hear a message she needed to hear.

It does make me laugh when I look back at that night, thinking of the impression that was left behind of the crazy foreigner who came and tried to sing and speak. Who knows, someone who was in the audience struggling with getting up publicly to do their ministry, might have thought, "If she can get up and sing and speak like that publicly, I can do it!

*

Other missionaries told us it couldn't be done, yet the Lord put it on our hearts to step out and invite many of the local churches from different denominations to come together for one month to labor in the migrant camps around Guasave. Instead of going from church to church, encouraging each pastor to allow their congregation to be part of the ministry, George asked permission from the pastor who was in charge of a monthly alliance gathering (a group of pastors who met together to discuss community issues) if he could present the work that the Lord was doing at the meeting. The pastor showed favor toward George and the ministry we were involved in, and gave him his consent.

After a half hour presentation, silence fell over the room. One pastor stood up, breaking the stillness. He began to address the group by telling them how ashamed he felt about their work for the Lord. He went on to say that Guasave was filled with Christians, and to his knowledge, no one was laboring in the camps that were practically in their own backyard. He was embarrassed that the Lord would have to place it on an American family's heart to travel all the way down to Mexico to do the work that they could be doing. Suddenly the whole assembly began to "Amen" to what this pastor had to say. The group was quickly moving into the direction that we had prayed it would go. By the end of the meeting, most of them wanted to be a part of it. When it was time to put their words into action, we ended up with five different churches willing to join us. We were pleased with the outcome, knowing that it was the hand of God, especially when we saw the variety of churches we were working with. From conservative Baptist to Pentecostals, they were willing to put their differences aside for the sake of the gospel.

Word got out that we were doing a month-long outreach among the indigenous peoples. A Yaqui church from Obregon, a town about one hundred seventy-five miles north of Guasave, came to participate. Then, when we didn't think it could get any better, a mission group from Culiacan sent their students to help. Most of that mission group was from Norway, which gave our team an international twist.

One of the churches opened their property, allowing anyone from out of town to stay inside, while we parked our fifth wheel next to the church. We had up to eighty people meeting at the church every afternoon.

We used both of our vehicles, and several volunteers from the different churches used their trucks and vans as well, totaling eight in all. The teams were broken up according to each one's talents and skills. Some were singers, others played instruments, and many were prayer warriors. There were evangelists, preachers, puppeteers, actors for a drama team, and crafters. We also had those that wanted to be involved with the cassette tape distribution. Each team would show "The Jesus Movie" or another Christian film.

My favorite part was the time before breaking up to go into the camps. We all gathered together for a time of devotion and sharing. We always ended by reminding the group that "They will know us by our love" (John 13:35), and to put our differences aside, followed by a prayer.

It was such a powerful time. We all could sense the touch of God upon us. The testimonies that came out each afternoon proved it. Some of the stories that were shared were phenomenal.

One night George's team went into a camp. (I wasn't able to go that evening because I had too much to do at home.) As the team set up the equipment and started the movie, several team members noticed a young woman standing off by herself. She appeared to be interested in watching the movie, yet kept going back and forth, not sure what to do. They decided to go over to her to see if they could help in any way. When they approached her, they realized she was crying. She began to share with them her story. "I have been so miserable for so long. Tonight I had decided to go down to the canal and end it all. I was going to take my life by drowning myself. On the way over to the canal, I saw your movie, so I decided to stop and see what it was about. Do you think this Jesus could help me?" One of the team members asked her what was so difficult about her life that she felt like she needed to end it. Her response was, "I have an older sister who is involved in witchcraft. She is a witch. She is very controlling and continually tries to control me with her ways. I feel so oppressed I can't take it anymore." She assured the team that she was not a part of witchcraft and didn't want to be a part of it.

After sharing the gospel message with her that Jesus loves her, gave His life upon a cross for her sin, and that she could be renewed by asking Him into her life, the young woman didn't hesitate. She was ready to surrender her life to a God who was so full of love and who could restore her. She asked them if they would continue to lift her up in prayer. She believed her sister had placed a curse of oppression over her that she needed to be freed from. They prayed for her right there and then, assuring her that they would commit to pray for her in the future.

The next day, George and I began our family morning devotion (having also opened our devotional for anyone involved in the outreach). A woman from the church where we were staying, who lived right behind us, showed up. She happened to be one of the team members involved with this young woman the night before in the camp. As we went into a time of sharing what the Lord was doing in our lives, Victoria said, "Last night the Lord woke me up at three o'clock in the morning. He told me to pray for this lady. I stayed up the rest of the night because the burden for her was so great. I think there's a really evil presence that wants to hurt her." We all agreed to pray for her, and encouraged Victoria to get some rest.

The following day several of us met for devotions again, including Victoria. Her story was the same as she had shared the previous day. She was awakened by the Lord at exactly three o'clock in the morning to pray for this girl again. She hadn't slept the rest of the night. Once more, we prayed for Victoria and the girl.

Every day that week, Victoria came to our devotional and shared the same story. By Friday morning, she looked tired and worn out, but this time she seemed excited. She had something to share with the group. This particular day, we had a newcomer in our circle. Eduardo was one of the staff members from the mission in Culiacan. He had not heard Victoria's testimony throughout the week like the rest of us had. When she came in with a great big smile and informed us that she had wonderful news about her prayer sessions with the Lord, we asked her to first share with the group again what the Lord had been taking her through. This way everyone would benefit from her great news. After explaining her whole story, she told us that the Lord awakened her last night at three o'clock in the morning to pray for this young lady again. This time, while she was praying for her, the Lord gave her a vision. She saw this woman curled up on the floor with chains attached to her wrists. A demonic looking figure was hovering over her. Suddenly, while she was calling out for this girl to be released, the chains broke off of her, and the ugly figure disappeared.

We were all staring at her in silence, processing what she had just told us. Not another moment passed when our new guest jumped into the conversation abruptly and said, "I can't believe you said what you just said." All eyes now turned on him. "You see, last night I also was awakened by the Lord at three o'clock in the morning. He told me that someone was in dire need of prayer and that I needed to pray for this person. I had no idea who I was praying for, but I was obedient to the Lord. I saw the exact same vision that you just described."

All of us cried out in amazement. Another minute passed before any of us could say anything else. We just stared at each other.

No one in the outreach ever had any more contact with this young lady as far as I know, yet we believe through the faithfulness of Victoria and Eduardo's prayers, this girl was set free. We hope to see her in heaven one day.

*

Victoria never ceased to amaze me with her stories. Living right next door to each other, we were able to spend a lot of time together, building a unique friendship. She shared with me that she had the gift of prophesy. I don't know about you, but when someone tells me that it usually puts me on guard, being not exactly sure where they're coming from. Some Christians believe if you have the gift of prophesy you are able to praise the Lord through His word of events that have already taken place. Others believe that a prophet is one who brings up events that will happen in the future, while still others don't think that present day prophets exist, believing that they were only around in Bible times. My belief tends to go with the teaching that a prophet is one who brings up events that will happen in the future, yet not everyone who says they are a prophet is a true prophet of God. When she shared with me that she was a prophetess, I wasn't ready to embrace her gift right away.

One day while my son Jonathon and I were standing outside our trailer, she walked up and joined us in conversation. After a time of visiting, she threw out these words: "Jonathon, God told me that when you grow up, you are going to marry a girl from Mexico, and she's going to be from Obregon."

I'm sure the look on our faces was that of surprise. When she walked away, Jonathon's expression turned scornful. He said, "That lady needs help. That will be the day I marry a girl from Obregon." Victoria didn't know it, but Jonathon had distaste for Obregon for several years. Earlier, when we had spent time working on a reservation outside of Obregon, he really had an aversion to being there. When we left, he told us that if we loved him, we would never take him back there again. Now our friend was telling him that he was going to marry a girl from that very same place. To Jonathon, this was absurd. I wasn't sure what to think. I must have not thought much of it because over time I forgot.

Years later, when Jonathon went off to college in the States, he met a beautiful young lady from Mexico. He had forgotten about the words of Victoria as well. Six years had already passed. Jonathon asked Cristina where in Mexico she was from. When she replied Obregon, those prophetic words suddenly came back to him. He had only dated her a couple times and wasn't thinking marriage at this point. Feeling a little weird, he called me up. "Mom, remember that lady from Guasave that lived behind the church?" he said.

"Victoria?" I responded.

"Yeah, her," he answered.

"What about her?"

"Do you remember when she told me that when I grow up I'm going to marry a girl from Obregon?"

I had to think a minute before it came back to me. "Yes, I do remember that. Well, what about it?"

"You are never going to believe this, but I met a girl from Mexico recently and she's from Obregon."

I was just as surprised as he was. He added, "I'm not ready to propose to her, but I sure like her a lot."

The rest of the story: they fell in love and got married.

When I shared the conversation I had with Jonathon to George, he looked at me and said, "What else did she share with us about the future, anything?" When I thought about it, I remembered that she shared that she had a dream about big white ants leading a group of other ants into Mexico to do a work. She believed those ants represented George and me taking a group of people into Mexico to do a ministry. (Later down the line we would find ourselves doing just that.)

*

With all the wonderful things the Lord was doing in our lives, the enemy began to rear its head again. George got a gout attack. For those of you who don't know what gout is, let me explain. The body doesn't produce enough of the digestive enzyme uricase. As a result, uric acid accumulates in the blood and tissues, and then eventually crystallizes. When it crystallizes, the uric acid takes on a form like a needle, which pokes its way into the joints. It is excruciatingly painful. Gout usually attacks the big toe first.

George had been diagnosed with gout years earlier when we lived in Flagstaff working at the mission. Our doctor had told us it can be controlled by diet, so we tried to eat fairly well to keep attacks at a minimum. When he did get an attack, his joints would inflame, making it hard for him to walk.

This time it appeared in his hand. It had swollen up so badly that he could hardly move it. When our friend Angela invited us over for dinner one evening, George was reluctant to go because of the pain. Not willing to let this intrusion keep us from fellowshipping with our dear friends, we finally decided to go anyway.

If ever we had met a prayer warrior, Angela was the greatest. She told me on one occasion how she arose in the wee hours of the night, got down on her knees, and lifted her loved ones up to the Lord in prayer.

She noticed George's swollen hand and questioned him about it. After explaining his problem to her, she insisted she pray for him. She gently took his hand, covered it soothingly with both of hers, and began to pray.

Getting ready to leave, we thanked her for such a lovely evening, and we were on our way. Driving home, George noticed that the swelling was starting to go down. He even felt much better. By the time we got home, the swelling was completely gone, along with the pain.

It was so encouraging to experience the healing power of God on his own hand. Watching the healing take place in the camps and then experiencing the healing for himself was quite a blessing. He kept wriggling his fingers and moving his wrist around, all the while saying, "Wow!" We couldn't wait to tell Angela about the healing that took place in George's hand that night.

We continued that season in the camps with the outreach in full swing. The Bible says, "To everything there is a season, a time for every purpose under heaven" (Ecclesiastes 3:1). This was a time of healing to take place. After the experience of George's hand returning to normal, we witnessed another healing shortly after that.

A beautiful young lady came up to us during a night in one of the camps. She was desperate. "Could you pray for me? I've been sick and I don't know what's wrong with me," she said sadly.

"How long have you been sick?" I asked, out of curiosity.

"For months I have felt very weak and have been without energy. I don't know how much longer I can go on like this."

The group gathered around her as we had been accustomed to throughout the outreach. Because our group represented a mix of international languages, I explained to her that we would each be praying in our own language at the same time. We didn't want to startle her. With Norwegian, Yaqui, Spanish, and English going all at once, I'm sure it sounded pretty strange to those standing around watching us.

While we were all praying for this girl, who was placed in the middle of the circle, she suddenly fell to the ground. The indigenous people who were observing what was going on became quite frightened by all of this, especially when they saw her lying on the ground. Even the Christians who had been praying turned to me with fear in their eyes. To be quite honest, I was somewhat fearful too, not knowing what just happened to her.

"What happened?" someone in the crowd asked.

"I don't know," I answered back, trying not to show my alarm.

We all knelt down around her, hoping she would open her eyes and get up, but she just lay there, listless. Some of the crowd of indigenous people started running away from us. Fear came over me that they were going to start spreading word around the camp that we hurt her. I began to fervently pray that the Lord would awaken her; not only for her sake, but for the sake of our testimony in the camp.

She didn't come around as soon as we would have liked, yet we knew from her pulse that she was still alive. Soon after we prayed again she finally opened her eyes. She slowly got to her feet with our help. Looking around a bit befuddled, she assured us that she was all right. She walked away slowly, her loved ones on each side of her. We weren't sure what happened that night.

Three days later, several of us from the team walked to a nearby store in the same area where this young woman passed out that night. She happened to be walking on the opposite side of the street from us. "*Oye! Oye!*" she yelled (which means "Hey, you!" in Spanish). We turned to look as her calls caught our attention. I didn't recognize her at first until she explained who she was. She was very excited to tell us about the healing that took place several days earlier, right after we had prayed for her. She hadn't felt so healthy since she could remember. When we reminded her that we weren't the ones that healed her, it was the Lord Jesus Christ, she was able to acknowledge it was from Him. As she and her companion went one way and we went the other, we were all happy to hear of the great improvement in her health, since we had been left in the dark about what really happened to her three nights earlier. My hope and prayer is that she not only received a physical healing, but that she received a spiritual healing as well. How could a person not want to know a personal God after experiencing a personal touch from Him?

We continued to experience the power of God in the camps. The ones I've mentioned are only the ones that made an impact on me personally.

Not only were the indigenous farm workers impacted, the ministry team received revelation as well. For George and me, ours was seeing how well the Mexican church labored together in the Spirit of love. In spite of their doctrinal differences, they were all able to stick to the clear gospel message of salvation through the blood of Jesus Christ. This was evident to the non-believers, as we witnessed how they were drawn to this love.

For Miguel, Angela's son, the camp ministry impacted him so incredibly that throughout the outreach he believed God was calling him to give up his carpentry position to become a pastor. After the outreach, he and his family moved to Hermosillo, a city another three hundred and fifty miles north of Guasave, to attend a Bible college. When last we heard, he had graduated from school and is now pasturing a church somewhere in Mexico.

We don't know where most of our team members are today, yet we trust God is using them in different parts of the world to bring people into a knowledge that we truly do serve a personal God.

*

Returning to the U.S. again, we were stepping out of our usual routine of going to Baja to spend the summer in Guadalajara, Mexico. We were trying to expand our vision to allow other churches in Mexico to take part in an outreach that would give them opportunity for missions. By presenting the work, it was our hope that they would catch the vision too. After seeing how the Yaqui church from Obregon came to participate, why wouldn't others from the south take interest? Why Guadalajara? It was a big city, and it intrigued us.

On the way to Guadalajara, we stopped by to visit Jorge and Angelica's family. We invited their son Tomas to come spend the summer with us. He was a great help in the camps and had the gift of music. He would be a good addition to our family. As we went around presenting our vision to the churches, he could give the audience a taste of the music played in the camps.

Our trip down went quite smoothly. We pulled our fifth wheel down and found a nice R.V. park full of palm trees. It was expensive by the standards of Mexico, yet compared to the U.S. prices we considered it fairly cheap.

Within a couple of weeks, we discovered a church while driving past it. Wanting to experience a Sunday morning service, we made a point of being there the following week. Immediately, we connected with the pastor and a few friendly families. The pastor was interested in our ministry, yet cautious. He asked if we could meet together one afternoon to discuss more about the ministry. He then asked us to present the work to his congregation. We were thrilled at how quickly the Lord opened the doors for us.

Sunday morning came. George was feeling somewhat nervous, realizing that his presentation was going to be done in Spanish. He had shared in Spanish before, just not with this big of a crowd. When the pastor picked up on his uneasiness, he offered to supply him with a translator. George sprang to accept the offer, which set him at ease.

The church congregation was different from what we were accustomed to. We happened to be in a wealthier section of town, so our audience was on the well-to-do side. Going from the poorest of the poor now to the wealthy was quite a contrast, yet we knew none of it mattered in the eyes of the Lord. It reminds me of the scripture in James, chapter two, verses one through four, "For if there should come into your assembly a man with gold rings, in fine apparel, and there should also come in a poor man in filthy clothes, and you pay attention to the one wearing the fine clothes and say to him, 'You sit here in a good place,' and say to the poor man, 'You stand there,' Or, 'Sit here at my footstool,' have you not shown partiality among yourselves, and become judges with evil thoughts?" We never should feel any different between the rich and the poor.

What struck me funny that Sunday morning was what happened when George first began his message. After a good introduction, at one point in his talk George switched to Spanish and the translator to English. No one noticed it for a while, but then unexpectedly we all started laughing. George and the translator didn't catch on as to why the congregation was laughing until someone in the audience blurted out, "You're talking in Spanish!"

"I am, aren't I?" he said, half smiling. "Well, I'll just continue in Spanish. It will save us all a lot of time."

I was so proud of him. I had never heard him speak so fluently in Spanish as he did that day, nor since. We later found out that half the congregation knew how to speak English anyhow.

We continued to draw close to the church, spending most of our time with them. One man in the church volunteered to help George with Spanish lessons. He insisted he do it for free, so we received his generous gift as coming from the Lord.

As the summer was coming to an end, it was time to pack up and head home. Several members had showed interest in coming to Culiacan the next season, but unfortunately with cost factors and the great distance they would have to travel, it didn't pan out for any of them. We were a bit disappointed, and at the same time we wouldn't have traded our experience there, even if we knew no one would come to participate.

Our trip back home didn't go as smoothly as the trip down. Right before departing, we were hit by a horrific storm, sending down golf ball sized hail that left big dents all over our fairly new fifth wheel. A second storm came whirling through, ripping our awning and bending the poles that held it. At times like this, it's good to give thanks for what is good and not concentrate on the negative. It could have been worse for us. One trailer, right next door, had a huge tree fall on it, doing considerable damage.

Fifty miles outside of Guadalajara, all the lug nuts from one of our wheels came unscrewed and broke off. We don't know if someone deliberately loosened them while we were parked at the R.V. trailer park, or they just mysteriously came undone. Nevertheless, this dilemma stranded us out on the side of the highway.

George knew the only way to solve our problem was to hitchhike to the nearest town and try to locate an auto repair shop that would have these same lug nuts we needed. Leaving Tomas with us for protection while he went alone was the best option for all of us. We weren't sure how long we'd be out on the side of the highway, but this was one of those times to not lean on our own understanding, and trust God.

We were so relieved to see George return within the hour. He had all the lug nuts and studs; there was only one slight problem. The collars on the studs weren't the right size, so he would have to file them down to fit the axles. There were twelve of them. I always thank God for George's mechanical abilities. He seems to be able to make things work that normally wouldn't. Do you ever find yourself in a trial that becomes a Catch 22? In order to grind the studs with the tool he had, we needed electricity. We had a generator on board, but in order to use the generator, we needed gas. No gas, except in our vehicle. In order to get the gas, someone had to siphon it out of our gas tank.

Meanwhile, the heat of the day was hitting hard. Why I didn't fill our five gallon water cooler before we left is beyond me. With about a half gallon of water to share among the five of us, plus our dog, we were not happy campers at the moment. Looking on the bright side, thankfully our dog was a small Chihuahua. We had this running banter between all of us when things were looking up. "Oh, the life of a missionary!" we would say to each other in a contented tone. Today, Tomas was saying those words in a rather sarcastic tone as we were trying to make the best of our situation. We ended up out on the road for about four hours. As George was tightening up the last of the lug nuts, we were overjoyed to be getting back on the road again.

Nearing Culiacan, it was now quite late, and we were beyond tired. Laura and I were in the back seat getting ready to doze off when I heard Jonathon say to George, "Dad, what's that stream of fire trailing behind us?" George quickly pulled over. We had blown two tires without realizing it and been driving with no tread; just the rims were left. Once again, George was out on the side of the road, trying to make it work.

While he was changing the tires, a truck full of men with machine guns pulled up and got out of their vehicle, surrounding George. They were the Mexican *Federales*, part of the police force. It was rather intimidating, to say the least; yet when they saw our situation, they left us alone.

Feeling tired and beat up, we were more than ready to get home to Bisbee. If only I could tap those little red shoes in "The Wizard of Oz" and say, "There's no place like home!" The reality was that we weren't going anywhere until we found two tires. Unfortunately, our spare didn't fit either. We would have to park in Culiacan and hunt down the right size tires for our fifth wheel. At our wit's end, we parked for the night in the nearest gas station outside of town to get some rest. We would have to deal with this latest obstacle tomorrow.

As we were preparing to sleep for the night, Tomas seemed very nervous. "Tomas, why are you so jittery?" Jonathon asked.

"Look at the color of the sky!" he answered. "The last time I saw the sky that color, we were hit by a hurricane."

We were all so tired and burned out that we shrugged it off and went to bed. Thank God, when we awoke the next morning, nothing drastic had happened. Our trailer was shaken quite a bit throughout the night, but the storm Tomas predicted obviously took another path.

After taking Tomas back to his family, we returned to Culiacan where we parked at an R.V. trailer park to deal with our trials. George called every tire store in town. Not one place had our tires. Meanwhile we continued to pray for God's intervention. After an extensive search in the market, we were left with two options. Option number one was for George to fly to Los Angeles where the tires could be readily found in most tire shops, or to buy used tires here that were smaller and less durable than the ones we really needed, hoping we could make the five hundred miles home.

After much prayer, we decided to go with option number two. We bought the used tires and drove less than fifty miles an hour all the way home. Praise God! He got us back safely. Those turned out to be two strong tires! We ended up using them on a different vehicle for years after we purchased them.

We thought we were going to Guadalajara to drum up laborers for the camp work in Guasave, but looking back, we were really there for the people in the trailer park. The Lord opened many doors for us to help some desperate people who needed to know that there really is a personal God who desires to have a personal relationship with each of us. He gave us the boldness to share His love to several stubborn, hard core individuals. Someday, I expect to see them in heaven too!

With God, all things are possible (Matthew 19:26).

And let us not grow weary
while doing good,
for in due season we shall reap
if we do not lose heart.

Galatians 6:9

15
Ready to Throw in the Towel

Many times during our eleven years of ministry in Mexico, I questioned the Lord why certain trials had to come about. Why couldn't He just make it easy on us, allowing life to move along in a much more peaceful and simple fashion. Yet, that still small voice inside told me, "You're in training." For the most part, those words usually comforted me, but when we were held up at gunpoint, that was the last straw. I had had it with Mexico.

It was our tenth season of working in Mexico, mostly with the migrant farm ministry. As the season was coming to a close in Guasave, it was time to pack up and get ready to leave Mexico. Driving down to Culiacan, where friends allowed us each year to store our equipment until the next season, was becoming a tradition. After dropping our things off, we went to the bank to withdraw money to get back home, approximately three hundred and fifty dollars. Leaving Culiacan that evening around eight o'clock, Jonathon needed a pit stop. We didn't think anything about stopping on the side of the highway. That was a regular routine with us, since, as you've seen, our vehicles broke down regularly. As we pulled over, Jonathon jumped out of the truck and walked several yards away. The three of us were chit-chatting while we waited, and like any normal evening, had left the truck idling. Unbeknownst to us, two men had leapt out of the bushes and put a gun to Jonathon's head. They wanted all of his money. Since he didn't have any money on him, they turned their attention to us. With the gun still at his head, they forced him to walk toward our truck. As they approached our window, Jonathon, in English, began to explain what was going on. At first it was hard to believe that this was for real, but we quickly realized it was no joke. George pulled out his wallet and handed fifteen dollars to the man with the gun. The gunman grabbed the money, momentarily moving the gun away from Jonathon's head. Having waited for his chance, Jon quickly opened the back door of our truck and jumped into the back seat. Meanwhile, realizing that George had only handed over fifteen dollars, the gunman abruptly snarled, "What's this?"

George told the man that fifteen dollars would buy them what they needed for the night. The thieves weren't going for the deal. With angry tones and expressions, they demanded that we all get out of the vehicle immediately. At that second, the Holy Spirit spoke to my heart and warned me not to get out of our truck. At the same time He was telling George the exact same thing. We glanced at each other and in unison looked at the two men standing outside our window. "No, we're not going to get out," George said firmly. The lead man who previously had the gun pointed at Jonathon's head looked at his partner in bewilderment. I think we caught them totally off guard. They now had to make a decision: either shoot us or let us go.

George chose not to wait around to find out what they were going to do. As they were staring at each other and shrugging their shoulders, George immediately popped out the clutch and took off. He was moving so fast that our truck was almost sideways as we speedily regained the highway. Pebbles were flying everywhere as I screamed at Jonathon and Laura to stay down on the floor of the truck. At any second, I was expecting bullets to come our way. It all happened so quickly we didn't have time to think, only to act upon what the Holy Spirit had spoken to both of us.

When we realized we were out of harm's way, Jonathon popped his head up from the back seat and said with an excited tone, "Wow! What an experience! I can hardly wait to get home to tell my friends what we just went through!" Laura, on the other hand, handled the situation quite differently. She broke out into hysterical crying as she began to shake all over. Although I was pretty shaken myself, and tempted to respond the same as Laura did, my motherly instincts kicked in to bring comfort to her. "Now, now, Laura," I said as calmly as I could, "It's all right. We're all safe. God has protected us. We're going to be all right." I held her in my arms as I continued to comfort her. George and I stayed very calm and collected the rest of the way back to Guasave where our trailer was parked.

When we arrived, the pastor and his family were still up. We went inside to share with them what had happened to us earlier. The pastor shared that he had been robbed at gunpoint three different times in his life, sharing his experiences with us.

It wasn't until we went to bed that sobs overwhelmed me, but in a little while I was able to come to the same conclusion that I had shared with Laura in her time of fear. "We're all safe. You protected us, Lord." I couldn't quit thanking God. At last I fell asleep soundly, as did George.

It really wasn't until we were on U.S. soil that I started to get angry. Every time I thought about the incident, indignation arose. "How obnoxious that someone would dare put a gun to my son's head," I said, replaying over and over in my mind what had happened. "And to think what we sacrifice to go to Mexico to share the gospel." The more I kept reliving the scenario, the more embittered I became. Full of pent-up anger, I finally went to George to tell him exactly how I felt. "I have had enough of Mexico. I'm never going back. If you want to go back then you'll have to do it alone." Expecting a fight, and, truthfully, ready for a good one, he shocked me by his response.

"Honey, if you can't go back to Mexico, I understand. I'll go look for a full-time job here in the U.S.," he said as calmly and gently as he could.

That was the best thing George could have done at that time. Knowing me as he did, if he had jumped into the fight I was expecting, he knew I would have diverted all of my anger and frustration onto him. It's the ones we love most that we lash out at when we're hurting.

Over the next several weeks, feelings of guilt started to take over as I pondered the decision I had made to never return to Mexico again. There was no peace in my heart about it either. When I was finally ready to bring it up before the Lord in prayer, tears overflowed. God is so full of love and compassion, and at the same time, all knowing, ready to give us understanding when we're prepared to listen. "The safest place in the world to be is in My will," the Lord gently spoke to me.

The realization that, no matter what country or what city we're in, anything can happen, is what I needed to see. Being exactly where God wants us to be is where real peace exists. "I could be in a fast food restaurant eating and minding my own business, and someone could come in and open fire," I thought to myself. I knew right then that the Lord wasn't calling us out of the Mexican ministry. Being guided by my own fears and worries was what had directed me to respond in the way I did.

I went to George that day and described to him my conversation with the Lord. He confessed that all along he knew that God wasn't yet through with us in Mexico. He had been praying fervently that the Lord would reveal this to me and was quite relieved to hear my testimony.

This was a good time to take the summer off from missions. Even though George was working building cabinets, here in the U.S. he was able to spend quality time with our children. Jonathon loved playing soccer so we encouraged him to join a local team. Laura's interest was in gymnastics, so we signed her up for classes. It was a busy summer with all the driving back and forth to soccer games and gymnastics, yet I wasn't complaining. I saw the benefits and joy that the kids experienced, and it was all worth it. They were both very gifted in their abilities in sports. We supported them in every way we could.

Although we were off the mission field for a few months, but it didn't mean the Lord placed us on the shelf for that time. He still used us in people's lives to encourage them and bring them to a saving knowledge of Him.

One such event that particularly sticks out is the time Jonathon's team was competing in a tournament in Tucson, Arizona, for the weekend. He was so excited about going. Instead of driving back and forth from Bisbee to Tucson, we decided to make it a weekend getaway. We planned to book a hotel room and then attend his games.

Awaking early Saturday morning, the first thing on the agenda was to go to his first game. It was fun to see Jonathon playing on an American team and enjoying himself so much. They were now all ready to play their second game after doing a terrific job in the first game. The second game was across town, so we drove quickly over to the field since there wasn't a lot of time between the games.

When we arrived, in all of the excitement, Jonathon realized he had forgotten his sports bag with his soccer shoes in it. Knowing he wouldn't be able to play his best with regular tennis shoes, we had to think fast. We didn't have time to go all the way across town and back to get his bag without him being late, so we decided to take him to a nearby sports store. Hopefully, they would have a pair his size.

Remembering having seen a sports store close by, we headed there quickly. We didn't have time to waste. We were able to find a used pair of shoes in his size, which was awesome, considering our circumstances. We bought them and quickly returned to the field, just in time for the game to start. Unfortunately, we weren't going to be able to stay for the game because we still needed to go back across town and get the bag Jon had left behind. We weren't willing to just leave it there to pick up later, since the bag also contained some of his clothes, his jacket and other things of value. We would probably only be able to make it back to pick him up from the game since it would be a full hour's drive to the first field and back.

By the time we reached the park where Jon had his first game, it was filled with other players. We looked all around, but his pack was nowhere to be found. No one in the vicinity had seen it. It seemed we would just have to take the loss. Wishful thinking made us hope possibly one of his team members picked it up and just forgot to tell us that he had it. Oh, well, you win some and you lose some.

On our way back across town to the second field, we passed a Chinese restaurant. We could smell the scents lingering in the air, enticing us to pull into their parking lot. We justified our stop, agreeing that we would all eat quickly so we could possibly get to Jon's game before it ended. We finished eating and were back in the car within twenty minutes.

As George tried to start the car, nothing happened. The battery was totally dead. He jumped out of the car and lifted the hood to see what the problem was. The battery posts seemed to be fine. He didn't know what the problem was. He continued to check other areas that possibly could be the culprit, with no luck.

After ten minutes under the hood and still no answers to why our car wouldn't start, I started to panic. My fear wasn't over the car not running; it was over the fact that we had no way of contacting Jonathon and telling him why we weren't there. He would be stranded at the park. He didn't even know the location of the hotel where we were staying. "George, we need to get to the park within twenty more minutes. The game will be ending and Jonathon will be worried about where we are," I said anxiously.

"The only thing I can think of doing at this point is calling a taxi," George said, distracted by the problem. He decided, "You and Laura take a cab over to the park while I continue to look for the problem with this car. If I can't figure it out within the next hour, I'll have our car towed to the hotel and work on it there." His idea seemed the most logical thing to do.

Within five minutes the taxi pulled up. As Laura and I started walking toward the cab, feelings of anxiety began to grip me. The driver's profile fit that of someone you might see in a murder movie. He was very rough looking. When we got to the door of the car, I didn't know what to do. Out of fear, I said, "Just a minute, I need to talk to my husband." Laura and I immediately turned around and went back over to George. "George, do you see what this guy looks like?" I said, concerned. "I'm scared to get into the cab, but I don't know what to say to him. And how are we going to get to the park if I don't take this ride?"

George, a little put out, looked at me. Trying to be patient and loving with me, he turned back to the car, saying, "Maybe you could trust the Lord to protect you."

I snapped back, "Yeah, well the Lord gave us a brain to use too, you know!"

"I don't know what to tell you, Jennifer. You can't go around stereotyping people either," was his final response.

I had to make a quick decision. The taxi was waiting, and Jonathon would be waiting for us soon too. I felt safer if Laura went with me instead of staying with George. At least if anything happened to me, she could give the police a good description of the man. We both went back to the cab and got in. I told him the park we wanted to go to.

For the first five minutes, there was silence. In my nervousness, I figured it was better to strike up a conversation and show ourselves friendly. If he was a wicked man, at least I might be able to create a nice atmosphere to change his mood. "So, where are you from?" seemed to be an appropriate place to start out.

"New York City," he answered.

"Do you like Tucson?" I asked.

"Not really."

"What brought you to Tucson?" now starting to sound a bit nosy.

"Well, I'm going through a divorce and I'm fighting a custody battle. My wife lives here, so I had to come and get a job while I go through all this."

It was then I sensed a great sadness in his voice. Before I knew it, the driver began to open up to me and share his heartache and his loss of hope for the future. Feeling bad for him, I found myself sharing that there is a hope and a future even though it looked like the floor was dropping out from under him. "Do you know that God loves you so much that He's trying to talk to you and get your attention?" I said. "He broke my car down in the parking lot of that Chinese restaurant where you picked us up so I could share with you these words." I added, "He wants you to surrender your life to Him so He can begin to restore you."

"I went to a church a few times and heard a salvation message, but I'm not sure I'm ready to give my life to the Lord quite yet. I was thinking of yielding to God someday down the line, maybe before I die."

I had heard this in the past from other people with the same mindset as his. Feeling it was appropriate to share with him what had happened to one of the employees at the rescue mission years earlier, I began to tell him the story. "Kathy was the cook at the rescue mission I once worked at. One day a woman came in to get a nice warm meal and a place to sleep for the night. Kathy and this woman struck up a friendship during her stay, and she was able to share the love of Jesus with her. The woman responded the same way you did. She wanted to live a life of what she thought was pleasure. The woman left the mission with that same mindset: someday when I'm ready to die. Two days later, Kathy opened the newspaper and read about a woman who was hit and killed by the local train down the street. It was this very woman who she had just talked with days earlier. She could only hope this woman changed her mind before the accident happened." I ended the story with these words: "Now is the day of salvation (2 Corinthians 6:2b). None of us is promised a tomorrow. We need to look at this day and live it to the fullest."

We were now pulling up to the park. I paid the taxi driver and we got out. "Thank you for sharing what you shared with me. I needed to hear that," he told me. As Laura and I were walking over to the field, I was overjoyed, knowing without a doubt that the Lord had set that whole scenario up.

Jonathon's game had ended just minutes before we arrived. I explained to him everything that had happened. He was so glad we had appeared when we did, because his coach had asked him if he needed a ride, and he didn't even know where to tell him to drop him off.

Gathering my thoughts together, I realized that we still needed to get to the hotel. I should have asked the taxi driver to wait, but I hadn't even thought of it. It was necessary to call the taxi company again, so we borrowed a cell phone and made the call. Within minutes a taxi showed up. It was the same guy! We all laughed when we got into his cab again. Humbly, I explained my absent-mindedness. Personally, I don't think he was finished asking me questions about the Lord. We discussed a few more important issues that concerned him before we arrived at the hotel.

This just shows you how perfect God's timing is. When we pulled up, there was the tow truck, hauling our car into the lot of the hotel. Feeling a little discouraged that George hadn't been able to get it running, I still needed to trust the Lord. This meant we would be spending time fixing the car, or I should say, George would be fixing the car.

We watched as the tow truck unhooked our car, thankful that we had free towing attached to our insurance. As the tow truck pulled away, George got into the driver's seat again. He stuck the key into the ignition and turned it over. Immediately, the car started up with no problem. We both looked at each other in amazement. He turned it off and then turned it on again. We were puzzled, yet at the same time thanking God.

Tired from the day, we decided to relax in our room for the night. We would deal with the car issue in the morning. Meanwhile, as we were walking to the room, talking a mile a minute, I told George everything that had taken place with the cab driver. "You don't suppose the Lord allowed our car to break just so that taxi driver could hear about Jesus, do you?" I asked.

"That's just what I believe happened," George said. "Don't you think it's ironic that our car starts right up after the tow truck left? Jennifer, I checked everything under the hood I knew to do and nothing seemed to show up. Now the car just starts. It will be interesting to see if it starts up tomorrow morning."

The next day, we all got into the car. Sure enough, it started right up. I have to admit, I was somewhat skeptical, thinking that it would die any minute. Thank God, it ran fine. We drove around Tucson the rest of the weekend, and then drove to a gas station in Tombstone, Arizona (about twenty miles outside of Bisbee) before we had any problems. We had bought cheap gas and the car let us know. It sputtered a few times, but other than that, we had no other difficulties.

God is right on time. I expect to see that taxi driver in heaven someday too!

*

Getting ready for our next season in Mexico was always strenuous, especially with repacking and trying to stock up with supplies. This next trip didn't prove to be any different. As a matter of fact, it seemed worse than usual. Even the spiritual attacks that came our way during preparation time appeared to be stronger than normal. We predicted through our difficulties that this was going to be one good season of ministry. The enemy was working overtime to discourage us.

I was clued in when we had a falling out with some very close friends. Not only did we lose our friendship, we walked away from a large part of our financial support. It was stressful to the point that I was wavering in my faith to return to Mexico. Finding faith to believe we could still go to Mexico, and also live on very little, was an old door that I didn't want to have to walk through again. Living with a steady amount coming in monthly had been comfortable.

My spirit was also crushed by the loss of our friendship; my heart was heavy. We couldn't change what happened. Remembering the words in the Bible, "If it is possible, as much as depends on you, live peaceably with all men" (Romans 12:18), we still didn't know how to make it right. Each day, in faith, I had to turn my broken heart over to the Lord just to get through. Between finances and the broken friendship, my heart grew heavier and heavier every day.

One morning, getting into my car to pick up the mail, I started crying. I turned on the radio to take my mind off my problems. It was tuned to the Christian station, on which a well-known speaker was giving an awesome message. I couldn't believe what was coming across the waves. It was as if God were talking to me personally. The message was on broken relationships and what that looked like in the spiritual realm. As I continued to listen, great peace filled my car as the Lord assured me of His love, reminding me not to trust in man, but God and God alone for our provision. He took my burden at that very moment and released me.

Pulling up to the post office, I got out of my car, skipping and praising the Lord all the way in the building, soaking in the spiritual awakening that had taken place. Collecting the mail out of my box, suddenly another disturbing thought came to mind. "Lord, I know I can trust You in this relationship issue, but it still doesn't resolve our financial problems," I prayed. "Please give me peace about going to Mexico again with a lot less money."

Getting back into the car, I began to rifle through each envelope before starting the engine. I noticed a letter in the pile that came from an old friend that I had lost contact with for a couple years. Excited to receive her letter, I quickly opened it. A check fell out of it onto my lap. As I picked it up, I could see that it would make up the finances we needed. I was astounded! If it had come from one of my more well-to-do friends, it wouldn't have been as amazing. What was so stunning about it was this friend had struggled financially. As long as I had known her, she was barely able to raise five children, and part of that time as a single parent.

I looked up. "Lord, how can this be?" I asked. His answer was so comforting as He spoke to my heart.

"Jennifer, I am your provider, not man. I can give you money through whomever I wish, even your poorest friend." It almost took my breath away. I don't mean that figuratively either. God's presence and love so enveloped me at that moment that I found myself taking deep, slow breaths.

Pulling away from the post office, I turned the corner to a park down the block. I stopped the vehicle and got out. Looking up to the sky, my attention turned to the Lord again. "Thank You, God! You are so awesome!" I remember walking around that park at least three or four times, all the while repeating, "You are so awesome, God!"

It was finally time to get into my car and go home before George might start to worry. What had started out that morning with despair, turned out to be a very Spirit-filled day. The Lord showed Himself faithful and real to me again.

Packing up and preparing for Mexico was now looking good. I was actually looking forward to going, knowing the Lord had something really special awaiting us. The Lord replaced my feelings of failure, weakness, and lack of faith with expectations, confidence, and strength.

Little did we know, it was going to be our last year to minister to the migrant farm workers. I thank Him that it was a grand and memorable last year for us, and it began the first week we returned to Culiacan.

We had decided that this particular season we would leave our fifth wheel in Bisbee and rent an apartment or house (still not aware that this would be our last trip). One of our friends, the director of a mission group in Culiacan, was interested in buying the school bus that we had brought down in previous years to use in the camps for our recording and puppet ministry. He was interested in turning the school bus into a mobile dental clinic for the camp workers, and also for the Mexican community in general. He had several rented apartments available, so we had made an agreement to trade our bus in exchange for one of the apartments for a season.

The plan was to meet him and a group of Norwegian students from his school at the border of Arizona and Mexico, in Nogales. Several of his students had to come up to renew their visas, so the director would travel with them. He and his wife were heading for Norway, planning to fly out of the United States once at the border. He had designated one of the Norwegian men to drive the bus to Culiacan. This way we could drive our own vehicle down.

We fell in love with Ray and Riley right from the start. Ray is a robust man, a typical Norwegian: tall and blonde. He has a gentle disposition, a strong accent, and is fun to be around. Riley, on the other hand, is very outgoing and outspoken, able to communicate well. I love her honesty and the way she expresses herself. Needless to say, their family is definitely a gift from God. Ray was the designated driver for the school bus. Our introductions took place in a hotel room, all of us exchanging names and shaking hands with one another. Soon we would all be caravanning five hundred miles together down the Mexican highway.

This wasn't a leisurely, relaxing trip. Most of us were in a hurry to get to Culiacan, especially the students, because they needed to get back to their classes. The bus needed to be driven much more slowly on the highway because the engine was getting old. It had to be driven no more than fifty miles an hour. We agreed to caravan at a slow pace with Ray so he wouldn't be left alone on the trip back.

Starting the caravan, we were all delayed at the border because one of the students had credit card problems. Ray decided to drive on since it was going to take him longer to travel. We weren't worried since we knew we'd see him somewhere on the highway. Driving only fifty miles an hour, he wasn't going to get that far ahead of us.

A couple hours later, we were free to leave and get on with our trip. Yet after traveling a couple hours and not catching up with Ray, we began to wonder what happened to him. Finally when we did catch up with him, he was pulled over on the side of the highway, stranded, unfortunately with a blown motor. To top it off, the temperature was at least one hundred degrees in the Sonoran desert.

We were able to call a tow truck, which came within the next hour and pulled us back to the nearest town,

Hermosillo. We quickly remembered that our friend Miguel from Guasave was attending a Bible college in this town. We called the school to make sure he hadn't graduated yet, and to our surprise and pleasure, not only was he still a student, but the director of the school gave us permission to park the school bus on their property while it was being repaired. They also invited the team to stay in one of their empty dorms, allowing us to save money on hotel accommodations. Their hospitality towards us was generous and kind.

Looking at the budget, we quickly realized none of us had the money to pay for the replacement of the motor. George was willing to do the labor on the mechanical end, but we didn't think it was our responsibility to pay for the damages, especially since we had given them explicit instructions not to drive the bus over fifty miles an hour. The director did finally agree to pay for the motor and parts, yet if my memory serves me right, he wasn't too happy about the whole situation. Ultimately, Ray and Riley jumped up to the plate and offered to foot the bill for the motor to take the stress off the mission's budget. It was one of those difficult situations, and like all trials, they do eventually pass, only to be followed by a new set of circumstances down the line.

With tribulation, there's usually something good that comes out of it too. In this case, we drew very close to Ray, as we all spent three days together replacing the motor. This was especially beneficial, since this next season in Mexico was going to be spent periodically with Ray and Riley, showing them the open fields of harvest in the surrounding area of Culiacan. Once more, what the enemy meant for evil, God meant for good (Genesis 50:20).

When we arrived, the apartment proved to be much more spacious and comfortable than our trailer. Unpacking and trying to decorate before starting ministry was the plan for the first week. We were already making plans to go south with the Norwegian mission group. Hearing that a group of businessmen, all Korean, from the Los Angeles area were coming down to join us in the camps as well, we were thanking God for such a wonderful provision of laborers.

Days before the group arrived, it was on my heart to pray and fast for a day, laying out the most common needs I could foresee. In addition, over time I had become increasingly concerned about a bump that was lodged inside my leg. It had started out really tiny, but over the years it had grown to a point where it was getting quite bothersome. In the past I had addressed the Lord about this bump, asking Him to just miraculously heal me, thinking it would save us all the hassle of getting it removed, but that didn't happen. When we were in the States, I had called a doctor's office hoping to get in for an appointment. I was discouraged when I found out that it would take over a month to even get in for a biopsy of it, and perhaps another month before the lump could be removed. The cost factor was even more of a discouragement, so I put off doing anything more until we had the money and time. During this day of fasting and praying, I decided to bring it up again. "Lord, I'm at a standstill on what to do about this bump in my leg. I never have the time or the money to get this taken care of in the States. Please heal me miraculously, or bring a surgeon into my life that can deal with this." I left it at that, in the Lord's hands.

Within the next couple of days, after the Korean group arrived, we traveled to the mission site we planned to evangelize. Ceuta, a small town fifty miles south of Culiacan, is surrounded by numerous migrant camps. It was off the beaten path, and a great spot to reach people for the Gospel of Jesus Christ.

While surveying the area before we all headed down, George had met a local businessman that owned a hotel right in the middle of town. They hit it off from the onset, which turned out to be a grand blessing for the group. He offered free accommodations for all of us during the week we did the outreach.

The Koreans were fabulous to work alongside. Anything that needed to get done, they were right there. Several of them wanted to get involved with the children's ministry, and I was thrilled to train them in the different activities. Lin, a vibrant, intelligent, meticulous man, sticks out in my memory as one of those eager to jump into the work. He absolutely loved the people in the camps and the ministry we were doing. He was a great asset to the team.

One afternoon before going out to the camps, we all gathered for fellowship and a meal at the home of a pastor who lived in the area and wanted to be part of the ministry. As we were eating and enjoying ourselves, Laura suddenly felt ill. I had her lie down for a while, hoping that would help, but she felt no better. Thinking that perhaps one of the Koreans might be a doctor, since I knew they were all professionals of some sort from the Los Angeles area, I inquired of the group whether any of them happened to be a doctor. One of the women in the group responded, "Three of us are doctors. We have an eye doctor, a surgeon, and a pediatrician. Why do you ask?"

I quickly responded, "My daughter isn't feeling well. Could I ask the one who is a pediatrician to come look at her?"

One of the women stood up and said, "I'd be glad to take a look at her." She followed me to the back yard, into a motor home. An American family who were guests of the pastor had their trailer parked behind the home, and had allowed Laura to lie down on their couch.

After checking Laura out thoroughly, the doctor assured me it was just a flu bug that would pass. Thanking her for her services, I suddenly was reminded of the response from earlier when I had asked if there was a doctor in the house. I seemed to recall the word "surgeon." I pondered for a minute. "Excuse me, did you say there was a surgeon in the group?"

She replied, "Yes, Lin is a surgeon."

Entering the living room together, I turned to Lin. "Excuse me, Lin, I heard you are the surgeon in the group."

"Yes, I am," he answered with a smile.

I didn't immediately focus on my prayer of days earlier. Out of simple curiosity, I asked him if he could take a look at my leg and be able to tell by sight if the bump was just a cyst. He assented, and after observing it closely, he calmly assured me, "It's nothing to be worried about. It is only a cyst." A few seconds later, he nonchalantly added, "Do you want me to remove it for you? I brought my tools to do a surgery like that." He caught me completely off guard.

I said in amazement, "Now? Here… in this place?"

"Yes, I can do it within fifteen minutes," He answered.

George jumped into the conversation immediately. "Yes, Jennifer, you want to do this. You just got done praying the other day for God to put a surgeon in your life, and here he is!"

Funny, but when I was praying, I didn't exactly envision being at a pastor's house, with a group of people getting ready to go into a camp, when I underwent surgery. I mean, the environment didn't seem comfortable, or even safe for that matter.

The doctor, sensing my hesitancy, grabbed his surgeon's case, opened it up, and began to assure me how safe it really was. Still somewhat skeptical, yet reminded of my prayer to the Lord just days ago, I leaned on my faith. "What are the chances for this kind of opportunity to arise?" I thought. "All right," I consented, "Just let me change into a skirt to make this easier for you."

As I walked toward the bathroom to change my clothes, Lin stopped me, saying, "I will do this under one condition." I turned around and looked at him. "You have to be willing to let all of my colleagues watch so they can experience what I do as a doctor." I thought about it and agreed with his condition.

As I lay on the couch, with twenty or so people surrounding me, Lin carefully began numbing my leg. During the surgery, I couldn't watch what he was doing, especially when hearing the sound effects from the onlookers with their oohs and aahs. This was probably the first time for most of them to observe something like this. One man actually pulled out his camera and started taking pictures.

Lin's estimation of time for the surgery was right on. He had that cyst out and my leg sewed up within fifteen minutes. I felt hardly any pain other than when he inserted the needle to numb my leg.

Thanking him from the bottom of my heart for his service to me in removing that nasty bump, I shared with him my conversation with the Lord before coming on this outreach when I asked God to put a surgeon in my life. Then Lin told me that before leaving Los Angeles, he had asked the Lord to allow him to use his surgical skills in Mexico to help a missionary or pastor, or whomever God would put in his path that needed help. When he mentioned his prayer, I realized once again what a powerful, awesome God we serve. Here is Lin in Los Angeles asking the Lord to allow him to do surgery, while I'm down in Mexico praying, "God, please put a surgeon in my life." At the exact time and place, our Lord put us together to bless both of us tremendously.

Whenever I look at the small scar on my leg, it's a reminder of how loving and personal my God is.

*

Another blessing on this trip to Ceuta was discovering another American family who had a vision for working in the migrant camps. They had arrived earlier in the summer, months before we had returned. A local pastor introduced us to them. What stood out about this family was when they heard from the locals that other missionaries came down each year to labor in the camps, they wouldn't set foot there, because they lived by a teaching of scripture that speaks of not building on another man's foundation (Romans 15:20b). They actually waited until we arrived to ask permission of us for them to labor in the same camps alongside us. From our experience in the past, we had not seen this teaching practiced among Christian brothers and sisters; many times the enemy uses a situation like this to drive a wedge between them. It was encouraging.

As I mentioned earlier, we didn't know this was going to be our last year working in the migrant camps, yet in the Lord's perfect and precise timing, this was all in His plan to replace us with this wonderful family. We were delighted to have other missionaries join our team. They were exceptionally talented. Katie played the guitar and sang beautifully, and had a knack for children's ministry. She and her husband, Jim, spoke fluent Spanish, and had many years of cross-cultural experience. There weren't many things on which we needed to train them other than the tape distribution, and even in that area they caught on very quickly.

Besides discovering our new friends and their love for the camps, we had our Norwegian friends, Ray and Riley, who wanted to come down to stay with us for a week to also look at the area for ministry. They were more interested in the surrounding villages.

Because we didn't have our fifth wheel this year, having planned only to stay a short time, we began to see a dilemma. We really needed to stay for a month or so in Ceuta to help Jim and Katie feel comfortable enough to do the ministry alone. We didn't like the idea of going back to the States to get our fifth wheel to haul it down for just a month.

After much discussion, George came up with a solution. Instead of hauling our big trailer, we would try to purchase a small, cheap trailer for about one thousand dollars that we could then sell when we returned to the States. We laid our fleece out to the Lord. If it was His will for us to return to Ceuta to help out Jim and Katie, and Ray and Riley, everything would all come together. If not, we wouldn't be returning.

We shared our fleece with our friends, in hopes we would be back in a week. If not, we were saying our good-byes until next season. Now it was in the Lord's hands to reveal His will. Saying our farewells, we didn't waste any time, knowing we only had a week or so for our hunt for the trailer. We were on the road and back in the States by late evening.

The next morning, by searching the papers, we realized we would need to head toward Flagstaff to continue our search. If we couldn't find a trailer between here and there we would abandon our quest, and be content with the Lord's answer.

We no sooner left Bisbee when we saw a small trailer being pulled behind a medium-size car stopped in front of us as we all waited in line to pass through a border patrol checkpoint. "That's about the size trailer we need for Ceuta," George said, as we were staring at it. Then all at once, we both saw it: a "For Sale" sign posted on the trailer's side window. Trying to wait patiently to get pass the checkpoint, once we passed through, George accelerated the car so he could get even with the driver of the vehicle to wave him down. The driver appeared to be in deep thought, so George started honking the horn as we all waved our arms out the window to get his attention. Finally he looked over at us. We were pointing for him to pull over. Before getting out of the car, George and I both agreed that if the price was over fourteen hundred dollars we wouldn't buy it.

George got out of the car alone to negotiate with the owner of the trailer. It wasn't long before he was returning to the truck. "It's no deal. He wants eighteen hundred dollars for it," he spoke, disappointedly.

"Well, did you bargain with him?" I asked.

"No."

"Why not?"

"Because that is what he wants, and I don't want to talk him down," George told me.

"But most people expect you to wheel and deal with them," I persisted.

"Well, then you do it if you feel like that's what you're suppose to do," George retorted.

I quickly jumped out of the car and ran over to the man's car before he drove away. "Excuse me, but we want to know if you'll take fourteen hundred dollars for your trailer," I asked, hoping for a positive response, yet trying to act calm at the same time.

He hesitated momentarily, and then came back with his answer. "Okay."

Waving for George to get out of the truck, I was thrilled that he actually said yes. "He said he'll take fourteen hundred dollars," I told George, excitedly.

"We have a check, but if you want, we can go to the bank near here in Tombstone, and give you cash," George said. The man felt more comfortable receiving cash so we agreed to meet him at the bank.

Once inside the bank, we saw a long line of people waiting to do business. We would have to wait a while. This gave us time to get acquainted. He told us that he was traveling to Oregon to see his sister. Not having to haul his little trailer all the way up there was a blessing for him, while we shared with him the blessing of hauling this little trailer down to Mexico for our ministry.

Right before approaching the bank teller, the man turned around and said to us in a kind voice, "I really only want eleven hundred dollars for the trailer; you can keep the other three hundred dollars."

"Why are you lowering the price when we were willing to give you fourteen hundred dollars?" I asked, befuddled.

"Because it's only worth eleven hundred dollars," he answered. I took a deep breath, not sure if it would be right to give him less. He added, quite firmly, "I'm sure. This is all I'll take from you." Now at the teller's window, we obtained the cash and handed him eleven hundred dollars. We left the bank, all feeling pretty content.

We went back to the trailer. It was cram-packed with junk. Imagine a sixty-something-year-old single man who had probably lived in the trailer for some time. Not only was it filled with stuff, it was also going to need a good scrubbing!

We all helped him unload, since we were in a hurry ourselves to get back to Bisbee. It wasn't long before we noticed that not all of his belongings were going to fit into his car. He suddenly began to get really generous with his possessions. "Here, take this television, and... you can have this too... and, oh, take the microwave too. Do you need some dishes?' Most of his things we didn't need, but we took them and then donated them to a local charity in the area, since he didn't have room to haul them.

We were back in Bisbee within hours from our search to find a trailer. I have to admit we were amazed that the whole trailer adventure happened so quickly. That same day George bought new tires with the extra money the man so generously gave back to us. I had the trailer cleaned inside and out within a couple of days.

We found ourselves back on the road heading down to Ceuta in less then a week. Our friends were just as surprised as we were at our quick return, or even that we returned at all for that matter.

We were able to spend quality time with Jim and Katie for one month as planned. We stayed a little longer to help a church in the area erect their brick walls for their future church building. Ray and Riley were also able to come for one week as we surveyed the surrounding area of Ceuta for their future ministry. Riley shared with us that she had an exact dream of the corn fields we were driving through before they came to Mexico. In her dream she didn't know where she was. At last, the Lord was revealing to her the interpretation of that dream: the corn fields of Mexico.

A side note: Ray and Riley returned to Norway after serving several months at the mission's school in Culiacan with a great vision for Mexico. Their home church sent them out one year later and they have been laboring in the Lord in Culiacan and the surrounding area since. God is using them in great and mighty ways for His kingdom. That's something to praise the Lord about!

*

From years of experience, George and I recognized a pattern of events that would occur when the hand of God was working in mighty ways. Torrents of spiritual warfare would come swooping through our lives in the midst of praise and glory. This time it was the thieves. One early morning, waking from a good night's sleep, we looked out of our window and noticed the window of our vehicle had been broken out on the front driver's side. Unfortunately, thieves had taken a box full of George's favorite, most-used tools, along with several other pieces of equipment we used in the ministry. We must have discovered the break-in before the thieves were finished, because there were other valuables in the car still intact. Feelings of dejection filled us that morning; however, we knew that wasn't going to bring back our possessions.

In times like this, the Lord always knows the perfect words of encouragement to send our way to help us to keep on keeping on. In the midst of reevaluating whether our ministry was really worth all the headaches and hassles we had to encounter, we would question the Lord on the validity of our labors. "Lord, are we really being used to change people's lives? Are they truly coming to a saving knowledge of You?"

During one of our times of doubt, we were blessed with a visit from missionaries we had met in Culiacan several years earlier. Sharing with us all of their adventures, they wanted to tell a story of interest, seeing that we were connected to tape distribution in the camps.

While they were up north in a town called Navajoa, they contacted missionary friends who lived there and decided to spend some time in the village with them. Their hosts had another guest staying with them at this time, a young indigenous lady from a southern state of Mexico. Teresa came from an abusive home. Her father regularly lashed out at her, not only verbally, but also physically. He would come home each night after drinking all the family's money away and get in a rage. She lived in fear day in and day out, and finally had enough. She planned to secretly leave her village and go North in hopes of finding a better life. Along the way in her travels, she came across the missionary family in Navajoa who took her in, their compassion leading them to help her start a new life.

When her father discovered that his daughter had left home, he was even more enraged. Getting word that his daughter headed up north, he set out to find her, determined to get her back, even if it took the rest of his life. No daughter of his was going to pull this on him. He left Guerrero, a southern state, on the journey to find her, which led him to

Culiacan. Running out of resources to continue his hunt, he decided to work in the migrant camps to get enough money to continue. During his stay in one of the camps, a team of people came in to show the Jesus Movie. He remembers a *"gringo"* man giving him a cassette that was in his own language. One night, while all alone, he decided to listen to the tape. For the first time in his life the words of God permeated his heart. He found himself crying and repenting before the Lord. The Lord revealed the wretchedness in his behavior toward his family. How could he blame his daughter for wanting to run away from him?

In the next few days of his life, he came to realize that he still needed to search for his daughter, yet this time to ask her for forgiveness. He left Culiacan and continued to head north. Once he arrived in Navajoa, he inquired of her through different sources. When he shared his conversion to those he came in contact with, and of his plans to find his daughter to reconcile their relationship, those who heard were skeptical. However, word got back to the young lady and the missionary family. Was this really the truth what they were hearing, or was this just a scheme to get her back? After petitioning to the Lord for wisdom, the father had received the information of her whereabouts. He came to the house in a very humbled state. Meanwhile, his daughter was filled with fear, not sure what to think. The father began to cry as he shared his story. "Please forgive me for all I've done to you. I love you so much. God is changing me. Things will be different now. If you don't want to go back home with me, I won't force you. I just need your forgiveness."

Our missionary friends who were now visiting us had experienced all of this firsthand. I started to cry when they finished the story. I needed to hear this story for my own encouragement. For the word of God is living and powerful, and sharper than any two-edged sword, piercing even to the division of soul and spirit, and of joints and marrow, and is a discerner of the thoughts and intents of the heart (Hebrews 4:12). I know that is what changed this man.

I am blessed because once again I am reminded that He uses us when we're willing to bring His word forth. This is the answer I needed when I asked, "Lord, are we really being used to change people's lives?"

It was now that time of the year to go back home to give our report to our church family. Something was different this time as we traveled back. We had a sense we wouldn't be returning, yet we couldn't put our finger on what it was. We decided not to lean on our feelings; we would wait on the Lord as we trusted in His guidance for us.

Trust in the Lord and do good;
dwell in the land, and feed on
His faithfulness.
Delight yourself also in the Lord,
and He shall give you the desires
of your heart.

Psalm 37:3,4

16
Epaphroditus

O̲ur usual routine upon arriving back to the United States was to go to Bisbee, Arizona, unwind for a week or two, unpack our Mexico gear, and repack to travel to our church family and friends, and those that supported the ministry.

Within a short period of time, we found ourselves in Albuquerque once again. Our mission's pastor asked us if we would share the ministry of Mexico with the weekly prayer group and those interested in missions. We were delighted to speak.

We shared the blessings and difficulties of the season down there. When we came to the close of our talk, the pastor asked how they could pray for us in the future. George opened up to the group about our feelings of perhaps not returning to Mexico the following season. He felt God could possibly be opening other doors, moving us in a different direction for ministry, but we weren't sure what it was, nor of the timing. They agreed to lift our request up to the Lord as we waited on Him for the answer.

After our time of prayer together, Todd, the mission's pastor, took us aside as the crowd was leaving. "So, if the Lord were to take you out of Mexico, what is your heart's desire for the next ministry?" he inquired.

George spoke up. "Jennifer and I have talked for some time about ministering to missionaries. We noticed in the last year or so that we've had several missionaries come to us with needs that they feel uncomfortable about bringing up to the church office back home. You see, many of the staff members that work in church buildings have never been missionaries before, so they don't understand or even know how to deal with some of the problems that arise. Some in the office may think these missionaries need to come off the field and regroup. What they really need is someone who can come alongside them and encourage them. We already have a shortage of missionaries, without taking them off the field."

Todd's expression was priceless after George expressed his thoughts. "You're not going to believe this, but Paul (the senior pastor of the church) and I have had that same vision for two years now. We have been praying the Lord would bring a couple to us that had the same vision." He went on to say, "We never felt like we wanted to advertise that we were looking for someone to fit this ministry, out of concern that too many people would come forward, because it's a glorious ministry. But... you know what? I think you two are the couple we've been waiting for."

We were as stunned. Doors were opening faster than we had imagined. Still, we didn't want to jump into this commitment too hastily. George spoke up again. "What exactly does the church have in mind for us to do?"

"We would like to send you to each of our missionaries throughout the year to minister to them personally. Since each person is very unique, as well as with being in a different area, the Holy Spirit will show you what their particular needs are in hopes that you can help them. Basically," Todd added, "you will be representatives of the church. We want our missionaries to know that we care. We'll meet them where they're at."

We loved the idea. This was right up our alley. The more we talked about it, the more enthusiastic we became. Could this really be what the Lord wanted us to do next? George suggested to Todd, "Why don't we try this out with one missionary family before we make any long term commitments. You send us out, and if we can see the anointing of this ministry upon us, we'll move forward in faith and make plans to do this." We were all in agreement. We ended our conversation with prayer. In the next few days Todd would give us our first assignment.

While we waited on the Lord, George and I prayed fervently about this new adventure. Would the Lord truly count us worthy to be involved in such a great responsibility as this ministry entailed? The next thing I pondered was, "Where will we be going?" My hope was Israel. I have always wanted to travel there.

We waited patiently, or I should say we tried hard to be patient, for the direction from the church. After three days, Todd called to let us know where we would be going. "South Dakota! We're going to send you to South Dakota!" He told us that the team in the mission's department had also been praying diligently and felt like this was where the Lord would have us go. So, South Dakota it was.

He requested we call the missionaries personally and explain to them our ministry and intentions on coming. Our assignment was to spend at least one week with them to help out in any way we could. The goal was to gain their trust so that if there was anything personal to deal with, they would feel comfortable enough to open up to us. We also made an agreement with the church that anything the missionaries shared with us stayed with us. Our missionaries needed to know that confidentiality was of the highest standard concerning our ministry to them. The only exception was that, if we came across a situation where our missionaries were involved in deep sin, defaming our Lord and the body who supported them, this then needed to be brought to the attention of our leaders. We knew without a doubt that

345

wasn't going to be the case with the majority. We were also still planning on our tour to visit family and friends, so the church agreed to let us visit my family in Minnesota when leaving South Dakota.

After calling the missionaries in South Dakota, we felt encouraged that this was the Lord's doing. They received us with open arms and were thrilled that we were coming. Our trip up was uneventful; however, our stay made up for it. We hit it off with the family immediately. They were involved with the local school graduation, busy doing the activities that were required of them. We jumped in and helped in all the areas that we were able. Laura quickly made friends with their children, who were close to the same age. Most of the week was all business, with evenings for fellowship. It wasn't until the last few nights left with them that they felt comfortable enough to share difficult areas; once they did, we really saw the validity of this new ministry. We also experienced the anointing we were looking for, feeling confident that God was leading us into this new work.

Observing their hard work and labor of love toward the people they ministered to, I was interested in the outreach they do every year. Each summer a team of short-term missionaries come to distribute new shoes to those on the nearby reservation who can't afford to buy them, for all ages from children to adults. They start the process by sitting each person down, washing their feet in a bucket of clean water, drying their feet, putting new socks on them, and finish by fitting them with a new pair of shoes. All the while they share the love of Jesus with the person they are ministering to.

Throughout the whole week I kept praying the Lord would use me in a way that would bless the mother of the family. After she shared the shoe ministry with us, I felt this nudge from the Lord. "Since Sharon is involved washing other peoples feet, it would be nice for you to serve her in this same way by washing her feet." I really tried to ignore that thought, yet the harder I tried to put it aside, the stronger the nudge got.

"Oh, Lord, this is too weird for me, not to mention humbling. Besides, she'll think I'm really strange if I even suggest that I wash her feet."

I recalled the time I was at a church service in Arizona, when all the elders got up on stage one Sunday morning and did a foot washing among each other. I left that day thinking it was all a bit unnatural for my liking, yet I never forgot the message behind the image of what they were portraying. They were emulating the story in the Bible where Jesus washed the disciple's feet (John 13:5). This scene is the very picture of humility. Washing feet was a job for slaves. In this same passage, Peter couldn't understand why Jesus wanted to do it, but Jesus told him that even though he didn't understand it now, he would later. Peter grasped the meaning of humility when he mentions in I Peter 5:5 that we must all be clothed with humility. I was now being challenged by the Lord to be obedient to His request that I minister to my sister in the Lord through humility. As I was debating with the Lord about how peculiar all of this seemed, He spoke to my heart. "Jennifer, it's nothing more than a present day pedicure. Offer to give her a pedicure and she'll love it!"

"Yes, I can do a pedicure! That's what I'll do," I thought, feeling much more at ease. It's amazing how my emotions changed just by having it reworded.

The night before we were ready to leave, I asked Sharon if I could bless her by giving her a pedicure. At first she seemed somewhat embarrassed that I wanted to do it, but when I shared with her that, as she ministers year after year washing people's feet, I wanted to give back to her what she gives out, she was more inclined to let me bless her this way too.

It was a humbling experience for the both of us, yet somehow through that experience we drew together emotionally like sisters. The Lord had a purpose in all of it. When we're able to come together in fellowship with a humble heart toward each other, God's love is brought forth in a deeper way.

We left South Dakota on cloud nine. We were convinced this was our next mission field. When we returned to Albuquerque, we would accept the position the church was offering us. There were still details that needed to be worked out. We would have to move to New Mexico and find a new place of residence, but we knew it would all come together if this was the Lord's will for us. Meanwhile, we first had to finish out our visit with our family in Minnesota.

While in Minnesota, I received a phone call from my close friend, Judy, in Bisbee. At first it alarmed me that she would be calling me at my sister's home, knowing she wouldn't ordinarily just call to chit-chat while we were traveling. She let us know that the owner of the property where we were living in Bisbee needed us to relocate since his mother-in-law was in need of a place to live. I could tell Judy was struggling with her words, trying to break the news as easily as she could. We had been there for over ten years and made it our home. My response was the total opposite of what she had expected. I was so thrilled because to me it was a confirmation that the Lord was relocating us to Albuquerque. The timing couldn't have been more perfect. In all the years we had lived on that property, we were always welcomed and felt at peace about staying there. Now they needed us to move, at the very time that we were wondering if we should move and where we should live. This was our answer! Moving to Albuquerque was our next step. Still asking where, and not yet knowing, we knew this was a trust issue with God. He would open the doors for us.

Thinking about living in our fifth wheel long term wasn't the answer either. We would already be living out of suitcases in our new ministry. Having a house in which we could unpack and unwind seemed to be in order. This would definitely take waiting on the Lord because our budget couldn't afford paying for rent.

After we got back to Albuquerque, we shared with the church how anointed and blessed we felt on our trip to South Dakota. We were ready to make a full-time commitment to this new ministry, and to move to the vicinity and say good-bye to the Mexico ministry.

The ministry we were now officially a part of was called "Epaphroditus". The name came about through the man, Epaphroditus, who was Paul's helper in the Bible (Philippians 2:25, 4:18). He was the man the Philippians sent to encourage and to bring financial assistance to Paul. Todd (the mission's pastor) and Paul (the senior pastor) thought the ministry fit the title. We liked it too.

Our next step was to go to Bisbee and move off the property. We owned a moving box trailer that we had used for storage in the past. We planned to pack up our belongings from the house and bring them all to Albuquerque. A friend of ours owned some commercial property there and gave us permission to park our storage trailer on it until we found a place to live. Meanwhile, we decided to continue living in our fifth wheel.

Driving down to get our first load went smoothly. We loaded up the trailer box and did a turnaround all in one day. Before going down for the second load, our friends with whom we had been staying told us they had received a phone call from someone in the church. They had left their number and a message about a house they wanted to talk to us about.

The call came from a family we had met in a home fellowship earlier that year. They heard we were looking for a place to live, and thought we should go look at a house about twenty-five miles outside of town, between Albuquerque and Santa Fe. We weren't too excited about living so far away, yet we didn't close the door since we were asking the Lord for His direction. I don't know why, but after the owner of the house explained to me it was a manufactured, double wide home, my first impression was that it would need work. My imagination went so far as to envision a place that had been inhabited by a couple of bachelors who liked to party, leaving the place all trashed out. I was already gearing up to the thought that it was going to need tons of repairs.

After pulling up into the driveway and getting a first look at the house, however, hope sparked in my heart that I had been totally wrong. Going inside, I was even more delighted to discover it was only a four-year-old home, in very good condition. Still, after taking the tour, I didn't think we would be able to afford the rent for someplace so new and big. To my surprise, the woman told us that they were going to let us live in it free of charge. I had totally missed that part when we had talked earlier. They had set aside this house for the availability of anyone that needed it who was involved in the ministry. The only thing they asked is that we take care of it. Because it was out in the boonies, somewhat isolated, they didn't like leaving it vacant.

We were elated! The Lord came through for us again. We hadn't even finished our move from Bisbee and already we had a house to go home to. We accepted their generous offer, and hurriedly went down to get our last load, able to bring it right to our new home.

I couldn't thank God enough for His tender loving care for us. We were now more than ready for our new adventure.

How much better to get wisdom than gold!
And to get understanding is to be chosen
rather than silver.

Proverbs 16:16

17
Overseas Adventures

Many years ago, by the prompting of the Lord, George and I contacted a group of people who knew us well. They committed to pray for us regularly while we were in the mission field. Once a month, taking turns at each of their homes, they gathered to pray for us. As time went on, they found other ways to support us, along with their prayers. One family took on the labor of sending out our newsletters and took on the responsibility for receiving donations and making deposits for us. Others gave to us financially, also jumping in when there were unexpected expenses. With the diversity of the team, there was always wisdom and counsel for us to call upon. We knew we were always covered in prayer. We give credit to our "care team" to the victories for the ministry. We have been so blessed by their love and support all of these years.

Seeing how blessed we had been by having our support team, when we introduced the concept to the mission's department as we started out in this new ministry, they thought all of the missionaries from our church should have that same kind of care. We also held mini-conferences to introduce the idea to the church congregation in hopes of getting them involved in missions. We were overjoyed to see the enthusiasm that spread through the church. Many of the churchgoers ran with the notion right away. As we set off to visit each missionary family, we were excited to be able to tell them about the zeal back home.

It was easier and less expensive to visit missionaries closer to home, so our missionaries in Mexico were visited first. Within months the opportunity to travel overseas entered the picture. I had never been abroad before, nor had Laura (by this time, Jonathon was away at college), so we were eager to take a two-month assignment to Africa and Europe. Much planning and preparation was on the agenda, considering the timing of when to visit each family. After mapping, calculating, contemplating and plotting out this whole trip, plans were set in place. Uganda was first on the agenda, with a stopover in London. After leaving Africa, we planned our next stay in Jerez De La Frontera, in the southern region of Spain. From there, the train would take us across Europe to Hungary, to visit yet another missionary family. Traveling back, it seemed a good idea to take another route to see other sights, taking us to France, which would come at the halfway point of the trip. The church had requested we take a few days off in the middle of our trek before beginning the second leg of the trip, and it would be convenient to plan to spend our three days off in Paris. Leaving Paris, our flight would take us to England, where three different families lived. After ending our excursion in England, we would fly back to Albuquerque after all-in-all two months of visits.

Most everything went as planned as far as our scheduling was concerned, but the Lord had lots to teach us and many things to show us. For those of you who are world travelers, you understand jet lag, language barriers, and cultural differences in matters such as food, customs, dealing with exchanging money, and trying to remember the value of each coin. It can be a real challenge, to say the least.

After leaving Uganda, I still had shillings left in a cloth money purse I wore around my neck, tucked nicely inside my shirt. When we had arrived in England, I needed to buy stamps to send out a few letters. Exchanging dollars for pounds, I threw the coins in my money purse. Next we went to Spain. When we left there, I had lots of Euros to add to my collection. On a train in France, hunger hit, so we bought food with dollars, getting our change back in Francs.

Then we arrived in Switzerland. After the train unloaded its passengers, we planned to transfer to another train to get to Hungary. As we got off the train, I suddenly realized I needed to use the restroom. It didn't seem like such a difficult task to accomplish. Was I wrong! There wasn't a restroom in sight. We walked back and forth, turning down one hall to the next. My situation was becoming quite grave. Then I saw one! Running frantically to reach it, to my dismay I was met at the entrance of the door by an attendant that didn't speak English. It appeared that he was there to collect fees to get in. I was beginning to turn green. I could hardly think. I pulled out my coin purse as fast as I could, spilling all the coins in front of him. He was looking at me oddly as I tried to explain my dilemma to him in English. "Take what you need and give me back my change, and be honest about it!" I held out my hands with an array of francs, euros, shillings, pounds, and quarters, dimes, and nickels. We both had to smile at the humor of the situation, but I had no time to try and work out the language barriers between us. Thank God, he let me through without any more questions. He probably saw the urgency in my eyes, or my green colored skin.

When I came out he handed me my change. I could only hope he was an honest man. I guess I'll never know what it really cost me to use that restroom that day. I learned a valuable lesson on that trip: never get off the train before using the restroom, especially if you don't know where you're at.

I think some of the Swiss people thought we were crazy. When I returned from the restroom, I asked George and Laura what country we were in. At this point in our long journey, none of us were sure. I went up to the ticket booth and politely asked, "Could you tell us where we are?"

"Geneva," he responded briskly. Until this moment I thought I knew my geography, but suddenly I found my mind a total blank.

"And what country might this be?" I inquired, trying to appear sophisticated.

He didn't even bother to answer me, giving me a snide look as if I were purposely being sarcastic with him. To give him the benefit of the doubt, maybe he didn't understand my English. At any rate, when I walked back over to George, he had found out that we were in Switzerland.

I could write about all the little quirky, funny, crazy experiences that happened to us in those two months; however, my space is limited, so I will focus on the presence of God and a few of the supernatural experiences we encountered overseas. It is a comforting thought to know that no matter where we go, God is always there (Psalm 139:7-10).

Our first encounter of amazing "happenings" on this trip took place in the Dallas airport before we even arrived overseas. We were all hungry, not having planned ahead where we were going to eat. When we saw the expensive menu prices, with a fast food meal costing ten dollars per person, we realized the predicament we were in. Did we want to wait until we got on the plane in hopes that they would serve us a meal right away, or should we splurge and pay nearly thirty dollars for the three of us to each get a meal? While we were contemplating our options, unexpectedly and out of the blue, two men approached us from the crowd of people that surrounded us in front of the restaurant. "Excuse us, but we were wondering if you would like these two meal tickets we have for this restaurant. We just ate and we're quite full. Since we're getting on a plane soon, we won't be able to use them," one of the gentlemen explained.

"You want to give them to us?" George asked, incredulously.

"Yes. That is, if you want them," he replied.

"Sure!" the three of us said, simultaneously.

They handed us the two tickets and turned to leave. "Thank you!" we all said in unison. As the three of us looked around at the crowd of people pushing in around us, we were awestruck. Why did these two men choose us in this large group of people? "God is sure watching over us!" was our conclusion. We felt great relief at only having to spend ten dollars to eat lunch that afternoon. Somehow that meal tasted a lot better than if we had to spend the thirty dollars. The Lord was helping us with our budget. However, it wasn't until we arrived in Africa that the Lord revealed to me His strong presence.

Our church had asked us to check in with them by e-mail as often as we could, to keep them informed of our whereabouts and give them a short report of our encounters. There was an internet café a mile or so from the mission base we were staying at that supplied computers, so we made a point of walking down there every few days to send our updates. (The missionaries had a computer, but it wasn't working for part of our visit.)

One particular day while I was inside writing to the church, George sat outside the café at one of the quaint little tables arranged in the front of the building. The computers in Uganda weren't as modern as the computers back home, so it ended up taking me over an hour to get a letter written and off. Meanwhile, as George was enjoying a nice hot cup of coffee, an elderly man came up and started a friendly conversation. George invited him to sit down at the table with him. George listened to the man for over an hour, until finally the man observed, "Usually Americans want to do all the talking. I'm surprised you let me talk and have said hardly a word. I really appreciated you doing that." He then went on to say, "Well, the real reason I stopped to talk with you is because as I was walking down this street, the Lord talked to me and said, 'I have a word I would like you to tell this man sitting at the table.' So, I have a word for you from the Lord." George was somewhat surprised, especially because this man didn't know us at all; he hadn't even mentioned to him that we were Christians. The elderly man continued, "God is going to use you all over the world to help His people. He also wants you to know that He will protect you on your journey." Stunned by what he said, especially since this described what we were already doing, George quickly thanked him for the message. Little did we know, there was much more depth to that statement.

About the time the two of them were finishing their conversation, I walked out of the internet café. George stood up and walked over to me. "I would like you to meet my wife, Jennifer," he said, putting his arm around me. Focused on me, he continued his introduction. "This is Brother James. We met out here at the table." We shook hands. The man called me "Mama Jennifer." (I've been told that in Uganda traditionally they add "Mama" to women's names as a designation that they have borne children.) After a few words of courtesy were exchanged, we departed and went back to the mission base. Walking back, George was biting at the bit to tell me what Brother James shared with him. "You'll never believe what Brother James told me before you came out of the café," he said excitedly. Relating in detail their conversation, I was just as surprised as George, since the man's message so accurately described what God was already doing in our lives. He concluded by telling me that James had said he worked in an orphanage in the area.

A few days after our encounter with James, we decided to take a walk to the marketplace to get outdoors for awhile. Laura joined us. Assuming that he knew the way, George took us on a shortcut to save time. However, fifteen minutes into our walk, I suddenly realized that not only did Laura and I not know where we were, but George didn't have a clue where we were either. The neighborhood where we found ourselves didn't look very safe. Here we were, having lost our way in a strange land, none of our friends knowing where we were, and unable to communicate with anyone around us. Glancing at the people standing outside their little modest abodes staring at us, a sudden strong fear came over me that we might get jumped and stabbed to death at any moment. Without saying a word, I looked up and began to pray silently, yet fervently, "Lord, please protect us, have Your guardian angels surround us this very instant because I think we are in some serious danger." Although I was trying to act as calm as I could, my heart was pounding a mile a minute.

We made it to the next block still alive, but I was not having victory over my fear. As a matter of fact, the anxiety in me was gaining momentum, especially when I saw an opening on the next street crowded with a lot more people, which gave me an even greater sense of being closed in by the throng. As we got closer, I felt some relief to see what appeared to be an outdoor bus station, with many buses and taxis parked along the curb. Again glancing up to the heavens, with more eagerness in my tone, I prayed, "God, help us! We're lost, and... and... I really don't like the situation we're in."

I turned around to get my bearings, when suddenly standing in front of me was Brother James. He took me completely by surprise. It didn't seem possible that he should be standing there at that precise moment. The whole scenario seemed out of place. I was thinking to myself, "Why are you standing here?" As we stared at each other, I sensed he could see the fear in my eyes. In a slow, gentle voice, he opened his mouth and said, "Mama Jennifer, how nice to see you all here." Still staring intently into my eyes, he articulated the following words clearly: "You don't need to be afraid. Don't you know that Jesus is right here with you?" With those reassuring words, and the comforting look in his eyes, a strong sense of peace permeated our surroundings. With each moment, his eyes grew more piercing, full of passion and love. I saw the eyes of Jesus in this man! It was astonishing! This look was so incredibly surreal, I started to cry. He continued, "Jesus has his protection all around you. His angels are surrounding you." He pointed to the far distance. "They are all around the mountains. So, you need to trust in Him, not just now, but on the rest of your travels too."

I was so amazed at what was coming out of his mouth. Nodding my head in agreement, I responded with confidence, "All right."

Looking down at his watch, his countenance changed. "I must go. I have a meeting I need to be at and I don't want to be late. It was good seeing you again." And off he went.

I looked at George and said, "Honey, did that just really happen?" It was like something out of a movie.

Continuing to search for the marketplace, feeling much more assured after our unexpected meeting with Brother James, George's perspective of where we were suddenly came into focus. "I believe the marketplace is right down this street," he pointed. His instincts were correct. We found our way and were on track to where we had planned to be in the first place.

I couldn't help but ponder our encounter with Brother James. "I wonder if he was an angel," I kept thinking. The scripture from the Bible that talks about entertaining angels penetrated my thoughts. "Do not forget to entertain strangers, for by so doing some have unwittingly entertained angels." (Hebrews 13:2).

When we got back to the base, we sat down to visit the missionaries we were staying with. In our conversation, we brought up the story of Brother James, and how we met him at the internet café. George told them he had said he worked at a nearby orphanage. All of the missionaries were certain that they had never heard of a "Brother James" in the area. "Besides," they told us, "We know all the Christian workers in the area, and we're in tune with the local orphanages around here. There is no one by that name that works at any of them."

I'm still not sure if Brother James was an angel or not, but George is convinced he wasn't because he gave him an e-mail address. "Angels don't have e-mail," he told me. After discussing it quite extensively, we decided to write to him. The strange thing is that we lost the address before we could write. One missionary mentioned, "Angels don't lie. He told you he worked in a nearby orphanage which wasn't true." My thoughts on that remark were that maybe he really did work in an orphanage, just in 'angel' form. Only God knows. However, Brother James was an awesome man to meet and his words of encouragement at a time of need blessed me tremendously. His words continued to resound through the rest of our trip when I found myself in uneasy situations.

Believe it or not, when we got to England, I believe we had another "angel" encounter. We were now in York, England, a small, quaint, beautiful place, visiting a wonderful missionary family. After our visit with them, our plan was to catch a train north to a place called Harrogate. We planned to arrive at three p.m. to meet up with our next missionaries at the train station. It was all set. They would be there to pick us up.

The day we left York, our new missionary friends drove us to the station. Mike told us it was only a fifteen minute drive, so he suggested we leave right on time to prevent us having to sit around needlessly waiting for our train. We didn't foresee the traffic jam we found ourselves in. Unfortunately, when we arrived at the station, we only had ten more minutes before the Harrogate train was to leave. We still needed to purchase the tickets and get our luggage out of the vehicle and checked in, so George suggested I run in and buy the tickets while he dealt with the luggage. Running into the station, it dawned on me that I had no idea where to go to buy them. I saw a receptionist at a window, so I quickly made my way over to the counter and asked, "Excuse me, but could you tell me where to go to purchase train tickets?" He pointed to a glass door across the hall where we were standing. "Thank you," I responded, hurrying to the door.

As I opened the door, dismay set in. The room was filled with lines of people in each lane, also waiting to buy tickets. I threw up my arms in defeat. We weren't going to make the train. We'd have to try again tomorrow.

Wondering how we were going to manage to contact the missionaries we were scheduled to meet at 3 o'clock in Harrogate, I was interrupted by a tap on my shoulder. Turning around, I saw standing in front of me a clean-cut man dressed in a full conductor's outfit, even to the conductor's hat, just like you would imagine from a movie. While I stood there mesmerized by his attire, he spoke up. "Do you need to buy a ticket for the train?"

"Yes," I answered, surprised.

"Well, come with me over to this machine and we can get you one a lot quicker," he said, in a friendly tone.

I looked across the room, and in the corner stood a machine all by itself. Following him, my thoughts were running in every direction. "Why isn't anyone else using this machine if it's so fast," I thought to myself.

"Hurry, give me your credit card, we're losing time," he said briskly. I wasn't about to hand some stranger my credit card. He must have sensed my reluctance because he started explaining to me how it worked.

"But I think we've already missed our train," I interrupted.

"If you don't make this train, I'll refund your money," he replied.

My thoughts were spinning, but I went with my instincts that this man was legitimate. Besides, there was no more time to waste. Taking my chances, I pulled out my credit card and stuck it into the machine. He started pushing buttons, meanwhile asking me for the information he needed. Three tickets popped out of the machine, and my credit card was back in my possession before I knew it. "Come now, we must move quickly if you're going to make the train. I'll take you to the platform where you need to be," he said kindly, rushing me out of the door.

George and Laura were standing back in the hall with the luggage. Running over to them, I quickly explained who this man was, and how he was going to get us to the place our train was. All of us practically ran down the hall to the elevator the conductor directed us to. The elevator took us down a few flights. We came out into another floor where the man instructed us to hurry down the hall and get into another elevator that was going up. As we were moving upward, the conductor began to give us explicit instructions on what we were to do. "When this door opens, I want you all to run as fast as you can to platform number seven. You don't have any time to waste, so move as quickly as you can." We were ready to run. The doors opened, and the conductor darted out in front of us. As he was running toward the platform, he was shouting to another man standing toward the end of the train. "Hold that train, hold that train," he yelled, "don't let it leave!"

The man must have been in his late sixties or early seventies by the looks of him, but he could sure run. We were amazed. He got to the train before the three of us did. We were actually out of breath, breathing hard. The two men grabbed our luggage and began throwing it into the train. Jumping aboard, we quickly turned around and sat down in the seats facing the door. As we watched the two men standing outside the train, the conductor who had helped us get the tickets saluted us, saying these words, "God bless you!" The doors shut. The train took off within five seconds of our entering and sitting down.

The three of us looked at each. The only thing that came out of my mouth before I burst into tears was, "I can't believe that just happened." George and Laura hadn't yet heard of my dealings with the conductor in that huge room full of people, and the details of how we got the tickets from some little machine tucked away in the corner of the room.

Whether this conductor was an angel or not, only God knows. These things simply don't happen on an everyday basis, yet when they do, they are reminders that God is truly watching over His people. Brother James words resounded again. "God's angels are surrounding you." All afternoon as we traveled to our next destination, I couldn't quit thanking Jesus. His love for us is quite evident!

*

After two months overseas, we were ready to come home. Our travels to each missionary family blessed us beyond measure. Although we were there to minister to their needs, we were filled and encouraged as well.

Our flight back landed us in Albuquerque from London after a ten hour flight. When we got off the plane and were nearing the baggage claim area, our care team was all there to welcome us home. We were very surprised to see them, especially since it was during working hours and most of them worked. They got the time off just to be there for us. What love!

We all hugged and chatted for a short time when one of them said, "We wanted to all be here to greet you and to let you know how happy we are to have you back home, but we also understand that you are probably experiencing jet lag and want to go home to sleep, so we're going to leave." They hugged us one by one and left, except for one couple who were the designated drivers to take us home.

Traveling home, our friends, thinking we were probably hungry, suggested we get a bite to eat. They had guessed right. Thinking our house had been sitting vacant for two months and with no food stored away, we agreed it was a good idea. They also volunteered to take us grocery shopping, but we were too tired. Even the thought exhausted me.

Pulling up to the house, we were all so happy to be home. As we were walking up to the door with our friends helping carry our baggage in, Laura noticed first the bed of flowers that had been freshly planted along the front of our home. "Mom, look! Do you think the landlord planted these while we were gone?" Observing the smiles on Tyler and Rachel's faces at Laura's question, we turned to them with eyebrows lifted. "Did you plant those flowers?" we all asked.

"Yeah, we did," they said humbly.

"That was so thoughtful of you to plant those," I said, as I was opening the front door.

To our astonishment, our care team had come out and cleaned our home, filled our refrigerator with food, put bouquets of fresh flowers on our dining room table and Laura's bedroom, and stocked our cupboards with dry food and toiletries. They also hung up a banner that read, "WELCOME HOME!" Along with the banner, they put up pictures of each care team member printed from computer paper. It was a great understatement to say that we were overwhelmed by the love they had displayed, and I was moved to tears.

Tyler and Rachel quickly left us alone, concerned that we needed some sleep. After they left, we discovered cards placed throughout our house hidden in various places. It was so much fun finding and reading the messages from many dear friends in the church, letting us know that we were missed and that they were glad we were back home.

Before retiring for the night, we found another card lying on our pillow. Opening it up, we found three hundred and fifty dollars in cash. The card read, "Just thought you might need a little extra to get started up again." Our friends had taken up an offering for us. They showered us with so much love; I couldn't quit thinking and talking about all they had done for us. They definitely had the definition of "care team" down.

If that wasn't enough, three days after our return was our wedding anniversary. We received a phone call from one of our care team members letting us know that they had reserved a hotel suite for us for our special day. Their abundance of love was humbling us greatly.

Arriving at the hotel, we walked in to find chocolates wrapped in romantic paper placed throughout the room. Next to the Jacuzzi, they had placed lots of other fun food to munch on. They were treating us like royalty when we hadn't deserved any of this kind of treatment. Don't get me wrong: we were very appreciative of all the thought and love put into our return; however, we found it very humbling being on the receiving end, to say the least. Sometimes it seems easier to give than to receive. After that, whenever we did our mini-conferences at the church on "Care Teams", we couldn't help but brag about what a wonderful care team the Lord blessed us with.

*

As we traveled, we began to see great needs for the missionaries we ministered to. We decided to organize periodic garage sales to raise money for them.

Many of us are more than glad to get rid of excess accumulation in our homes. In our case, we advertised, offering to pick up people's unwanted items, and soon found this ministry was becoming quite lucrative. We had an old single wide trailer in our yard where we were able to store the items, and throughout the months the trailer was always full to the brim. Before we held each garage sale, we would ask the Lord for a specific amount, knowing ahead of time where the money was going and who is was designated for. What amazed me most of all was how the Lord would give us close to the amount we asked for, give or take a few dollars. Experiencing this, we knew the hand of God was on this ministry. Not only were we blessed to make the money for the missionaries, we also had so much fun doing it. I didn't particularly enjoy the cleanup afterwards, but it was all worth it.

The Lord also has a sense of humor. That was the case with George and the Christmas box ministry. As long as I have known George, he has always been of the sort that doesn't like the "Christmas hype". To him that means all the shopping for presents and buying a tree to decorate. Every year as we start nearing the holiday season, he comes up with his reasons for not enjoying it. Most of our friends are aware of his attitude, and could see the humor that came our way when the mission's department asked him if he would take over the Christmas program they had planned that year for missions. They asked him to lead a group of people down to Mexico in an outreach, handing out eight thousand Christmas boxes to the children in the community. They only wanted him to be in charge of phase one, which didn't include giving out the boxes. His responsibilities would be to set up the outreach before bringing the group down. It also entailed finding a hotel, making reservations for a big group, locating a person who was willing to cook for the group, renting a stadium for speakers and singers to perform, setting up advertisement on the local radio station in the community, and visiting all the churches in the area, inviting the pastors to get involved in hopes of creating an interdenominational event for everyone in the community. This part of the ministry he liked, since it was right up his alley to organize an outreach. Giving out the boxes was another thing.

George was going to be quite busy for the next month, spending a lot of time with Mexican pastors. We thought it best that Laura and I fly to Minnesota to free him up to do what he needed to get done.

When George arrived in Mexico, everything went quite smoothly. One of the missionaries from our church was a pastor in the area George would be working in, so that helped out a lot. The pastor was able to introduce him to many of the pastors and set him up with the connections he needed to make this all work. One of those connections was with the president of the community. He happened to be a believer in Jesus Christ, and loved the idea of this Christmas program coming to his city, especially the blessing of all the children with Christmas presents.

George and the president bonded in friendship quickly. They put their thoughts together to come up with an awesome event. Making a list of all the things our church would be responsible to pay out financially, George knew we would need prayer for provision. They were expecting at least six thousand people to attend each of the two nights, and would need an ambulance on the premises, ten port-a-potties placed around the stadium, trash barrels, and a clean up crew. They also needed to rent extra chairs for seating, plus a stage, and to hire security for such a big event as this. George agreed with the president that we would pay for it all upon returning for the outreach.

When he came back to the church and presented the budget, the leaders realized that the money would have to come partly from those that signed up to go on the outreach. Certainly, God would work it out.

The big part of George's ministry was completed. The church was responsible for phase two of the outreach, or so he thought. A month before the outreach was to take place, the mission's pastor in our church had an unexpected change occur in his plans. He asked George if he would be willing to take over phase two, which meant taking the group down to Mexico to pass out the Christmas boxes personally. George agreed to do it, but with one stipulation. "I'll do this outreach only if you allow me to lead the group under my direction. We can't have several different people in charge or it won't work." They agreed to let George lead the way.

One of his first changes of plan was to lower the price for those that wanted to sign up for the outreach. His rationale was that way more people would be able to afford to come. When he laid out an amount of two hundred and fifty dollars per person at the meeting, he could immediately sense the disapproval among some of the group. However, when he reminded them that they agreed to go with his direction, they all unanimously went along with his idea. Even though there might have been an underlying concern about where the finances would come from if we didn't get it from the group, George felt assured that the Lord would provide it all if this was His will.

After the meeting, one of the men that attended offered to make up any difference. George was quite blessed that this man was so generous to back him up. The day of departure, there were thirty-five people who had signed up to go. It was a great group, zealous to do the work of the Lord.

During the first week, before the big two-day event was to take place, the team did a couple of short medical outreaches with a doctor. They also put a dinner together for pastors that were going to be part of the outreach, along with their wives. After the meal, two American pastors in the group taught on specific subjects through translators. It turned out to be a wonderful get-together. All the while, the president of the community was observing the works of our group.

The turnout for the outreach was phenomenal. The stadium was packed with people in all the services. Approximately eight thousand people came forward and responded to the gospel call. The pastors from around the city helped counsel those that came forward.

On the second day of the outreach, the president came up to George. "I am so delighted to see all of these pastors working together in unison for one cause," he commented. "I've also been watching your group of people and am so pleased at what you all have done for our city. Because of this, I've decided to pay for the cost of renting this stadium, including the trash bins, toilets, security guards, the advertisement for the radio time, and the chairs and stage." If that wasn't enough, he continued with blessings. "Not only that, but I'm also going to pay for your group's hotel bill and food bill. Just let me know who and where to go to pay the bill," he said. What generosity! To top it off, he invited the team out for a dinner on him.

George was ecstatic. So was the group when he called them all together for a meeting and shared the president's news. "Now that the president has paid for every expense we have incurred down here, we have another area to look at. The money we have in our money bag belongs to you all, minus the traveling expenses and deposit money we had to put down ahead of time for the hotel and meals," George shared. "Now we as a team need to decide what to do with the money we have left over." After talking it over together, the group unanimously agreed to give the money to the missionaries for the projects they were involved in.

Being able to come back to the church and share the provision of the Lord and the thousands of people whose lives would be changed forever was delightful. All the honor and glory goes to the Lord for the great things He has done. And giving out Christmas boxes to little children that had next to nothing wasn't so bad after all. It brought joy to

George, especially when he saw the happiness in the eyes of the ones that looked and acted as if it were the first time they ever received a gift in their whole lives.

Then you will call upon Me and go
and pray to Me,
and I will listen to you.

Jeremiah 29:12

18
Between Ministries

After what I considered our best three years of ministry, there was a change. Our church decided to eliminate certain programs, one of which was the "Epaphroditus Ministry". They were still willing to back us financially as missionaries, just not with the agenda we were currently involved in. Although I felt somewhat discouraged because we were in a realm where our spiritual gifts were being used, nevertheless I knew that if the Lord was closing this door, He would open another for us.

In the next few weeks after the news of Epaphroditus closing down, we did a lot of prayer walking. Early every morning, we arose and hiked down the dirt road right outside our home. We did this regularly throughout our marriage and found it to be a wonderful way to start each day. We would hike close to one-and-a-half miles one way, sharing with each other what was on our mind or what or how the Lord was working in our lives. On the return back home we would each take turns praying. The Lord always met us out on those many dirt roads we hiked as we felt His presence and guidance, being assured that He would give us direction, sometimes just to get through the day.

During this time our church allowed us to take six weeks off to seek God and His word, since this was going to be another big change for us. Being a missionary and then suddenly finding yourself with no mission field is hard. One needs to be called by the Lord; otherwise it's all in vain. Unless the Lord builds the house, they labor in vain who build it (Psalm 127:1). We would wait on the Lord during our furlough.

Several of our friends knew we had time off, so they called George to ask if he would be willing to help with projects. He was more than happy to help them out, but it took us away from what we really should have been doing: spending time in the word and prayer. After three weeks of repairing cars, replacing roofs, and building decks, we knew that if we didn't leave Albuquerque and find a quiet place, we wouldn't be spending that time with the Lord. We decided to take off in our fifth wheel trailer and head toward Flagstaff. We were very familiar with the surrounding forests and believed this would be a good place to hide out. Just before leaving, we were offered a position as mission's director at a small church (not so small, but little compared to the mega church we were previously involved in). This church was connected with the medical outreach we had formerly done in Mexico among the Tarahumara village where fourteen people gave their lives to the Lord. The pastor had a vision to get his people more involved with missions. He was asking us to assist him in taking teams down throughout the year to build up this village of new believers as well as help the church catch the vision for world missions.

We loved the idea, yet we still felt that we needed to seek the Lord concerning this new ministry. We told the pastor that we were going away for three weeks and when we returned we would give him our answer.

The first week out in the woods went just as planned. We found an isolated spot to park our trailer among the pine trees. Each day we read the word, prayed a lot, and took hikes into the forest. There's just something about being out in the wilderness that seems to make me feel so in tune with

God and nature. We were having a wonderful time. One day toward the end of our first week's stay, as we were taking one of our hikes we came upon a man standing by himself on the dirt road next to a huge tree. We could tell by his countenance that he was not happy. By the looks of him, we guessed he was indigenous, very similar to the people groups we had worked with in the past. Stopping to see if he needed help, George quickly engaged in conversation with him. We realized he didn't understand a word that was said, so George switched to Spanish. Instantly we could see from the stranger's face a spark of delight. He was excited to discover the two '*gringos*' in front of him could actually speak his language. To top it off, after talking a few more minutes, we discovered that he was a Christian too. He had come up from Peru and was hired by a local rancher who needed help with his horses. He confided in us that he had just lost one of the horses that morning and needed to find it. After conversing back and forth for awhile, George offered to drive around the forest area and look for a horse running free. Unfortunately, we didn't see any free roaming horses that morning.

He had shared with us that he was staying up the road in a tiny trailer parked next to an old abandoned house. We decided to drive over that evening to see if he had any luck finding the horse, and also to satisfy our curiosity about where he lived. We were happy to hear he had found the lost horse. Standing outside his little abode, we noticed that his water supply, a big fifty gallon plastic container, was about to run dry. He seemed very lonely and really needed fellowship so we invited him to go to town with us the next day to get him some supplies. He told us he didn't know when the rancher would come out to the property again.

The next day we were over there bright and early to pick him up, as well as the fifty gallon tank for water. Although we had planned to be alone for a time, we knew that we couldn't just leave our Peruvian friend stranded without water and supplies. Off we went to town. While gathering up supplies, my cell phone rang. I wasn't sure if I should pick it up, but that voice in the back of my mind reminded me that it could be an emergency. To our surprise it was our Norwegian friends, Ray and Riley, who lived in Mexico. They had time off for vacation so they decided to come to the U.S. and visit the Grand Canyon. We told them where we were staying and that they were welcome to join us out in the woods. They came, bringing tents, and they fit right in.

By that evening, we found ourselves in front of a big comfortable campfire with our Norwegian friends and our new Peruvian friend. The fellowship was so rich, yet again we realized that we weren't alone, and that probably wasn't going to be the case for the next week. We just couldn't say "no". George and I concluded that the one week was all we were going to get alone, and now we would trust God to give us direction for our future before we left to return to Albuquerque.

Soon after, we were going to leave the forest and check into an RV park in Flagstaff to spend a few days with our children and friends. Neither of us had any idea yet what we were supposed to do concerning the mission's job that was offered to us before we left. All we could think of was, logically, if this was what was offered and nothing else was in our path, we should take it. That particular morning, still lying in bed, I could hear Riley and their children down in the living room area talking with George. I knew we wouldn't have any time for prayer alone so I prayed by myself up in bed. "Lord, I'm feeling like we've run out of time. We're returning to Albuquerque soon and we don't know what we're supposed to do. I just ask You to intervene between now and the time we get back. If we're supposed to do something other than this mission's position, please make it known to us." I no sooner ended that prayer when my cell phone rang. It took me by surprise when it happened because our cell phone hadn't been picking up a signal very well the whole time we were in the forest. I quickly answered the call. It was our friend Bill from Bisbee. He was calling to offer George a job working as a carpenter for him. He thought George would be perfect for the position. Not only was he offering him a job, he also had a house he had just bought and told us we could live in it. The house payment would be deducted from George's pay. It was the words that he said next that enticed us. "I know you both love the mission field. I would be willing to let you take off four times a year to do missions." After hanging up the phone, I shared with George what I had just prayed a minute before Bill's call came in. We were both intrigued by the timing of that call. We didn't want to make our decision based on the fact that the call came in right after my prayer, though, knowing that sometimes coincidences can be a distraction from what we really should be doing. Still, it was another option to pray about. The next week we mulled around our two choices, asking several friends for advice. I felt strongly that George was the one who needed to make the final decision no matter how I felt.

By the time we returned to Albuquerque, George was leaning toward working for Bill. He just didn't feel like the timing was quite right to jump back full-time into the ministry as a mission's director. He did like the idea of helping the church by taking down the groups the four times a year though, an opportunity that Bill's offer had left open for us. This way, we still had our foot in missions, and at the same time taking a break full-time. I liked his plan; we both had a peace about his decision. When we talked to the pastor that offered us the position of taking groups from his church to Mexico four times a year, he was all for it.

George and I both believe in and have experienced times in our lives when the Lord gives us choices. I think God wants us to make decisions and then move forward with them. Of course our decisions need to line up with scripture. But if a time comes when we don't get a direct answer from the Lord and it's time to make a move, we believe you move on it. So that's what we did. No matter what, as a Christian we have the promise: "All things work together for good to those that love God, to those that are called according to His purpose" (Romans 8:28).

We were excited about our new direction, and yet at the same time sad to leave our friends in Albuquerque. Somehow we knew we'd stay connected; our doing missions four times a year would hopefully involve many from the Albuquerque area.

Our care team once again jumped in to help. Most were able to travel with us to Sierra Vista, Arizona. We had more than one vehicle to drive, so we really needed the support. Of course, the trip turned out to be an adventurous one, as usual. The care team got to experience firsthand what it was like to travel with us. Nothing goes smoothly. Something is bound to happen, which it did. We borrowed a tow dolly from Larry, the pastor of the church we would be working with, to pull Laura's car behind the truck. One of the tires blew out on the tow trailer, the impact of the blow damaging the fender wheel. It delayed our caravan by a couple hours. We pulled off the side of the highway and found a piece of property that looked suitable to park the moving van, our vehicles, and the car our care team would be returning home in. Seeing a house next door, we thought it was only right to get permission from the homeowners to park our caravan on their property until we could obtain a tire from a nearby tire shop, and then repair the trailer there. A couple of people from our group approached the owners, who turned out to be very hospitable and willing for us to stay there until we fixed the problem.

As George and one of the men went to look for a tire, we noticed the beautiful field in front of us with a nice big shade tree out in the distance. We hiked over to the tree and plopped ourselves down. It was proving to be a comfortable waiting place, up until I started sneezing. Unbeknown to us, we were sitting amongst a patch of ragweed plants, which I am highly allergic to.

Meanwhile, George and our friend found a tire shop that turned out to be the only tire shop in town. Business was getting ready to close for the day. They happened to have one tire in the size we needed. The Lord is so good, even in the little things of life. George bought the tire. The caravan was up and moving in no time at all.

We were so blessed to have our group along. It always seems a lot easier to handle a trial when there's more. Having many hands to help move all our possessions into the house was another blessing.

Most of us camped out on the floor for the night. Waking up early the next morning, after we got a bite to eat, our care team prayed over us and then got on their way back to Albuquerque. We were ready to begin a new phase of life once again. This time it would be a lot different than what we were used to: an eight-to-five job! It all seemed so odd. We hadn't lived like this in twenty years. Would we be able to adapt to staying put?

*

All seemed to be going fairly well in our new lifestyle. George enjoyed building cabinets and learning new carpentry techniques. We had always wanted to join a health club but never could because we were always traveling. Taking advantage of our "stay put" status, now was the time to do it. As it was my last year of home schooling Laura, I wanted to make our time together memorable. Meanwhile, the church that offered us the position in New Mexico continued to contact George to plan for an outreach to Mexico among the

Tarahumara Indians. I could tell George's heart was still in the work of the Lord. He lit up every time he talked about going. Every spare moment, he was mapping and planning the outreach. The pastor was a pilot, so he was able to fly in to visit us and to make plans with George. Three months into working with Bill, it was now time for George's first of four trips a year.

Needing time to first survey the area in Mexico, George was looking for two extra weeks of time off. Bill was gracious enough to give him more time than the agreement stated, since his heart was into missions also. I decided to stay home with Laura, because it seemed easier to home school her in the States. Besides, she was working at a local mall. She couldn't just pick up for two weeks.

Arriving home from the outreach, George was floating around on cloud nine. That's all he could talk about. The trip had turned out to be such a success, totally anointed, and the team of people he went with was very nice to work alongside. Fourteen Tarahumaras had given their lives to the Lord. This is a very conservative indigenous tribe. They don't easily get moved. During the outreach, the team also provided a medical and dental clinic and many people were helped physically. Everyone involved was stoked with excitement as they saw the hand of God mightily at work. George could hardly wait for the next mission's trip he could go on. Waiting three months to go on another trip seemed so far off. Meanwhile, plans were moving along quite rapidly on the other end. The tribal community wanted to donate a piece of property to the church in the hope that they would build a community building. They were willing to allow the building to hold church services for the new believers. Meantime, the church outside Albuquerque was looking for George's time to set that all up.

George approached Bill once again to explain what was going on in this little Mexican village. Bill was excited as well to see what God was doing down there, so again he let George go a little earlier than planned. Yet as the demands to be in Mexico to plan the next outreach with medical teams approached, George was realizing that once again he needed to be there ahead of time. Trying to juggle cabinetry work and deal with the mission field, it soon dawned on us that we couldn't have both and do a good job with either. Bill at the same time was recognizing that it wasn't working out. He came to us one night and opened up. "George, I have realized that your heart is in missions. I should have known better than to try and hire a missionary. You'll never be fully satisfied until your back into the work of the Lord one hundred percent of the time. You need to go back into missions full-time."

We knew it too. We enjoyed the house, the regular weekly paychecks and the health club, yet we didn't feel quite complete. Going back on the mission field was a draw that we couldn't ignore. By June the following year, we made a commitment to move back to the Albuquerque area and work with the east mountain church.

It was time for Laura's graduation weeks before our move. She planned to move to Flagstaff and live with Jonathon and his wife, Cristina, so we had the empty nest fast approaching us too. Going back into missions full-time was going to be a busy time for us, so the transition, I thought, would keep me from dwelling on my loss of not having her around.

Plans were set. The move would take place in June, with us going back to the same house we previously lived in before going to Sierra Vista. We were ready for the mission field once again.

Therefore we do not lose heart. Even though
our outward man is perishing,
yet the inward man
is being renewed day by day.
For our light affliction,
which is but for a moment, is working for us
a far more exceeding and eternal
weight of glory,
while we do not look at the things
which are seen,
but at the things which are not seen.
For the things which are seen are temporary,
but the things which are not seen are eternal.

2 Corinthians 4:16-18

19
Cancer Journey

The next six months with the mission's department at the east mountain church was truly a gift from God. We met so many beautiful people. The fellowship was rich, to say the least. Our survey trips and outreaches were equally rich. The word "missions" became a common phrase in the church. Old and young alike got involved. Missions were running thickly through our veins. By January, we realized that the church was capable of doing missions on its own. Several people had been down in the area we had been targeting throughout the last half year.

There was a growing need in the nearby Mexican village that happened to be the first village we visited back in 1984 with our friends Aaron and Theresa. Our hearts were tender toward them. On one of our survey trips we visited a missionary couple that lived in the village. Our eyes were opened at this time to the lack of food in this area throughout the winter months. The people's diet consisted of corn and chilies. When the missionaries shared with us that they would be leaving this village soon and moving to the other one, we saw the vision to help not only spiritually, but also to help the people develop a diet of fruits and vegetables. This vision would take up a lot of time and energy, yet we were willing to dedicate the rest of our lives learning the Tarahumara language, developing relationships, and helping the people to build a better life for themselves. If this is what the Lord wanted for us, we were committed to give it our all.

We prayed about it. The Lord wasn't saying "no", so that must mean it was all right to follow our vision. However, making plans to leave Albuquerque and move to Mexico full-time was going to be a leap of faith on my part.

The first phase of the ministry would entail learning the language. This language was not an easy one to learn, yet with the Lord's help, it could be conquered. Meanwhile, during our time of learning, we would have a good opportunity to build relationships with others. There was a nearby village a few hours from where we planned to plant ourselves. It was quite a bit bigger, so it seemed to offer more of a chance of hooking up with someone to teach us the language. Starting out in this town, improving our language skills and learning to understand more about the culture, would give us the time to make our way slowly into the village we had our hearts set on.

We were two weeks away from leaving the United States again to start our new adventure in Mexico. I was compelled to fast and pray about our new ministry, among other things. It was Monday morning. This is what I prayed: "Lord, George and I are ready to jump into this ministry that will probably take us until we're old. I want to do this ministry with all my might. I want to give it my all. If somehow this is not what You have for George and me, if You have another plan for us, I ask that You intervene between now and two weeks from now and stop us from going." Sometimes when we pray we don't realize nor understand the depth of what we're asking. It was that following Sunday that George was diagnosed with cancer and given only a short time to live.

As I sat alone in the hospital room next to George, wrapped in my thoughts, staring out the window, I now recalled my prayer to the Lord. Mexico was not the plan God had for us. That was not the place we would be pouring the rest of our lives into. I pondered many things. It wasn't until the doctor came into George's room and told me that we would receive the results of the bone marrow test the following day that despair started setting in. I couldn't drive home that evening because I don't see well at night, so Tyler and Rachel invited me to stay with them at their home.

The next morning, as I awoke to face another difficult day, I felt I just couldn't take it any longer. Fear and loneliness set in like never before. I felt so alone, and the thought of dealing with George's death was more then I could bear. Have you ever cried so hard that you found yourself gasping for air because you can't breathe? I was in that state. "Lord!" I cried out from the depth of my heart, "Help me!" The Lord, as usual, met me right where I was at. In His soft loving way, He spoke to my heart. "Jennifer, what are you asking of me?"

"I need You to heal George!" I said.

"Why?" He said ever so plainly.

"Because I love him," I responded.

"Go a little bit deeper with that thought. Why do you really want Me to keep him here and not take him home to be with me?" my Lord spoke in a still, quiet way.

I suddenly realized that if the Lord took George home he would be in glory land for eternity. For me to ask God to keep him here came from a purely selfish motive. Yet I couldn't bear the thought of going on without him. I began to dialogue with the Lord again. "Lord, even though I know he would be a lot better off with You, You have brought us through so much so we could be used in ministry. We work so well together. We make a good team." Imagine that! I found myself trying to convince God how important it was to keep George here on earth. Then the Lord showed me something incredibly awesome! He took me to a scene in the Bible where Jesus was in the garden of Gethsemane. Even though Jesus is fully God, He was fully human. He knew what was before Him: being crucified on the cross. I cannot imagine how overwhelming this moment was for Him. He prayed before the Father, "Oh My Father, if it is possible, let this cup pass from Me; nevertheless, not as I will, but as You will" (Matthew 26:39).

At that moment, I saw the omnipotence of God in a new light. God is God and I'm not. He knows all things! What if I was asking Him to keep George alive, yet it was really better that He takes him home now? This was a pretty profound moment for me. Then, just as soon as I came to grips with this new knowledge, the Lord reminded me that we can ask Him anything in His name, and if it's His will, He'll give it to us (John 14:14). I knew without a doubt right then that God would let George stay here on earth with me if this was the best plan for both of us. I also knew God wanted the best for our lives and I could trust Him to be in control. From the sincerity of my heart I looked up with confidence and prayed this prayer: "Lord, I ask in the name of Jesus to heal George from this cancer, and in this healing let people around us see how real and powerful You really are, but God, nevertheless, not my will but Your will be done."

Immediately following this prayer, I felt the peace of God envelop me. I knew I could go on. In my weakness He was made strong (2 Corinthians 12:10b). You know that nice popular Christian footprints story many of us have heard, about how Jesus picks us up and carries us in our deepest trials, and how the person who was lifted could see only one set of footprints in the sand? This was actually my experience the rest of our cancer journey.

That morning, I got out of bed and prepared myself for the day. Before going back over to the hospital to see George, I stopped by the local department store to pick up a few items for him. As Rachel and I were standing at the checkout counter ready to pay, the cashier asked us the most random question. "Are you two teachers?"

With baffled looks, we both at once answered, "No".

After a few seconds of silence, curiosity got the best of me. "Why did you ask us that?"

"Because I have noticed some of the happiest people in life happen to be teachers." She paused. "So then, why are you so happy in life?"

I couldn't believe those words just came out of her mouth. Just an hour earlier I was in the depths of despair and now someone is actually asking me why I'm so happy in life. I knew the hand of God was on me; she was seeing His presence covering me.

Good thing the Lord was carrying me because I was going to need it for what I was getting ready to go through. The doctors told George and me that he must have surgery at once to remove the tumor in his brain. The continuing pressure of that tumor would cause continued seizures. We agreed to go through with it. Meanwhile, the doctor took me aside and explained that even though he was a good experienced surgeon, this kind of surgery was quite dangerous. He told me to prepare myself with the fact that George just might not come out of this alive. Before the surgery, I remember sitting in the waiting room asking myself, "Now, how do I go about preparing myself for this?"

Talk about a blessing! Most of our care team, along with George's brother and another close friend, showed up to be with me during the five hour wait it would take for the surgery. Trying to assure myself and the Lord that if George didn't come out of this alive, I was ready to receive what He had for me for the future. Yet I kept adding, "Lord, my flesh is weak. You'll have to get me through this next step if you decide to take him home, moment by moment." George was covered in prayer by many people. This was no time not to trust in God. (Is there any time in life not to trust in God?)

The five hour wait was almost up. I was now calling on the Lord for His strength more than ever as I could feel my heart pounding against my chest. As the surgeon walked through the door, I instantly knew George had pulled through the surgery by the expression on his face. "It went quite well. He's going to be all right," were the sweet words that I had longed to hear. Grabbing hold of him and hugging him tightly, with tears flowing down my cheeks, I couldn't thank him enough. And then deep within my soul, I cried out to my Lord with a heart of thanksgiving for giving me more time with George.

The doctor then went on to explain to me that this surgery might have paralyzed the left side of George's body, noting that even if that did happen, with some physical therapy he might be able to gain much of his strength back. He added that radiation was next in line, since many cells left in the blood could still be cancerous. Meanwhile, as George was in intensive care, the oncologist began talking about a second surgery to remove his kidney. "As we're talking, the cancer in his kidney is spreading throughout his body," were her words. "You don't have time to waste."

I didn't have peace about putting George through another surgery, especially after what he had just undergone. We would need to wait until he was able to discuss this next phase of treatment that they wanted to do.

It was wonderful to see how quickly he came around, a bit detached and very tired, and yet coherent enough to hold a normal conversation. The surgery did leave his left side paralyzed just as the doctor had suspected, yet I was very hopeful that he would gain it all back in due time through physical therapy. Peace was at my side concerning this area.

What was consuming my thoughts during this time was the next decision that needed to be made about his kidney being removed. George was very compliant and went along with whatever the doctors thought he needed. I was not. I needed to talk directly with the kidney surgeon. My biggest concern was if they removed his kidney and the cancer cells had moved into the other kidney without yet being detected, where would this leave him? What would be the next step? Nonchalantly, the doctor said, "Of course, we would then take the other kidney out and put him on dialysis." This doesn't sound bad in itself, to go through all the painstaking sacrifice to get there, if we were talking about a person who would then be free of cancer, but they were telling us that even if he were to have these procedures done there was still no hope of him living. The oncologist told George's brother that he had less than three months to live.

I was extremely uneasy about this whole idea of removing his kidney or kidneys. George asked me what "Plan B" would be if we didn't go along with "Plan A". Days earlier, I had been pondering the notion of going to Mexico to have George treated there. I remembered reading a book on health some years ago. At the end of the book, it had mentioned a Christian hospital in Tijuana that treated cancer patients. What impressed me about this place was that not only did it treat the physical body, but it also talked about treating the patient emotionally and spiritually. After reading it, I remember saying to myself, "If I ever get cancer, that's where I want to go to get treated." The name of the hospital didn't come to mind, just the memory of it being in Tijuana. So I brought up my thoughts to him about going there. Since the doctors here only gave him a short time to live anyway, it seemed only reasonable to take another course: to go to a hospital that offered a different agenda, one of totally detoxifying his body of all impurities, putting him on an all-natural organic diet, and receiving more prayer from the missionaries that ministered there. We would make him as comfortable as possible until the Lord took him home.

George didn't buy my idea. He felt more at ease about going with "Plan A". He assured me that until he felt strong enough for the next surgery he would wait. For some reason, I couldn't accept what he was saying to me. I just knew: you know that gut feeling one gets when you are sure without a doubt this is not what is supposed to happen. Trying to convince him of this wasn't working. The stronger and firmer the communication from me, the more apt he was to do it his way. My hope that our friends would see it my way and help me to change George's mind didn't help either. Some of them thought I had gone over the deep end. Yet when one of my friends who shares the same interest in natural health and healing as I do came to visit and brought a book for us to read that happened to be about the very hospital I was talking about, I was more convinced than ever that God's hand was in this. I even read the book to George. His final words on the subject were, "The doctors are professionals. They know what's best for me. I'm going to do what they say." I was so frustrated. Leaving his room, feeling totally defeated, I sat outside his closed door and started to weep. "God, why can't anyone see what I see? I have no support here!" In the middle of my pity party, two of our dear friends came up to the door. They had come to visit George but instead found me crying my eyes out. They tried to console me, assuming that I was crying over George's condition. When I explained to them why I was really crying, my friend, who has lots of wisdom, spoke these words to me. "Jennifer, this is George's body and his life. He needs to make the decision for what he believes is right. If he has a peace about going through with the surgery, then you need to support him as his wife. You need to bring as much comfort and support to him as possible, especially right now while he is so weak." His words penetrated my heart. I received his counsel fully.

My next thoughts that followed were, "What if I talked George into going to Mexico and he died there." I'd never be able to forgive myself. I knew it would be a hard thing to live with. My friends and his family might always hold that against me too. My friend was right. It was George's decision to make, not mine. I thanked them for their advice and wise counsel.

Alone in the room with George after our friends had left, I felt an apology was in order for the way I had behaved in trying to bully him into seeing it my way. From here on out, whatever he wanted done, I would support his every decision one hundred percent. Whatever the request, I would be there to back him up. Although my thoughts still hadn't changed about going to Mexico, I still saw that this was the better choice; only God could intervene now. My prayers turned inward to ask God to please change George's heart if this was His will for him. "Let him see this on his own and be convinced this is what he's supposed to do," I pleaded. I left it at that.

God works in mysterious ways. Early the next morning, at around 4 a.m., George couldn't sleep. He turned on the television to pass the time away. As he was flipping through the channels, he came upon an advertisement on health. A woman doctor was talking about how she was healed of cancer. It caught his attention. She went on to say through eating wholesomely and changing her lifestyle, besides surrendering her life to the Lord, she had been healed from cancer.

I was sound asleep in one of those hospital chairs that fold out into a bed. Awakened by my husband trying to get my attention before the commercial ended, I heard George saying loudly, "Honey... Honey... Wake up! You need to hear what this doctor is saying!" Sitting up in bed and trying to concentrate as much as possible after coming out of a deep sleep, I was quite pleased to hear what she was saying: almost exactly what I had been trying to tell him for days. Maybe because she was a doctor her words had more credibility. Anyway, it didn't matter. Suddenly, George was saying to me, "I want to go to Mexico. Call them up today and get all of the details."

As I lay down, I silently prayed, "Thank you, Lord!" I knew that I knew that this was the right avenue for us to follow. And it was George's decision (of course, with the help of the Lord).

We didn't plan to tell anyone about our change of plans to go to Mexico until all the arrangements were made, having a sneaking suspicion we were going to get a lot of flack for our decision. I called the hospital in Tijuana as George had requested. They were very informative on what the protocol would be. They would detoxify his body through various alternative treatments, and put him on a good healthy diet. They had Christian missionaries who would be there to pray for us during the treatment. It was such a delight to hear them echo what I had believed the hospital would be able to do for us, until they mentioned the price: twenty thousand dollars! They would need the money up front. There was no payment plan. My heart sank. Hanging up the phone, I looked over at George a bit despondent. "Well, it looks like we won't be going to Mexico after all," I said.

"Why?" George asked, surprised.

"Because it costs twenty thousand dollars to do the type of treatment we want for you," I answered.

"Now, honey, since when is twenty thousand dollars a problem for the Lord? If He wills for us to go to Mexico for treatment, He'll give us the provision to go."

The faith George displays has always put me to shame. To tell you the truth, at that moment I didn't have the faith to carry me through on this one. I shouldn't say I was completely without faith. I looked up and said silently to the Lord, "Lord, I believe you can give us ten thousand dollars, but not twenty thousand dollars." Don't ask yourself why I thought the Lord could only provide ten thousand dollars. To this day, I shake my head at my unbelief. The only thing that comes to mind that gives any justification to my behavior is that the Lord gives us each a measure of faith (Romans 12:3), and this is the measure of faith I had for the day. Anyway, I knew if I shared my feelings with George that afternoon, we would end up getting into one of our "faith" arguments. He was so physically weak, so I didn't want to stir him up. Appeasement seemed like the road to take. "Honey, you're right. If God wants us to go to Mexico, He'll give us all the money we need."

It hadn't been two hours after our conversation on Mexico when we received a visit from some friends we hadn't seen in a while. We all greeted each other with a round of hugs. As they were sitting down and getting comfortable in the chairs situated next to the bed George was lying on, one of them handed me a card. We continued to talk while I was opening the envelope. I couldn't believe what I was looking at upon opening it: a check written out for eleven thousand dollars! Suddenly, I heard the small still voice of the Lord speaking to me. "Jennifer, your faith went to ten thousand dollars. Here's eleven thousand dollars. Now make the reservations at the hospital. You're both going to Mexico." I broke out in tears, happy tears, because of the tremendous blessing that was just bestowed on us, and at the same time feeling the shame and lack of faith for not believing the Lord could provide for us. "Lord, I'm just like the Israelites who were out in the desert for forty years. You continued to bless them daily and they continued in disbelief when things got tough. I'm no different," I was saying silently. Nobody, not even George, knew what was going on in my heart with God. Turning my attention to our friends, I asked them the purpose of the eleven thousand dollars. (They had no idea we were planning to go to Mexico.)

They answered, "Well, you know, this morning we were praying to the Lord and He told us to give you this money. So, it's for whatever God tells you to do with it."

I handed the check to George and tears quickly welled up in his eyes too. We decided to tell them about our plans to go to Mexico to get treatment. We were also happy they were accepting of our decision to go.

After they left, I confessed to George my lack of faith in believing the Lord could only give us ten thousand dollars. He thought it was just as ridiculous a notion as I did, but nonetheless was excited to know this was the Lord's will for him. The call was made and reservations secured for us to come in two weeks. Meanwhile, we would need to concentrate on physical therapy and go through the radiation treatments (only in the brain) that the doctors at this hospital had suggested he do. The timing was perfect. The treatments would take exactly two weeks. Our departure was on the same day his last radiation treatment would take place.

The day before they were ready to release George from the hospital is when the reality of his condition really hit me, and it hit me like a ton of bricks. The therapist asked me to come to a room with her so she could show me what would be required at home to take care of him. The room was filled with different devices such as half of a car with the passenger side of the door displayed, a bathtub with a chair inside used to help those in need of bathing to accomplish it more efficiently, as well as wheelchairs, walkers and the like. Walking over to the tub, she assured me that this was a purchase that I would definitely need for George. Showing me the walker display, she suggested we use the cane with the four feet. It was when she began talking about a wheelchair that I suddenly found myself beginning to panic inside. For a moment I wanted to find a closet and go hide so I could cry my eyes out by myself and have a pity party, yet I knew this was no time to be a coward. I needed to be strong, especially for George's sake.

With the directions in hand to the store that sold these different items, I needed to get on my way before they closed. What a blessing it was to have my friend Rachel along for moral support through this whole process. When we arrived, the salesperson was so kind and helpful. She found the best bathtub seat for the price available, and gave the four-legged walker to me for free. They were going out of business and had a few things up for donation. When it came to looking at the wheelchairs, my emotions locked up. I couldn't accept the fact that George was going to need a wheelchair. "I don't think I'll buy the wheelchair today," I said politely, moving away from the door to the room that stored them all. Rachel looked at me somewhat surprised, yet didn't say a word.

Once we got into the car, I explained to her that I just couldn't get myself to purchase the chair. "Maybe tomorrow I'll buy it," I said in an unsure voice.

"George is getting out tomorrow. You'll need it then," she said, trying to help me make the right choice in the moment. Still feeling locked up inside emotionally, I drove away.

Once we returned to the hospital, I related to George the two items I was able to obtain, sharing the excitement about getting the walker for free. "What about the wheelchair?" he asked. I was hoping he wouldn't bring up that subject.

"Well, honey, I didn't buy you one," I said sheepishly.

"Why?"

I could tell from the tone of his voice that he was not happy with my decision. "I don't know. I just couldn't emotionally go through with it. Tomorrow I'll buy you one," I promised, still upset inside.

He wasn't too happy with me, but he let it go until the next day. As the nurse was wheeling him to our vehicle parked outside, seeing the necessity of a wheelchair, George brought up the subject again. "We'll buy one later," I assured him again. "We can use the walker in the meantime." He did manage to stand up and get into the car, then get back out of the car and walk into the house with the aid of the four-legged walker. I could see how well he had progressed in his physical therapy classes. I was sure he could at least make it to the bedroom with the walker, and he proved me right.

Each day as George got up to go to the hospital for his therapy classes and radiation treatments, he just used the walker. By the end of the two weeks, now ready to go to Mexico, he was walking just fine. Thanking our Lord was in order for such a quick recovery of the use of George's left side. He had improved considerably since his discharge from the hospital. We knew his left side would get stronger and stronger, and my dread of having to purchase a wheelchair subsided. And added to the blessing of his physical recovery was that the Lord was faithfully bringing in the rest of the money we needed to go to the hospital in Mexico in two weeks' time. We even had fifty dollars extra for spending money, and two round trip plane tickets purchased for us to fly to San Diego. We hadn't even thought of flying. We were going to drive there and back until some dear missionary friends offered to buy our tickets. So much love and kindness was poured out on us through our friends and family. We were now ready to go.

On the day we arrived in Mexico, the hospital had more patients than usual. We were placed on the intensive care floor until another room became available upstairs. We didn't care; we found our room comfortable enough in the meantime. We also were pleased that they had placed us across the hall from a lovely couple from Australia we had met on the shuttle van on the way to the hospital.

Looking at the schedule of events planned for the patients for the following day, we noticed one of the programs was a question-and-answer session hosted by the president of the hospital. This was one class we wanted to sit in on. So we went. As the doctor opened up for questions, without hesitation George raised his hand. When the doctor pointed at him to speak, George brought up a question pertaining to kidney cancer. The question prompted the doctor to ask, "Are you George Swanson?"

"Yes, I am," he replied, surprised.

The doctor answered George's question and then added at the end of his dissertation, "We can't find any evidence of cancer in your kidney, or anywhere in your body for that matter, so we need to run some more extensive tests on you." Then he said, "Next!" and pointed to someone else.

I wish someone could have captured the expression on George's and my face about ten seconds after the doctor said what he said. I leaned over to George and murmured, "Now, what did he say?" not sure that I had heard him correctly.

George leaned back over to me and said quietly, "I think he just told us that I don't have cancer."

"Oh," I responded, expressionless, not yet processing what was really said. Five seconds elapsed when both of us at the same time made a loud "uhh" sound in the room. Those that were watching us started to chuckle.

It was torturous to sit there for the rest of the meeting. We were both fidgeting in our seats, waiting to get more information on what the doctor actually meant by what he said earlier.

When the meeting finally did end, the doctor told us they would come to our room and talk with us. George hadn't even started on his treatment yet. How could this be? A million thoughts were running through our minds as we waited.

When our doctor came in to talk with us, he confirmed what the president of the hospital had told us in the meeting. They could not find a trace of cancer in George's body. He told us in forty years they had never seen a case like this. The brain tumor that was removed from his head was diagnosed as Renal Cell Carcinoma, which only comes from the kidney. They didn't even see scar tissue in either kidney, so they wanted to bring in a specialist from outside the hospital to run a more extensive CT scan throughout his kidneys. They also told us that after doing blood work on George, not only did he not have any tumor markers, but his blood showed no signs of gout. "You are a very healthy man," the doctor added before leaving the room.

"Well, what about my treatment here? Can I have my money back?" George said, half kidding.

"Yes, we will refund your money if you would like, but since you are here you should still go through the detoxification you were planning to do. It will boost your immune system. You'll be that much stronger," the doctor remarked. We decided to go through with the eighteen day treatment.

We didn't call anyone for the first week to tell them the good news. Still processing what was happening, we felt it was very important to make sure the doctors were absolutely positive there was no cancer before telling everyone God healed George. Meanwhile, as he was going through with treatments, he was completely wiped out. Mostly he just wanted to sleep and rest.

During George's times of rest, I left the room to find something to do. Since we were on the intensive care floor, each day I found people sitting in the halls crying for their loved ones who were in a serious condition or dying. Compassion swept over me. I knew exactly what the companions were experiencing, having been on the same journey. Words of hope and encouragement poured out of me as I shared the love of God and His mighty power. I was able to share first-hand what God had done for us. I did whatever I could to help encourage those that the Lord put in my path. A lot of prayer went out in those hallways.

One day, having left my room at nine a.m., the need was so great that I stayed out in the hall ministering until nine o'clock in the evening. By the time I arrived back in our room, exhaustion had taken over. Plopping myself down on the bed, I turned to the Lord. "You know, Lord, I'm so tired," then going on to say, "I paid twenty thousand dollars to come here. I shouldn't have to labor this hard."

The Lord spoke back to my heart. "No, you didn't pay twenty thousand dollars to come here. I paid twenty thousand dollars for you to come here."

"Oh, yeah, it wasn't me, it was You." I agreed immediately. It was at that moment that it all made sense to me.
I had earlier been pondering this whole Mexico trip. Why
didn't the Lord just heal George in the U.S? Why did we
need to come all the way here and go through this? Now I
knew why.

I brought up to George the idea of applying for the
missionary position at the hospital. Because God had healed
George, we knew He wasn't finished with him yet. He
immediately liked the idea too. It was settled between us.
We would talk with the missionaries that were on duty to
find out all the details.

The directors of the missions department happened to
be on vacation, but they were expected back days before
George's treatment would be finished. The timing was
perfect. They were willing to meet with us the day before we
left. We went through the interview, feeling that it went well.
Although they mentioned we were a good fit for the position,
there was one slight problem. According to their policy, any
former patient would have to be clear of cancer for two years
before applying. Still, according to their records, George
never had cancer when he came into the hospital. This case
would have to be left up to the CEO. Meanwhile we needed
to wait a little longer for George to gain more of his strength.
We felt confident that we could lean on God's perfect timing
if this was His will for us to minister there. As we waited, the
directors requested we send our resumes along with other
paperwork needed to complete the process.

After receiving the results of all the tests and blood work
the hospital had taken, we felt it was time to divulge to our
family and friends the news of George's miraculous healing
and what God had done for us. The responses from different
people were interesting to observe. Most of us are willing to
pray for others when they are sick. Yet when God decides
to answer that prayer, for some of us it's hard to believe it

really does happen. (This is the same God who parted the Red Sea in the Old Testament in Hebrews 13:8. He's the same yesterday as He is today and forever.)

Coming back to Albuquerque, we were overjoyed. We just couldn't quit talking about the mighty hand of God. Everywhere we went, we shared our exciting news.

Although George was healed of cancer, he still needed to work on the left side of his body. He checked into physical therapy again, several times a week. His strength was coming back more quickly than they had expected. We thanked the Lord daily as we watched him progress.

In the midst of all that was happening with us, our dear friend's son was killed in Iraq. Our joy turned into mourning as we grieved their loss. Wanting to be there for them through this dark time, we felt plans to travel to Flagstaff to attend the funeral took priority. Upon awaking the morning after we heard the news, however, we discovered some fluid coming out from the incision on top of George's head where the brain surgery had been done. After taking a closer look, I could see clearly that it wasn't healing properly. Reasoning that since radiation kills cells, it made sense that the cells around the cut would not be able to carry on their proper function; yet that still soft voice inside said to get his head checked out before leaving on our trip.

After waiting in the outer office several hours for the doctor's evaluation, he finally called us back. The expression on his face wasn't good. Without delay, he told us the bad news. George had contracted a serious staph infection. Concerned that it had traveled into George's head, the doctor insisted he take George back into surgery to reopen the incision on the top of his head and make sure it hadn't reached his brain. There was no time to waste. This needed to be done immediately; the surgery was scheduled for that very afternoon. It was dawning on me that our hospital journey was not over yet. Again, I called on the Lord for His peace, mercy, and grace to sustain us through this next phase of whatever we were about to encounter.

The good news was the staph infection had not gotten into George's brain; the bad news was that it had spread throughout the rest of his body. He would have to be placed in the acute ward of the hospital for two months while they injected him with high doses of a very potent antibiotic.

I remember gazing out the hospital window of George's room again, wondering how I was going to handle this trial for eight weeks, day after day after day. The Lord always shows up in our darkest moments. In my wondering, the Lord spoke to my heart. "Look at this experience as if you were checking into a school for two months' training. I will be teaching you and preparing you for the things you will need in life."

Looking at it from that perspective, it seemed like an easier task to overcome. "Lord, I can do anything in You," I answered.

Without the Lord I would have never endured the next two months. Each day I watched as George just lay there in bed, getting weaker and weaker. Not only did he lose his energy, he lost his appetite. He would take a few bites of his food and then push it aside. He obviously began to lose weight. Throughout the length of his stay, he lost approximately fifty pounds. He looked horrible. I just could hardly stand to see what was happening. Here God healed him from cancer only to have this take place. I knew I needed to take charge of what was going on. I had to become a companion who wasn't going to sit on the sidelines while he got weaker. He needed to be prodded and encouraged to get up and out of the bed even though he didn't feel like it. Those bones needed moving. For starters, I went to the health food store every day for the wholesome food needed to strengthen him.

At first George was quite resistant to my suggestions. If he were writing this story, he would have changed the word "suggestion" to "commands". He began to call me "Gunner Sergeant Jennifer". Every day I would tell him how important it was to get up out of bed and walk down the hall and back, and each day he would refuse. Yet when he realized I wasn't going to let up until he got up and walked down the hall and back, he would do it to just get me off his back. Then when he got back into bed, I pulled my guitar out and sang and played a song to bring calmness to the room. I spent many hours reading stories to him too. Even though his body said "no" each day, he was finding it easier and easier to get up and move around. Our prayers and the prayers of others were the real strength behind his gradual recovery. It blessed me the day the doctor's assistant told me that after they left our room one day, the doctor commented, "That room is not like the other rooms we go into. It's so bright and cheery and so full of light." He felt the presence of God in there.

Two months seemed like an eternity, yet the day finally arrived when the infection was cleared up. Now we faced another dilemma. The incision on the top of George's head still had not healed. What would prevent him from getting another staph infection? A plastic surgeon came in to look at his head. He suggested that making a new incision in the same area and then closing the incision again would help it to heal. Since we didn't have any more promising options, we decided to go through with it. Within days after being released from the hospital, we were in the surgeon's office having the procedure done. George came through with flying colors. Hopefully he was fixed and we could get on with some normalcy of life.

Once we got back into our home, I noticed George starting to bounce back much more quickly. Regaining his appetite was a good sign and gave me more confidence he was going to be all right. He didn't even need to be prodded to get out of bed anymore.

It was when we began to come out of that heavy duty cancer journey that we shared with one another the incredible, intimate times we both experienced with God. George was in such awe of his memories of how God manifested Himself to him in such real, deep, special ways, that he told me he would go through the journey again just to have the closeness to God that he had then. Even though he often has special close times with the Lord on different occasions, George was especially blessed to know that, through his very darkest moments, God was right there with him.

Another wonderful blessing George received besides being healed was the fellowship of the believers. He had known before that he had friends, yet when his doctor came to me privately and told me too much stimulation from all the people that were coming to visit was not good for his health, it was actually quite a compliment. The nurses said his room had more visitors than that whole floor had in two years. We recognized during this journey how rich we really are, and where our riches lie.

You will keep him in perfect peace,
Whose mind is stayed on You,
Because he trusts in You.

Isaiah 26:3

20
Thank You Tour

As George's health continued to progress, so did his energy level for ministry. He came to me one day and expressed his desires of going on the road again to visit our family and friends across America to thank them personally for their prayer support. I was more than ready to go along with his plans.

We had sold our fifth wheel the year before, so we would need to purchase another one. Knowing it would be costly to stay in hotels and eat in restaurants, we knew this was the answer for us. We only had two thousand five hundred dollars in the bank, so the Lord would have to intervene once again. The faith was there on both our parts to wait upon God to see if this was His will for us or not. It was just a matter of waiting.

We always enjoy looking, even if we don't have the money. The fifth wheels we saw were either way overpriced or falling apart. Going for an older one wasn't out of the question, just as long as it was solid and could keep the rain out. Then one day it happened. As we were visiting with some friends, Peter mentioned to us a friend had offered to sell him a fifth wheel for two thousand five hundred dollars. Peter had no idea that we had just about that much in the bank. Our ears perked up. "I'm sure he would let you have it for the same price he offered it to me," he said assuredly.

"Give him a call; it won't hurt to look." We took his advice and called.

It was difficult to see what the trailer really looked like inside because the owner was using it for storage, yet after talking with him and looking it over very closely and seeing that everything was working, we knew it would be a good one for us. Especially the price! There isn't much we were going to get for two thousand five hundred dollars. Looking at the market beforehand as we had done, we were well aware we were getting a good deal. So we reduced our bank account to zero and again became the proud owners of another fifth wheel. It would take faith for this one, because the trailer was in desperate need of tires before going much farther than Albuquerque. Once again, we planned to wait on the Lord. Meanwhile, we started to clean it out. That was free!

Our wait didn't turn out to be a long one. Within the week, the Lord provided all the money that was needed. We had decided to gather a few close friends over for a potluck luncheon that following Sunday. Just about the time everyone was saying their good-byes, several friends wanted a tour of our new rig. We were eager to show them; as they all came inside we told them all about our wonderful bargain the Lord had given us. When one friend walked outside and noticed the bald tires, she exclaimed, "Before you go, you must change out these tires, they're terrible." We agreed, assuring her that it was on our agenda to do so before leaving. She spoke up again. "You know, I would like to pitch in and help you buy those. How much do you think they'll cost, about five hundred dollars?" As she was talking, she was writing out a check. She folded it and handed it to us. We felt so grateful for her generosity, but even more blessed by the love she demonstrated.

After everyone left, we went inside and began to talk about purchasing tires, both of us very excited. Our sense of the Lord's confirmation about going on this trip became even more prevalent to us when we opened the check and realized there wasn't just five hundred dollars for tires. She had written the check out for two thousand five hundred dollars, exactly the amount we had in the bank before we bought the fifth wheel! These plans were now becoming a reality.

The following week, we purchased the tires, loaded up our clothes, dishes and other miscellaneous items, and were on our way. Back on the highway again!

We first headed to the Midwest to see our families, stopping to see friends on the way. By the time we came back down to the Southwest we still had the same amount in the bank as when we left. If that wasn't astonishing enough, one of the most phenomenal things that occurred on this trip was finding ourselves in fellowships where, unknown to us, the people we were visiting had been praying for us. In one instance, we were in southern Arizona visiting some dear friends. In a nearby town there was a couple we also wanted to visit. The only problem was that this particular family could only visit with us on the upcoming Sunday afternoon. They were involved with a Bible study, so they invited us to go with them and visit after the study. We wanted to be supportive, so we agreed to meet them there. Little did we know, it was a home church. The upstairs of the house was set up just like a church building. They even had their own worship band. Before the church service started, our friends introduced us to the group as the family they had been praying for to be healed of cancer. The pastor was excited to hear about George's healing. He asked us both to get up and share our journey. Here was a group of people we didn't even know and yet they had been praying for us. We were on a "thank you" tour and the Lord was leading us to the ones He wanted us to thank personally.

It kept happening to us this way. We were thrilled to experience the leading of the Lord. I've learned when we're a part of the family of God there's a whole network of people out there praying because God puts it on our hearts to do so. What a blessing to be a part of the family of God!

*

We only planned to be on the road for the summer. We also wanted to resell the trailer when we got home. It wasn't until the hospital in Mexico called us and asked us to come to work there that we knew we wouldn't be going back home until October. We parked our trailer on a friend's property and headed to Tijuana to begin a new adventure, and what an adventure! This was our first time back into ministry since the cancer journey. It was thrilling to be on the mission field once again, especially with my healthy husband by my side. George's energy level still wasn't back to normal, yet I knew in time the Lord would restore his strength little by little.

As we worked at the hospital, we found each day filled with new challenges. I realized immediately that if George and I hadn't gone through the trials the Lord had taken us through, there would be no way we could have ministered to the people there. Many patients would start out by telling us we couldn't possibly understand what they felt. It wasn't until we were able to share with them what the Lord had taken us through that we had a receptive audience. I was reminded once again the scripture where Jesus tells us that He allows us to go through tribulations so we can comfort others (2 Corinthians 1:4). This new ministry also taught me how much love and mercy our Lord really does have toward us. I have seen His grace and mercy in times past, yet it was magnified at this hospital beyond what I had known. He doesn't want any of us to die without receiving the redemption that He has provided through His son Jesus Christ. Even up to the last moment of life for some people, not until their last breath did they accept Jesus Christ as their Lord and Savior. To watch people on their deathbed as they struggle with their eternal state, seeing the transformation that literally takes place through an expression of hopelessness to one of peace when they surrender to God's love, is an incredible experience to witness firsthand. What an awesome privilege it is to be used by our Lord to help others find the truth and connect with our Lord during the last minutes.

As it turned out, we never did end up selling our fifth wheel when we left the hospital in Mexico. We were both comfortable living on the road again. We felt at home. We also started to see the Lord working through us to help others one-on-one. What would start out as a short visit somewhere usually would turn out to be much longer than planned, because the need is great everywhere we go.

Feeling guilty about the house that was lent to us back in New Mexico, we knew it was time for George and me to make a decision to either go back or give the house up for someone else to use. We never forgot that our friends had so graciously allowed us to live there, hoping that we would take care of it and protect it from being vandalized.

One morning the burden was quite heavy on my heart. Bringing up my concerns to George, he suggested we pray about whether we should go back and live in New Mexico or stay on the road. I just love it when the Lord answers our prayers rapidly. Within two hours of our prayer in seeking God's wisdom, our friend Lori, the landlord, called us. Before this phone call, we hadn't talked to her in months. It was good to hear her voice. She had called to tell us that her niece was getting married and needed a home to live in. She wanted to know if we were planning to come back to live in the house, or if not, would we be willing to give up the house. I was elated that her niece needed a place to live. This was the answer we were looking for. The Lord was giving us His blessing to be transient once again and live in our fifth wheel full-time.

Making plans to move needed to be thought out. We had a household full of things, so we planned to make this move in steps. Step number one was to find a place we could park our storage box and flat bed trailer. I was willing to have a garage sale and unload items that were easy to replace. Hopefully we could fit everything else into the box. This step was achieved quickly thanks to our friend in Sierra Vista who was a landowner and had no problem with us storing our things there. We went back within that week to get our first load.

Besides the storage box and flat bed trailer, we also had in our possession a small eight by eight box trailer someone had donated to us for the ministry. This would be our first attempt to get the trailer to Arizona. Loading it up went fairly well, and before we knew it we were back on the road heading to Arizona. It started out as a beautiful, sunny late October day. Coming to Lordsburg, New Mexico, about three hundred miles from Albuquerque, it was time to fill up with gasoline and make a restroom stop. Getting out of the truck, as I passed by the trailer I noticed the smell of grease coming from the back axle. Nonchalantly, I mentioned it to George as we entered the gas station. When I came back outside, George was bent over the tire, checking things out to see if there was any problem. When I came over to him, he informed me that the bearing on the right side of the axle was pulverized. He couldn't believe how we even got into the gas station without the tire literally falling off. We would need to pull away from the pump and park our rig in a better parking stall in order to fix it. As we were backing up, our tire actually did fall off. We couldn't even drive it far enough to get it to a parking spot. At this moment we happened to be smack right in the middle of their lot, not a good place to be. George kept putting the wheel back on and trying to inch our way to an out-of-the-way place, but it was becoming a ridiculously useless endeavor. Our only option was to call a tow truck.

After talking it over, we decided the best thing to do was have our vehicle towed to the nearest hotel parking lot, which happened to be right down the street from the gas station. That way we could spend the night and work on the problem that evening and into the next day. Unfortunately, it was Friday, midday. We didn't have much time before the parts houses would be closing. We needed to act fast.

George called the tow company while I sat in the fast food restaurant attached to the gas station. This seemed like a good time to read since we might be waiting a while. Glancing up, I noticed George was outside fiddling with the tire again. Suddenly, out of nowhere, rain clouds began to gather over us, bringing along gusty winds. Within minutes, the rain started to come down pretty heavily. George was getting drenched, and all the while I could see that he was fighting against the wind and trying to remove something from the tire at the same time. "Lord, when it rains, it pours," I said to myself, hardly believing the intensity of our dilemma. It wasn't until I heard one of the employees from the restaurant say, "I can't believe how hard the rain is coming down. We haven't seen rain like this in years; it just doesn't rain this heavy here," that I started feeling that this was just one big spiritual attack on us.

Finally George came in out of the rain. He informed me the tow truck was going to cost one hundred eighty dollars to tow us a half a block away. Personally, this seemed like highway robbery to me, and I resisted the idea of taking the tow truck option. George was becoming upset with me because I was so against going that route. In his frustration he said, "Fine, then you come up with a plan, because our vehicle isn't moving out of that spot without someone towing us."

I was frustrated too, to the point of tears. Just when I wanted to have a pity party, the Lord brought to my mind a couple whom George and I had met at the hospital in Mexico when we were ministering there. Their situation had been very grave. The wife of this couple was very sick with cancer, and they had spent every last penny they had to get the help she needed. They had been to the hospital several times, each time her situation getting worse. The last time we saw her, we weren't sure she was going to leave there alive. Her husband was so torn to pieces watching his dear wife go through so much pain. Suddenly, in comparison our situation seemed doable. If we were going to have a trial, this one was one we would work our way through with the help of the Lord. I was going to trust God!

I suggested to George that we unhook our truck from the trailer and get permission from the store owner to let us leave our trailer where it was parked for a few hours until we could locate a bearing from a parts house to fix our axle. Thankfully, the manager was very sympathetic to our situation and agreed to let us keep it there for a few hours. He even gave us directions to a nearby parts place. We needed to hurry because it was getting close to closing time. By this time the rain had let up. We unhooked as fast as we could and were on our way to the parts place.

Finding the parts house was no problem; the problem arose when we got out of the car and neared the door of the store. Posted in big black writing etched on a poster board were these words, "Sorry for the inconvenience but our store will be closed until Monday." We both looked at each other, trying to smile through our ever-present trial. We knew this was the only parts store in town and we would be looking at driving back to Deming, about sixty miles away, to find another one. Time-wise, we wouldn't be able to make it before that store would close. "We are going to get through this," I told myself. Trying to cheer us up, I said, "Hey, let's get something to eat. We'll be able to think better on a full stomach." George liked my idea too. We started off again, now looking for a restaurant.

Thank God, there were more restaurants than parts houses to be found. After eating a big delicious meal, we did feel more relaxed and comfortable, even though our trial was still facing us. Neither of us knew what to do. As we passed the hotel down the street from the gas station, George wanted to pay for a room for me to stay for the night. He volunteered to sleep in our truck and guard the trailer, not wanting to leave it unattended. Since I was the one fighting against paying for the tow, I insisted that we both stay in the truck together and keep each other company.

We pulled into the station and parked our truck next to our trailer. It was kind of humorous because at that moment there was still daylight, but nothing to do. George looked at me, put his seat back and said, "Good night." We both started to laugh. Just then a man, a woman and a young boy in an old beat-up pickup truck pulled up beside us. "Ya know, I noticed ya have a broken trailer there. I was wondering if ya'd all be interested in buying yourselves another one," the man said, politely. I immediately noticed the tattoos he had on his body, and his rough demeanor.

George responded, "No, I'm not looking for another trailer. I just want to fix the one I already have."

It was as if the man didn't even hear a word George had said. He went on. "I have these real nice trailers. I think you'd really like 'em."

George repeated himself. "No, thank you, I really don't want to buy another trailer. I just want to fix this one."

When the man started in the third time, I leaned over and said, "Sir!" He stopped talking and looked at me. Being in a playful mood, I came back with, "We're not interested in buying a trailer, but what we are interested in buying is a bearing for a trailer. Do you sell bearings?"

George looked at me with a smirk on his face. The man paused for a second or two and then responded. "Well, I think I do have a bearing I can sell ya. It's at my friend's house. You'll have to follow me." George and I looked at each other, not sure what to do.

"We don't have anything else to do, we might as well go look," George said to me.

"All right, let's go then," I said.

We took off, following the beat-up truck. It wasn't until we crossed the tracks and ended up in a rough-looking neighborhood that I started to get a bit worried. "What if he tries to kill us?" I said to George.

"I highly doubt he'd try to do that with his son and wife in the car," George reasoned. I wasn't really all that fearful, but I have to admit the thought did cross my mind.

We pulled up to a yard, overshadowed by an old, worn-out mobile home and a homemade pickup truck trailer, which gave the clear impression of abandonment. To our amazement, there was an axle attached to that pickup bed that looked just as old as the one on our trailer.

The man began to disassemble the axle while we waited. Within ten to fifteen minutes, he was handing George a used bearing. George looked it over closely as they exchanged a few words. Walking over to the window of our truck where I was sitting, he leaned in and said, "Write a check for twenty dollars."

"How do you know this is the right size bearing?" I asked out of curiosity.

"I don't," George remarked, "but the guy looks like he needs money, so we'll take the loss if it's not the right one." I wrote out a check. George handed it to the man and then thanked him. He got back into our truck and we waved good-bye.

All the way back we commented on how weird this whole scenario seemed. George was amazed that this bearing actually did look like the right one. The strangest thing about it was that our trailer was old, and this particular bearing wasn't the common run-of-the-mill you just find easily. It wasn't until we came back to our trailer and he assembled it, finding it fitting like a glove, when we really began to see the miracle in it all. What are the chances of this all happening like it did? A man drives up to our window and just happens to have an obsolete bearing that we need?

We were back on the road and home in our bed by midnight. As we headed toward home, I was thoroughly amazed that we were actually on the road again. I started to muse about the immensity of the size of our universe. Naming over country by country, I began to identify different ones: "Canada and Sweden, Egypt and Spain, there's Russia, and Israel, and there's Mexico... and Lord, here we were in little ole' Lordsburg, New Mexico. You reached down and said, "Oh, my little loved ones, you need a bearing, well... here you go!"

And upon those thoughts, along our way, we are reminded once again how powerful and loving our God really is. Then I remember the highway ministry and His provision after walking the walk for twenty-seven years in the supernatural. I am convinced that my God will keep moving us forward as we stay close to Him and obedient to His calling.

And so, our adventures go on!

Epilogue

Each of us has a calling on our lives that differ one from another. I don't advise the reader of this book to sell everything they own, buy a recreational vehicle, and live like we do, unless God is telling you to do so. You need to do what God is calling you yourself to do with your whole heart, not what God told us to do. This was God's path for us.

Although I enjoy sharing stories of my life and the awesomeness and faithfulness of my Lord and Savior, my goal for writing this book is two-fold. First, to reach an audience which has never experienced a personal relationship with the Creator of the universe, and second, to encourage my brothers and sisters who are in the family of God, reminding them how powerful and mighty the God we serve really is.

To the reader who has never had a personal encounter with God, I challenge you to tap into the supernatural realm that truly exists. The Bible, Old and New Testament alike, is replete throughout with stories and miracles from the hand of God. Many of us are familiar with such miracles as Moses leading the Israelites out of Egypt, the parting of the Red Sea, manna coming down from heaven to feed them, along with water pouring out of a rock for them to drink, the story of Jonah being swallowed by a whale and spewed out three days later, and God speaking through a donkey to a prophet. Then in the New Testament, God coming to earth as a man, namely Jesus Christ, through a virgin birth, to live among us, healing the sick, raising the dead, casting out demons, giving sight to the blind, and the biggest miracle of all, dying on a cross and raising from the dead three days later. This is as supernatural as it gets. The good news is that the same God of the Bible who did all these miracles is the same God on the scene today. He hasn't changed. He's the same yesterday, as He is today, as He is forever (Hebrews 13:8). Yet, the Bible is also very clear about the calling of God on our lives. To be called by God is to be one who has heard and answered the call that God makes to everyone: Look upon Jesus Christ, believe on Him, and be saved (John 3:16).

One of the most loving things our God does is giving us a choice to love Him. He doesn't force us. Practically speaking, who would ever want someone to love us by force? He wants us to love Him by our free will. What's even more wonderful is He loved us first. He came to earth to live among us as a man so He could identify with our humanity, then took the penalty of our sin which is death (separation from Him), and through His death on the cross, by the shedding of His blood, made a way for us to be reconciled to God. You see, in the Bible without the shedding of blood there is no forgiveness of sins (Hebrews 9:22). By forgiving sin, God enables us to enjoy fellowship with Him. Jesus paid the price! This is a free ticket out of everlasting punishment. We have been sanctified (made holy) through the offering of the body of Jesus Christ (Hebrews 10:10). Now, that's something to pay attention to!

There are those who believe that there are other ways to God, but if you listen to the God of the Bible, He tells us there is only one way to Him. Jesus Christ is the only way. God's word says, "I am the way, the truth, and the life. No one comes to the Father but through me (John 14:6). There is one God and one mediator between God and humanity, the Man Jesus Christ (1 Timothy 2:5).

Sadly, not all men or women will respond to the call of God. They flat out will not believe. They refuse to call on the living God who actually loves them and waits patiently for them to turn their hearts toward Him. They will never experience the journey and great blessings that otherwise await them.

If you have never surrendered your heart to Jesus Christ, today is the day of salvation. All you need to do is pray (talk to God) from your heart, recognizing you are a sinner in need of a Savior, repent of your sins, and ask Jesus Christ into your life. Then experience the change. He will empower you with the Holy Spirit, and meet you on a personal level.

This doesn't mean that all your problems will go away. Sometimes just the opposite can happen. God receives us just as we are, but loves us enough to not leave us where we're at. Faith requires us to take one step at a time. Even though we would like to see the whole picture before we get involved in doing what it is God is calling us to do, that's not the way faith works. If He did decide to show us the whole picture beforehand, our minds wouldn't be able to handle it. We'd still worry about how it's all going to work out. No, God wants us to move each step of the way with Him, which in turn builds our faith and trust in Him.

Below are some scriptures to help you on your way.

Romans 3:10
Romans 3:23
Matthew 9:13
Luke 13:3
Romans 10:13
John 3:16
Romans 6:23
Romans 5:8
Romans 10:9-10
1 John 5:10-13

To the believer who has already surrendered his or her life to the Lord, my hope and prayer is that this book has encouraged your faith and inspired you to keep fighting the good fight of faith, that you hold on to the promises of God and stand firm on them, as you finish the race with endurance.

For whatever is born of God overcomes the world. And this is the victory that has overcome the world – our faith (1 John 5:4).